STATISTICS AND PROBABILITY

An Introductory Course

p191 Pop's are destrib.   "score" p31

p218 Normal Population

p21 R.S. Each element of pop'n equal ch.

STATISTICS
AND PROBABILITY

An Introductory Course

LONDON
W. FOULSHAM & CO. LTD.
NEW YORK . TORONTO . CAPE TOWN . SYDNEY

W. FOULSHAM & CO. LTD.
Yeovil Road, Slough, Bucks., England

572–00678–0

PRINTED BY CAHILL AND CO. LIMITED

The Schools Statistics Panel

Panel of Teachers responsible for the
Preparation and Writing

DAVID L. OVENSTONE (*Convener*), Albert Secondary School.

PETER C. DICKIE, Crookston Castle Secondary School.

KENNETH J. DUNACHIE, Knightswood Secondary School.

JEAN K. FERGUSSON, Glasgow High School for Girls.

ROBERT A. FINLAYSON, Allan Glen's School.

ROBERT B. LOWRIE, The High School of Glasgow.

WILLIAM RUSSELL, St. Margaret Mary's Secondary School.

EDWARD TOLAN, St. Aloysius College.

JAMES C. WELSH, Bellahouston Academy.

ACKNOWLEDGEMENTS

We are grateful to the following Examination Boards for permission to reproduce questions from their recent examination papers with amendments where indicated:

The Associated Examining Board for the General Certificate of Education (A.E.B.)
The Institute of Statisticians (INST. of STAT.)
The Joint Matriculation Board (J.M.B.)
The Oxford and Cambridge Schools Examination Board (O.C.S.E.B.)
The Scottish Certificate of Education Examination Board (S.C.E.E.B.)
The University Entrance and Schools Examinations Council, University of London (LOND.)
The University of Cambridge Local Examinations Syndicate (U.C.L.E.S.)
The Welsh Joint Education Committee (W.J.E.C.)

In addition, we wish to thank all those Education Authorities, Schools and Teachers who participated in the **pilot scheme** and made this text possible.

Contents

vii

Foreword

THE subject of Statistics is being increasingly introduced by schools for examination courses, because a knowledge of this subject forms a useful part of general education. Besides having increasing applications in mathematics and the sciences on the one hand, it also applies to business, commerce, and economics on the other.

This book has been written by the Schools Statistics Panel, comprising nine teachers of mathematics, which was formed, with the active co-operation of Glasgow Corporation Education Department, with the aim of preparing an elementary introduction to Statistics which would be designed to:

1. Meet the requirements of the new syllabus in Statistics of the Scottish Certificate of Education 'O' grade examination.

2. Provide a suitable text for pupils preparing for examination in Statistics for C.S.E. or at 'O' level of the General Certificate of Education or the examinations of the Institute of Statisticians.

3. Be a useful self-study book for those pupils who wish to learn Statistics as a branch of another subject.

Several thousand copies of the text were printed and distributed to schools throughout Scotland on a trial scheme, and teachers participating in the scheme were invited to submit their suggestions and criticisms. This work is the result of the revision and re-writing of the trial edition in the light of the comments received.

The book is intended to provide a two-year course, though the more able pupils may be able to cover the work in one year. It requires a reasonable skill in Arithmetic, without requiring a knowledge of 'O' level Mathematics.

The aim of the panel throughout has been to present the subject matter in the simplest possible way. Accordingly, an experimental approach to various topics has been adopted, and pupils are encouraged to verify results and formulae by performing the experiments themselves.

Those formal proofs which are included are intended for pupils with an adequate mathematical background and can be omitted, if desired. The contents fall broadly into two categories: the techniques of elementary Statistics (occupying the first half of the book), and the applications of Probability to Statistics (occupying the second half of the book). The units used throughout are completely metric, and the book contains three-figure tables of Squares, Square roots, and the Area under the Standard Normal Curve. There are two sets of revision exercises, carefully selected from recent examination papers of the various U.K. examining Boards. In some cases, though the meaning has not been changed, the units used in the original questions have been changed to metric units.

Formulae

(*N, X, $\overline{X}$, s* refer to samples, and *n, x μ, σ* to populations)

Arithmetic mean: $\quad \overline{X} \;=\; \dfrac{\Sigma X}{N} \;$ or $\; \dfrac{\Sigma f X}{\Sigma f}$

$\qquad\qquad\qquad\quad \mu \;=\; \dfrac{\Sigma x}{n} \;$ or $\; \dfrac{\Sigma f x}{\Sigma f}$

Standard deviation: $\quad s \;=\; \sqrt{\dfrac{\Sigma (X-\overline{X})^2}{N}} \;$ or $\; \sqrt{\dfrac{\Sigma f(X-\overline{X})^2}{\Sigma f}}$

$\qquad\qquad\qquad\qquad \sigma \;=\; \sqrt{\dfrac{\Sigma (x-\mu)^2}{n}} \;$ or $\; \sqrt{\dfrac{\Sigma f(x-\mu)^2}{\Sigma f}}$

Standard variable: $\quad z \;=\; \dfrac{X-\overline{X}}{s} \;$ or $\; \dfrac{x-\mu}{\sigma}$

Binomial distribution: $\quad \mu \;=\; np \;;\; \sigma = \sqrt{(npq)}$

Samples of size N (N large) from an infinite population:

$$\mu_X \;=\; \mu \;;\; \sigma_X \;=\; \dfrac{\sigma}{\sqrt{N}}$$

The above formulae, which are used throughout the book, are reproduced from the Specimen Question Paper of the S.C.E. O-Grade Statistics Examination, with the kind permission of the Examination Board.

Several other extremely useful formulae which are also used in the book are given below:

Standard deviation: $s = \sqrt{\dfrac{\Sigma X^2}{N} - \left(\dfrac{\Sigma X}{N}\right)^2} \;$ or $\; \sqrt{\dfrac{\Sigma f X^2}{\Sigma f} - \left(\dfrac{\Sigma f X}{\Sigma f}\right)^2}$

$\qquad\qquad\quad \sigma = \sqrt{\dfrac{\Sigma x^2}{n} - \left(\dfrac{\Sigma x}{n}\right)^2} \;$ or $\; \sqrt{\dfrac{\Sigma f x^2}{\Sigma f} - \left(\dfrac{\Sigma f x}{\Sigma f}\right)^2}$

CHAPTER 1

Presentation of Data

1.1 Introduction

In the world of today, statistical data and diagrams are used more and more to illustrate items of news and current events. It is most unusual to read through a newspaper or magazine without finding some reference to a statistical table or chart.

Collect some copies of different newspapers and magazines and use them to try the following exercises:

(1) Find an advertisement which says, 'Nine out of ten film stars use . . .', or another advertisement like this one.
(2) Try to find the statement, 'The latest statistics show that . . ..'
(3) Find numerical data about some of the following:

    (a) The weather,
    (b) Education,
    (c) Politics,
    (d) Sport,
    (e) Cost of living,
    (f) Any other subject which has been investigated and described by means of statistical data.

The statistical study of a topic of interest usually begins with the collecting of raw data which is organised and tabulated in some way. Then, to make them more striking, results are often illustrated in the form of graphs or diagrams.

(4) Try to find some diagrams in your newspapers and magazines which illustrate statistical data.

1

The purpose of a statistical investigation is usually to establish facts which will assist in making decisions and planning ahead.

(5) As an example, why should a Director of Education be especially interested in the numbers of children who will reach (in the next year) the age of,

(a) 5 years,   (b) 11 to 12 years,
(c) 15 years,   (d) 17 to 18 years?

Suggest other numerical data which would be of interest to the Director of Education. For example, the numbers taking school meals, annual cost of supplying textbooks, etc.

The above examples of statistical investigation show us that data is:

(1) Collected.
(2) Displayed in tabular or graphical form.
(3) Studied in order to make decisions.

The science concerned with the collection and meaning of numerical data is called **statistics.**

1.2 Statistical diagrams

Example 1. A group of girls prepared a feature for their school magazine on the television viewing habits of pupils in their school. They asked every pupil whether he or she preferred to watch I.T.V. or B.B.C. The following table shows the numbers of those who gave a definite answer:

	First year	Second year	Third year	Fourth year	Fifth year	Sixth year
Number preferring I.T.V.	72	68	68	47	33	21
Number preferring B.B.C.	30	38	43	47	37	40

The girls decided to display the data pictorially. They prepared Fig. 1.1 and Fig. 1.2 and tried to decide which they preferred.

1. Pictogram

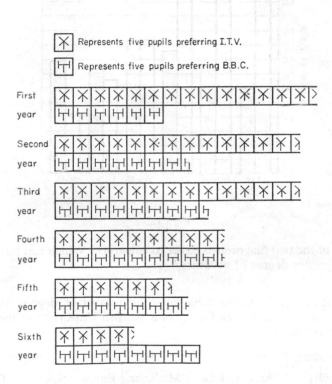

Fig. 1.1

2. Bar graph

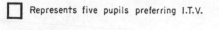

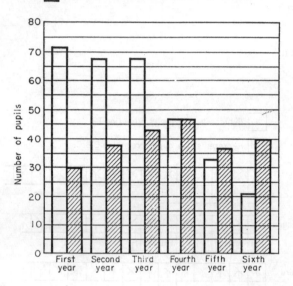

Fig. 1.2

Which of the two diagrams is easier to construct? Which can be drawn to the greater degree of accuracy?

Example 2. The following table gives the number of degree students (to the nearest ten) in each faculty of a Scottish University at the start of session 1968–69.

Faculty	Arts	Law	Medicine	Engin.	Science	Total
Number of students	2 430	270	1 170	630	1 980	6 480

What fraction of the total were, (a) Arts students, (b) Law students?

Calculate similarly the fractions for the other three faculties.

When data can be classified like this, it is often displayed in the form of a **pie chart** or **circle diagram**.

3. Pie chart

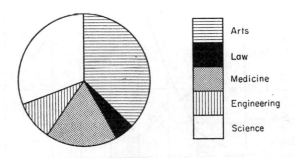

Fig. 1.3

Since Arts students make up $\frac{3}{8}$ of the total, they are represented in the pie chart by a sector which is $\frac{3}{8}$ of the circle. The angle of this sector is $\frac{3}{8}$ of one complete revolution.

That is, required angle $= \frac{3}{8} \times 360° = 135°$.

Calculate similarly the angles required for the other four sectors. Verify that the sum of the five angles is 360°.

Example 3. The following table shows production figures for Britain of radio receivers for the years 1958 to 1965. The table compares the production of valve receivers and transistor receivers.

	1958	1959	1960	1961	1962	1963	1964	1965
Number of valve receivers (thousands)	1 110	1 000	710	280	840	540	690	460
Number of transistor receivers (thousands)	120	380	1 250	2 420	2 520	2 200	1 870	1 240

Figures recorded at regular intervals like this can be illustrated conveniently as a **line graph**.

4. Line graph

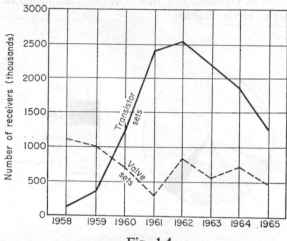

Fig. 1.4

Study the graph and answer the following questions:

(1) In which years were the following produced:
   (a) The smallest number of valve sets,
   (b) The largest number of valve sets,
   (c) The largest number of transistor sets?
(2) In which year did the production of transistor sets overtake the production of valve sets?
(3) What was the **trend** in the production of transistor sets from:
   (a) 1958 to 1962,
   (b) 1962 to 1965?

A line graph is easy to construct. It is most often used when it is desired to show a rising or a falling trend in a set of figures over a period of time.

The answers to questions (1), (2) and (3) represent some of the **facts** which can be established from a study of the data. A statistician is often asked to give reasons for past events and to make forecasts of future events. These may be difficult tasks, and findings are often treated cautiously.

Refer again to Fig. 1.4 and answer the following questions:

(1) Suggest a reason for the decline in production of valve radios from 1958 to 1961.

(2) Suggest a reason for the decline in output of transistor sets after 1962.

(3) Make a cautious estimate of the number of sets of each kind you might expect to be produced in 1966.

A possible answer to question (1) is that the newly developed transistor sets were proving more popular with the public.

A possible answer to question (2) is that foreign (especially Japanese) competition began to have a serious effect on the British radio market after 1962. It should be realised, however, that neither of these answers can be accepted as fact without a detailed study of further data than that illustrated in Fig. 1.4.

Exercise 1

(1) Make a simple table showing the number of periods per week which you spend on each subject at school, and illustrate the figures by (a) a bar graph, (b) a pie chart.

(2) Make a simple table showing the weekly total absences in your own class for the previous eight weeks. Illustrate the figures by a line graph.

(3) A motor insurance company investigated the causes of 1 000 accidents which resulted in damage to vehicles. A summary of their findings is illustrated in Fig. 1.5.

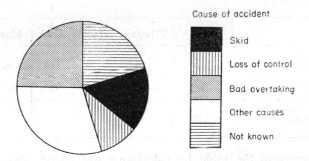

Fig. 1.5

Estimate (a) The percentage, (b) The number of accidents in each of the five categories.

(4) Copy the following table and headings:

Cars	Vans	Trucks	Buses	Motor-cycles	Taxis	Other vehicles

Observe the traffic on a busy road for fifteen minutes and make a mark in the table, noting each type of vehicle as it passes. When finished, complete the totals for all columns, and illustrate the figures by a bar graph or a pie chart.

(5) Collect data from your class on the popularity of regular television programmes as follows: Draw up an agreed list of ten (or more) programmes to be voted upon. Each class member should select from the list his or her **five** favourite programmes, and award one vote to each. Show the results of the voting in a table and illustrate by a bar graph.

(6) A monthly magazine estimated its sales for the next six months as shown in the first row of the table. The percentages by which the actual sales differed from the expected figures are shown in the second row.

	January	February	March	April	May	June
Expected sales (thousands)	160	170	175	180	190	200
% difference	+5%	+10%	+4%	−5%	−10%	−8%
Actual sales (thousands)	168					

Complete the table by calculating the actual sales achieved. Illustrate both the expected and the actual sales on a line graph.

(7) The following table compares the steel production in the years 1938 and 1962 of the six leading steel-producing countries of the world:

Production of steel ingots (millions of tons)

Country	1938	1962
U.S.A.	28	89
U.S.S.R.	17	76
Germany	22	36
U.K.	10	21
France	6	17
Belgium	2	7

Make a compound bar graph to illustrate the figures. Which country had the biggest total increase in production? What was the amount of this increase?

(8) Here is a bar graph issued by the ZYX T.V. Sales and Rental Company in their annual report.

Comparative diagram of sales and rentals

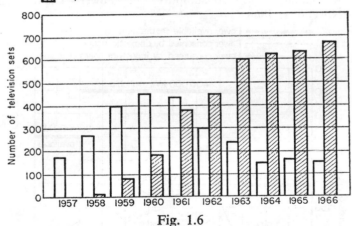

Fig. 1.6

(a) In which year was the largest number of sets sold? How many were sold that year?

(b) When did the number of rental sets **overtake** the number sold?

(c) For the year 1962, calculate the percentage of sets handled by the company which were (i) Rented, (ii) Sold.

(*d*) On the basis of the bar graph make a (cautious) estimate of the number of sets likely to be (i) Sold, and (ii) Rented in 1967.

(9) A new university in England began its first session with the following intake of students:

	Degree students				Diploma students	Totals
	Arts	Science	Engin.	Law		
Men	144	164	92	39	39	
Women	180	64	—	13	65	
Totals						

Copy and complete the table by putting in all totals. Which course attracted the largest number of students? What percentage of all students attended this course? Which course attracted the largest proportion of women students? What was this proportion? Make a compound bar graph to illustrate the figures.

(10) Study the graph and answer the questions below.

Loch Granite Power Station

Availability and Consumption of Power—Tuesday, 26th November, 1968.

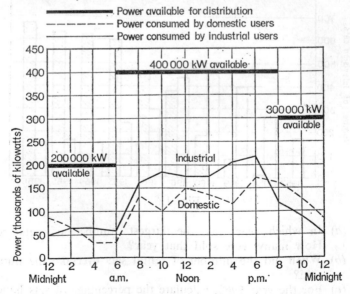

Fig. 1.7

(a) What were the peak times for domestic consumption? Explain why domestic demand is usually high at these times.

(b) What was the **pattern** of industrial consumption over the 24 hours?

(c) What was the total consumption of power (industrial plus domestic) at 12 noon?

(d) When was the total consumption (i) at its lowest, (ii) at its highest? What amount of the available power was unused at each of these times?

1.3 Misleading statistics

It has frequently been said that statistics can be used to prove anything. This is untrue. What is true is that statistical figures or diagrams are frequently used to mislead people who are not trained in the interpretation of such data. Here are some examples:

Example 1. A Building Society suspected of being on rather a shaky financial footing might attempt to attract investment by running an advertisement containing the following graphs:

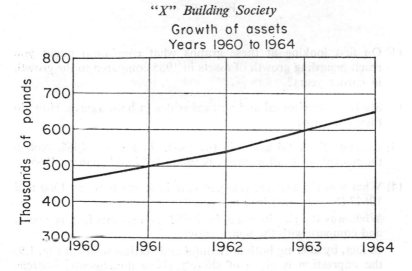

"X" Building Society
Growth of assets
Years 1960 to 1964

Fig. 1.8

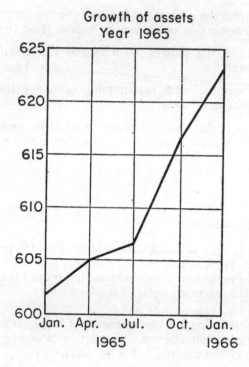

Fig. 1.9

(1) On first looking at these graphs what conclusion might you reach regarding growth of assets in 1965 compared to the growth in earlier years?

(2) Study the horizontal and vertical scales in both figures. How do they compare?

(3) Estimate the total assets in (a) 1964, (b) January 1965. Notice the unexplained fall in assets between 1964 and January 1965.

(4) What was the average rise per year in assets between 1960 and 1964? (Express this in £ per year.)

What was the rise in assets in 1965? Express this in £ per year, and compare with the figure above.

In fact, by altering both horizontal and vertical scales in Fig. 1.9, the impression is given of sharply rising investments, whereas the reverse is true.

Example 2. An article which appeared in a mass circulation daily newspaper began with the following headlines and diagram:

Brain drain causes alarm

Continued rise in graduates emigrating to U.S A.

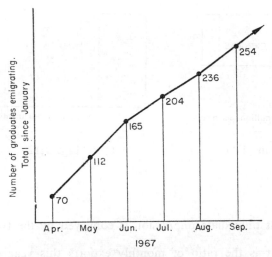

Fig. 1.10

(1) Since 70 graduates had left by the month of April and 112 by May, how many left between April and May? Write down the corresponding figures for June, July, August and September.

(2) What do you think is the purpose of the arrow at the end of the graph? From the answers which you gave to (1) above what is the **trend** in the numbers emigrating? Do you think the use of the arrow is justified?

Example 3. The comparative picture is a favourite device of government and industry alike. A new government after one year in office might produce the following pictorial comparison with the last year of the previous government:

Export drive to dollar countries gathers momentum

Average monthly exports last year   Average monthly exports this year
(under the previous government)   (under the new government)

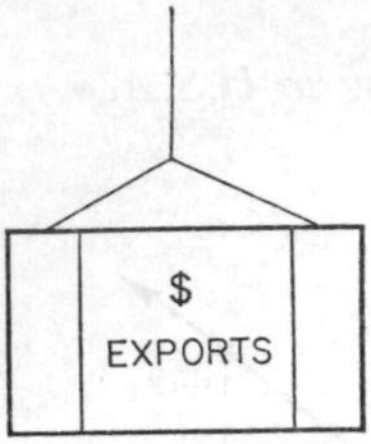

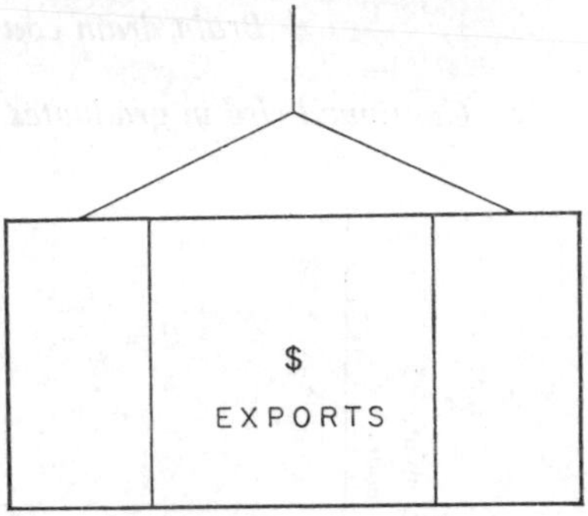

$120 million per month $240 million per month

Fig. 1.11   Fig. 1.12

(1) What immediate impression is conveyed by the two diagrams?

(2) What is the ratio of monthly exports this year compared to last year?

(3) Measure the lengths and breadths of the two 'crates' representing exports. What is the ratio of their lengths? Of their breadths? What is the ratio of the **areas** of the two crates?

(4) The crate in Fig. 1.12 is drawn with its dimensions twice those of Fig. 1.11, which makes its area four times as big. The impression gathered by a casual reader would be of a large increase in exports, certainly more than a simple doubling of the rate.

Exercise 2

(1) A few years ago, a County Council in England issued the following graph relating to its road-building programme:

Westshire County roads programme

Provision of dual carriageways

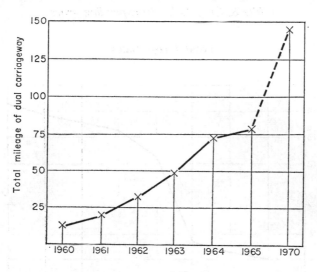

Fig. 1.13

(a) What impression is conveyed by the steeply rising dotted portion of the graph? Why is this portion drawn with a dotted line?

(b) Comment upon the horizontal scale.

(c) What was the average length of dual carriageway provided per year between 1960 and 1965? Express this in miles per year.

What was the estimated average length to be provided per year from 1965 to 1970?

Compare the two averages.

(2) Here is a chart produced by a multiple department store organisation, designed to impress readers with the amount of expansion of their sales:

White & Grey Ltd.—30 expanding years

Total Gross Sales

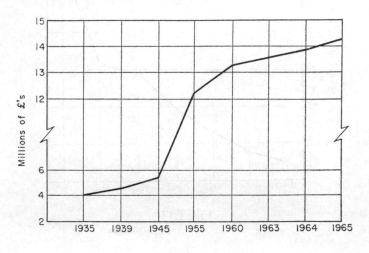

Fig. 1.14

(*a*) Comment upon the horizontal scale.

(*b*) What is wrong with the vertical scale?

(*c*) What was the value of sales in 1935? What was their value in 1965? Can you tell from these figures whether a larger volume of goods was sold in 1935 or 1965? Explain your answer.

(3) The following is typical of numerous articles, which have appeared in the press in recent years, on the difficulties of British ship-yards:

Britain's declining shipbuilding industry

1939 Percentage of world tonnage built	Shipbuilding nations	1960 Percentage of world tonnage built
34%	Britain	16%
15%	Japan	21%
16%	*West Germany	14%
7%	U.S.A.	7%
5%	Sweden	9%
8%	Holland	6%
15%	Others	27%
World tonnage built = 3 million tons approx.	*In 1939 the whole of Germany	World tonnage built = 9 million tons approx.

Is it true that Britain's shipbuilding industry declined? Japan's industry obviously increased, but by how much? What about other countries? To find out, calculate the approximate tonnages built in 1939 and 1960.

e.g. Britain in 1939:   34% of 3 million

$$= \frac{34}{100} \times 3 = \frac{102}{100} = 1\cdot02 \text{ million tons}$$

U.S.A. in 1960:   7% of 9 million

$$= \frac{7}{100} \times 9 = \frac{63}{100} = 0\cdot63 \text{ million tons}$$

Copy and complete the following table:

1939 Tonnage built (millions of tons)	Country	1960 Tonnage built (millions of tons)
1·02	Britain Japan *West Germany U.S.A. Sweden Holland Others	0·63
3 million tons	Totals	9 million tons

Illustrate the figures on a compound bar graph. Show the 1939 column for each country alongside that for 1960. Is it true that, **in terms of tonnage built,** British shipbuilding declined between 1939 and 1960? What is true of British shipbuilding in relation to the rest of the world?

(4) The table below shows the number of new school places provided for secondary pupils in Scotland in each two year period from 1952 to 1966:

Period	1952– 1954	1954– 1956	1956– 1958	1958– 1960	1960– 1962	1962– 1964	1964– 1966
Number of places provided (thousands)	22	23	31	51	50	46	54

Make a line graph to illustrate the figures, using the following scales:

Horizontal axis: 1 cm to each 2 year period.

Vertical axis: 1 cm represents 10 thousand places, starting at zero.

We can illustrate the figures in a more dramatic way as follows: We make a new table showing the **cumulative** total of school places provided since 1952.

Year	1954	1956	1958	1960	1962	1964	1966
Total places provided since 1952 (thousands)	22	45	76	127	177	223	277

This data is plotted as a line graph on a **perspective diagram,** as shown in Fig. 1.15.

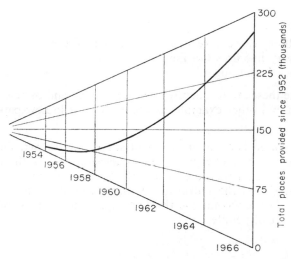

Fig. 1.15

What is the effect of presenting a set of data in the form of a cumulative perspective diagram, compared to an ordinary line graph?

CHAPTER 2

Population and Sample

2.1 Population

'Fourteen million viewers regularly watch Dr. Casey's Filmbook.'
'One car in every five uses Go Easy petrol.'
'Briter Batteries Last Longer.'

Statements like these are frequently seen in the press and on television. See if you can find other examples of similar claims in newspapers or magazines.

Each of these claims is a statement about some **universal set.** The first statement concerns the universal set of all television viewers, the second the universal set of all motor cars, the third, the universal set of all batteries. In statistics, the universal set under consideration is called the **population.** As the second and third examples show, the population need not be a set of people.

2.2 Sample

Assuming that a statement, like the one above about the number of viewers watching a particular programme, is accurate, how do the B.B.C. or I.T.V. obtain their information? Clearly, it would be too difficult and expensive to try to interview approximately forty million viewers throughout Britain.

Suppose the manufacturer of Briter Batteries claimed that every battery sold would have a working life of twenty hours. How could he be sure of his facts? Obviously, if he tested every battery for twenty hours to find out, he would have no product left to sell.

In cases like these, **samples** are selected from the population.

A **sample** is a subset of elements drawn from a population. From the information obtained from the sample, conclusions are drawn concerning the whole population. If the information obtained from a sample is to be of value, the sample should be representative of the whole population, and free from bias. Unfortunately it is not always easy to draw samples which are unbiased.

20

For example, if you questioned a sample of people on their attitudes to unofficial strikes, but selected your sample from the names in the telephone book, this would not provide a sample representative of the general public. Since few poor people have telephones, the sample would be biased by containing too many better off people.

Exercise 1

In the following examples, suggest some of the ways in which the samples might be biased.

(1) You wish to assess the attitude of people in general to music, both pop and classical. You question samples of people drawn from youth clubs in the district.

(2) You wish to assess the percentage of people in your town who regularly visit the theatre. You question samples of people as they enter a theatre before a performance.

(3) You wish to assess the attitude of the public to the motorway speed limit. You question samples of car owners as they enter or leave a car park.

(4) You wish to make a list of the six most popular television programmes. You question samples of pupils in your school.

2.3 Random sampling: some practical experiments

One method of drawing representative samples which proves adequate for many purposes is **random sampling**. Random samples are drawn in such a way that each element of the population must have an equal chance of being included in the sample. Following are some simple experiments in drawing random samples:

Experiment 1. To draw a random sample of 8 pupils from a class (i.e. a population) of 35 pupils.

Obtain the list of names of the class concerned and number them 1 to 35. Write the numbers 1 to 35 on counters or pieces of paper, mix well by shaking in a box, and draw 8 numbers from the box. Write out the names corresponding to the numbers.

Unfortunately, this method becomes very laborious when the population is large. Following is a simple alternative:

Experiment 2. To draw a random sample of 40 pupils from the whole school population.

Obtain the class lists for the whole school. Suppose there are 31 classes in the school. Number the lists consecutively from 1 to 31, and put corresponding counters marked 1 to 31 in a box marked A. Find the class list with the biggest roll. Suppose the roll is 42. Put counters numbered 1 to 42 in a box marked B.

To select a pupil for the sample, draw a number from box A and turn to class list with this number. Now draw a number from box B and read off from the class list the name of the pupil corresponding to this number. Return the counters to the correct boxes, shake well, and draw the next pupil for the sample. Continue until 40 pupils have been drawn.

If on any draw, there is no pupil on the list corresponding to the second number, or if the sample pupil is drawn twice, simply return the counters and continue. You will be given further experiments to perform with your sample in the exercises.

The sampling bottle. An extremely useful piece of statistical apparatus is the **sampling bottle** which can be made very easily from apparatus in the science room. For example, Fig. 2.1 shows a sampling bottle made from a chemical reagent bottle, stopper and glass tubing. Fig. 2.2 shows an even simpler model made from a plastic detergent bottle and a test tube.

Beads of different colours are put into the bottle as required. To draw a sample of 5 beads, shake the bottle, turn upside down, and note the colours of the first 5 beads at the bottom of the tube.

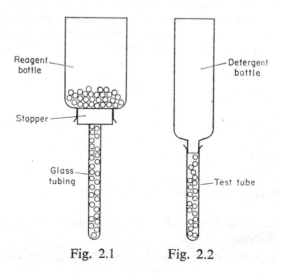

Fig. 2.1   Fig. 2.2

Experiment 3. Put into a sampling bottle an equal number of beads of two different colours, for example forty green beads and forty red. Draw a sample of ten beads and note the number of red beads in the sample. Repeat, until altogether thirty samples have been drawn and the results noted.

Calculate, to one decimal place, the average number of red beads per sample. How does this average compare with the sample size (ten)?

Experiment 4. Use a sampling bottle containing beads of two colours in the ratio 4 : 1 (for example eighty green, twenty red). Draw a sample of twenty beads and note the number of red beads in the sample. Repeat until altogether thirty samples have been drawn and the results noted.

Calculate, to one decimal place, the average number of red beads per sample. How does this average compare with the sample size (twenty)?

Experiment 5. To estimate the number of beads in a sampling bottle. Use a bottle containing about two or three hundred (precise number unknown) green beads. Remove eighty beads from the bottle and replace with eighty red beads. Perform the experiment of drawing thirty samples, each of twenty beads, noting in each case the number of red beads per sample.

Calculate the average number of red beads per sample and estimate the total number of beads in the bottle, as follows:

Suppose the average number of red beads per sample = 4·5. Let n represent the total number (i.e. the population). Then sample proportion,
    4·5 red beads per sample of 20
                equals
        population proportion,
    80 red beads per population of n.

That is $\dfrac{n}{80} = \dfrac{20}{4\cdot5}$

$\Leftrightarrow n = \dfrac{20 \times 80}{4\cdot5} = 356$ approximately.

Finally, check the accuracy of your result by counting the beads in the bottle.

Note. The symbol $\Leftrightarrow$ may be read as 'is equivalent to'.

Summary

Information should only be regarded as completely reliable if it is obtained from a complete survey of a finite population. In spite of the smaller reliability, information frequently has to be obtained using sampling techniques:

(1) If the population is very large or infinite.
(2) If the population is finite, but obtaining the information destroys the product.
(3) Even if a complete survey is possible, time, personnel, equipment and other resources may be limited.

It should be stressed that caution is required in drawing conclusions based upon sample evidence. As the course progresses, it is hoped that you will learn how much confidence to place on the results of tests.

Exercise 2

(1) Carry out the following experiment:
On the basis of a sample of 40 pupils to estimate the number of pupils in the school born in one of the first three months of the year.

Draw a random sample of 40 pupils, and note the number who were born in January, February, or March. Estimate the total number for the school as follows:

Suppose the total roll of the school is 600, and that 9 pupils in the sample were born in January, February or March. Then k, the required number, is given by,

sample proportion,
9 pupils per sample of 40
equals
population proportion
k pupils per population of 600.

That is $\dfrac{k}{600} = \dfrac{9}{40}$

$$\Leftrightarrow k = \frac{9 \times 600}{40}$$
$$= 135$$

Finally, if possible, find out the actual number of pupils with birthdays in those three months and check the accuracy of your result.

(2) At the same time as the above experiment is being performed, further information can be obtained about the pupils drawn in

The scores are arranged in order of their size, and we show by a tally mark each occurrence of a particular score. The total number of times each score appears is called its frequency. The table is called a **frequency distribution.** We can now get a better idea of how the pupil fared in the test with his mark of 7. Only six pupils, or

$$\frac{6}{40} \times 100 = 15\% \text{ of the class,}$$

scored a better mark. We can also see that thirteen pupils scored 4 marks or less and so failed the test.

Notation. We see from the table that the total number (N) of observations is equal to the sum of the frequencies (f).

i.e. $N = \Sigma f$

Here the symbol Σ is the Greek capital letter sigma, and means simply **sum of.**

If X is the symbol used to represent a variable, then $\Sigma f X$, the sum of the fX's, is the total number of marks scored. Using this notation, the table can be rewritten as follows:

Mark X	Frequency	f	fX
0		0	0
1	I	1	1
2	I I I	3	6
3	I I I I	4	12
4	++++	5	20
5	++++	5	25
6	++++ I I I I	9	54
7	++++ I I	7	49
8	I I I I	4	32
9	I	1	9
10	I	1	10
	$N = \Sigma f$	= 40	$\Sigma fX = 218$

Number in class, $N = \Sigma f = 40$.
Total number of marks scored $= \Sigma f X = 218$.

Example 2. Make a frequency table from the raw data:

29	25	28	22	24	25	28	26	26	24
23	25	26	21	23	26	27	23	28	30
27	27	24	26	25	25	24	21	25	22
25	25	27	24	23	27	25	26	23	26
23	27	25	24	26	25	24	22	24	26

Since the scores range from 21 to 30, these numbers are written in a column under the heading of **variable** X. Tally marks, corresponding to the first column of the data, are then recorded alongside the variable X.

Variable X	Frequency f	fX
21		
22		
23	I I	
24		
25	I	
26		
27	I	
28		
29	I	
30		
	$N = \Sigma f = 50$	1252

Copy the table in your jotter and make tally marks for column two of the data. Proceed tallying each column in turn until the table is complete. Check that $N = \Sigma f = 50$ and that $\Sigma fX = 1252$.

Exercise 1

(1) Draw forty samples, each of size 10, from a sampling bottle containing an equal number of red and white beads. Note the number of red beads in each sample. Make a frequency table of the data obtained.

(2) Think of a number between one and ten and write it down. Compile a list of numbers selected by the class and make a frequency table of them.

It might be interesting to try the same experiment with one or two neighbouring classes and compare the frequency tables obtained. You might find a tendency towards a **favourite** number or numbers.

(3) A road haulage firm recorded the number of breakdowns per month over a period of time. The record was as follows:

1	0	3	1	0	2	3	2	1	4	0	0
1	3	2	5	2	1	0	2	1	1	2	0
1	6	2	0	1	3	1	2	2	0	1	2
5	1	0	3	0	1	4	1	2	3	2	1

(a) Make a frequency table of the data.
(b) Over what period of time were the observations made?
(c) What was the total number of breakdowns over this period?
(d) Which **score** or number of breakdowns occurred with the greatest frequency? This score is known as the **mode** or **modal score** of the distribution.

(4) The numbers of S.C.E. ordinary passes obtained by pupils in a class were as follows:

3	3	4	3	5	3	2	2	4	3
2	3	1	3	4	2	6	3	5	3
4	3	3	0	3	3	3	4	2	4
2	1	2	4	3	3	2	2	3	3

(a) Make a frequency table of the passes obtained.
(b) How many pupils were there in the class?
(c) How many pupils obtained four passes or more?
(d) What percentage of the class obtained **at least** four passes?
(e) What was the total number of passes obtained?
(f) What is the mode of the distribution?

(5) Throw a die one hundred times, and record in a table the frequency of occurrence of the six possible scores.

(6) As part of a survey for a slot machine manufacturer, a sample of used pennies was taken and weighed to the nearest tenth of a gramme. The weights were recorded as follows:

9·3	9·3	9·3	9·4	9·3	9·4	9·3	9·4	9·4	9·2
9·4	9·2	9·4	9·2	9·4	9·2	9·4	9·0	9·4	9·4
9·2	9·4	9·4	9·1	9·3	9·4	9·4	9·2	9·1	9·3
9·3	9·4	9·3	9·2	9·3	9·1	9·3	9·3	9·4	9·4
9·1	9·1	9·3	9·4	9·0	9·4	9·2	9·5	9·2	9·4

(a) Make a frequency distribution of the weights.
(b) How many pennies were there in the sample?
(c) What was the total weight of the sample?
(d) What percentage of the pennies weighed 9·4 grammes?

(7) Forty batches of transistors were tested at regular intervals in a factory and the number of rejects in each batch noted.

```
0   0   2   5   4   2   0   1   0   2
1   1   4   0   1   0   0   2   3   0
1   0   2   3   0   1   1   0   1   2
0   0   3   0   1   0   0   1   0   1
```

(a) Make a frequency distribution of the number of rejects.
(b) What percentage of batches contained no defective transistors?
(c) What is the mode of the distribution?

(8) A machine is designed to pack soap powder in one-kilogramme cartons. A sample carton is taken from the production line at regular intervals, and weighed to the nearest ten grammes. The weights recorded in one day were as follows:

```
1·00  0·99  0·97  0·99  1·03  0·97  1·00  1·02  1·01  1·02
1·00  1·00  0·98  1·00  1·00  0·99  1·03  1·01  0·99  1·02
0·99  0·98  0·99  0·98  1·00  1·00  1·02  1·00  1·01  1·00
1·00  0·99  0·99  1·00  1·01  1·01  1·01  0·99  1·01  0·98
0·99  1·02  1·02  0·99  1·01  0·99  1·01  1·01  0·97  1·00
```

(a) Make a frequency distribution of the weights.
(b) How many cartons were checked during the day?
(c) Find the percentage of cartons checked which were different from the 1·00 kg advertised weight by more than 0·02 kg.
(d) What proportion of cartons contained less than the advertised weight?

Shape of a distribution

Before ordering dust coats the teachers in the technical department of a school measured the arm lengths of one hundred first year boys. The resulting frequency table was as follows:

Arm length (centimetres) x	Frequency	f
5 6	I	1
5 7	II	2
5 8	III	3
5 9	++++	5
6 0	++++ I	6
6 1	++++ ++++	10
6 2	++++ ++++ III	13
6 3	++++ ++++ ++++ I	16
6 4	++++ ++++ III	13
6 5	++++ ++++ I	11
6 6	++++ III	8
6 7	++++ I	6
6 8	III	3
6 9	II	2
70	I	1
		$N = \Sigma f = 100$

The tally marks give a rough picture of the pattern of the distribution of heights. This bell shaped pattern shows quite clearly a symmetry in the distribution centred on 63 cm, and thinning off at the end values.

Other distribution patterns which appeared in exercise 1 are shown below.

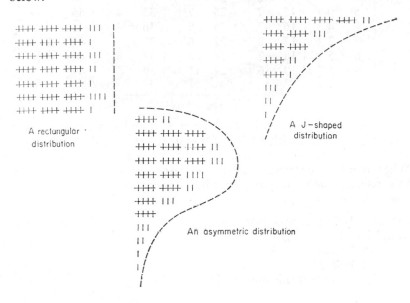

A rectangular distribution

An asymmetric distribution

A J–shaped distribution

Exercise 2

(1) Study the patterns in each of the distributions in exercise 1, and state whether any resemble:
    (*a*) The bell shaped, (*b*) The rectangular, (*c*) The J-shaped, (*d*) The asymmetric distribution.

3.2 Class intervals

Frequently we have to consider data in which the range of measurement is large. (The **range** of a set of numbers is the difference between the largest and the smallest number.)

Here is the frequency distribution of mathematics marks scored by first year pupils in a comprehensive school:

Mark	*f*	Mark	*f*	Mark	*f*	Mark	*f*	Mark	*f*
0	2	10	3	20	7	30	10	40	3
1	0	11	4	21	11	31	5	41	2
2	3	12	8	22	8	32	1	42	4
3	2	13	11	23	5	33	4	43	2
4	5	14	6	24	8	34	6	44	3
5	0	15	7	25	7	35	4	45	3
6	4	16	7	26	5	36	3	46	6
7	2	17	8	27	6	37	3	47	2
8	5	18	7	28	8	38	6	48	0
9	3	19	6	29	11	39	0	49	0

How many different marks have been scored by the pupils? Is it convenient to work with a table of this size? Try to find the pattern of the distribution. Does the table reveal the pattern?

When a table illustrating individual scores becomes unwieldy as in this case, it is better to group together numbers of marks.

Example 1. If the pass mark in the test was 25, how many pupils would have:
    (*a*) Passed,
    (*b*) Failed?
We might represent this information as follows:

Mark	Frequency
0—24	132
25—49	104
Total	236

Table 1

This table is certainly compact, but does it adequately represent the distribution? Suggest some disadvantages of this table?

Example 2. How many scored:
    (*a*) 40 or more,
    (*b*) Less than 10,
    (*c*) From 30 to 39?

To help answer these questions we might arrange the marks in groups 0—9, 10—19, and so on. Copy the table below and complete the column of frequencies.

Mark	Frequency
0—9	
10—19	
20—29	
30—39	
40—49	
Total	236

Table 2

Do you think that this table provides more information about the distribution than Table 1? Suggest one or two other possible groupings of the marks, and make a table similar to the above for each case.

When marks are grouped together in this way, each group is called a **class interval**, and the size of the interval is the number of marks which it includes. For example, in Table 2, the first interval contains ten marks so that the class interval size is 10.

When grouping data into class intervals we usually try to have at least six classes but not more than fifteen. In this case, since the range of marks is 47, perhaps the best frequency table would have ten class intervals, each of size five marks:

Mark	Frequency
0—4	12
5—9	14
10—14	32
15—19	35
20—24	39
25—29	37
30—34	26
35—39	16
40—44	14
45—49	11
Total	236

Table 3

In any class interval the largest value of the variable is called the **upper class limit,** while the smallest is called the **lower class limit.** Thus, in the third class, 10—14, 10 is the lower class limit and 14 the upper class limit.

Exercise 3

(1) The following questions refer to Table 3 above:
   (a) What are the upper and lower limits of the fourth class?
   (b) In which class interval does the greatest frequency of marks occur? This is called the **modal class.** Because the marks are grouped in class intervals we cannot pick out the modal score, but merely the class to which it belongs.

(2) Here is a table showing the number of goals scored by individual players in an amateur football league. Only those with five or more goals have been included.

22	15	29	28	5	11	13	23	12
5	5	15	18	14	9	5	33	11
10	7	30	18	21	8	9	23	15
23	18	15	6	15	5	11	13	26

(a) What is the range of the scores?

(b) Group the scores into six class intervals and make a frequency table of the scores.

(c) What are the lower and upper limits of the third class? Of the fifth class?

(d) What is the size of each interval?

(3) The percentage marks scored by a group of pupils in an examination were:

57	12	54	44	25	57	51	62	36	41
17	71	19	43	59	45	59	33	81	43
23	83	73	2	60	70	63	35	62	44
64	65	45	40	42	69	37	89	57	54
57	25	70	72	37	78	38	28	57	23

(a) Find the range, and decide upon a suitable number of classes.

(b) Using this decision construct a frequency table of marks.

(c) If fifty is the pass mark, what percentage of pupils passed?

(d) What is the modal class?

3.3 Class boundaries

Often a frequency table is made up from a set of figures which have been rounded off from the original measurements. In cases like this it often happens that some of the original measurements fall outside the class limits.

Example 1. Here are the weights, rounded off to the nearest kilogramme, of an intake of army recruits:

62	61	65	67	54	64	58	67	64	68
64	67	64	68	69	75	73	65	60	76
65	74	79	64	71	68	79	66	68	66
63	66	62	61	71	61	63	57	72	74

Make a frequency table of the weights using nine class intervals of size 3 kg, starting with 53–55 kg. Verify that the table is as follows:

Weight (kilogrammes)	Frequency f
53—55	1
56—58	2
59—61	4
62—64	9
65—67	9
68—70	5
71—73	4
74—76	4
77—79	2
	$N = \Sigma f = 40$

Because weight is a continuous variable, measurements can be made which **fall between** successive class intervals. For example, let us suppose that the recruit whose weight is entered as 61 kg in fact weighs 61·3 kg. Then his true weight would not be included in any class interval. For this reason, each class interval is considered to extend beyond its limits to the **class boundaries.**

For example, the boundary between the neighbouring intervals 53—55 kg and 56—58 kg is

$$\frac{55+56}{2} = 55 \cdot 5 \text{ kg,}$$

that is, midway between the upper limit of the first interval and the lower limit of the second. What is the boundary between the intervals 56—58 and 59—61 kg?

From the above we see that the lower and upper boundaries of the interval 56—58 are 55·5 and 58·5 kg respectively. What are the boundaries of:
 (a) The third class,
 (b) The fifth class,
 (c) The first class?

Add an extra column to your frequency table, and head it **class boundaries.** Complete this column for all classes.

Example 2. When a frequency table is constructed from a set of observations of a **discrete** variable, none of these observations can

fall between successive class intervals. Every observation must be contained in one or other of the intervals. In spite of this, when constructing a frequency table for a discrete variable, we often find it useful to consider class boundaries, despite their rather artificial nature.

Shown below are the numbers of cases of measles reported by thirty primary schools during an epidemic:

16	8	4	22	19	13	13	6	2	17
22	8	9	8	3	15	19	14	15	2
26	20	11	6	7	23	7	9	15	13

Copy and complete the frequency table below:

Number of cases	Frequency	f	Class boundaries
1–5	I I I I	4	½ and 5½
6–10	++++ I I I I	9	5½ „ (9½)
.	.		.
.	.		.
.	.		.

How many class intervals appear in the complete table? What are (*a*) the class limits, (*b*) the class boundaries of the third class? What is the boundary between the class 11—15 and the class 16—20? What are the class boundaries of the sixth class? The usefulness of class boundaries in discrete distributions of this kind will be demonstrated at a later stage.

Mid values
For the purposes of calculation, the mid value of each class is used as the representative of the class. In example 1 above, the first class interval is 53—55 kg, so that the mid value of the interval is

$$\frac{53+55}{2} = 54 \text{ kg}$$

What is the mid value of the interval:

    (*a*) having limits 56 and 58 kg,
    (*b*) with boundaries 61·5 and 64·5 kg?

We now proceed as though all observations in a class interval have the mid value. Thus, the total weight of the two recruits in the interval 56—58 kg is taken to be

$$2 \times 57 = 114 \text{ kg}$$

(Going back to the original data, the actual total weight of the two recruits in this class is seen to be 115 kg, so that using mid values leads to some loss of accuracy.)

Exercise 4

(1) Add two more columns to your frequency table of weights of army recruits, (example 1, page 37), using the headings shown below. The first row of the table has been completed to help you.

Weight (kilogrammes)	Ferquency f	Class boundaries (kilogrammes)	Mid values X	fX
53—55	1	52·5 and 55·5	54	54
.	.	.	.	.
.	.	.	.	.
.	.	.	.	.

Complete the table. Find Σf and ΣfX. What does the number ΣfX represent?

(2) Make another frequency table of the weights of army recruits, by grouping into seven classes, each with an interval of four kilogrammes. Find ΣfX from this table, and compare it with the result obtained in question (1).

(3) The distribution of wages in a small factory was as follows:

Weekly wage (£)	Number of employees f
7—9	4
10—12	5
13—15	9
16—18	16
19—21	12
22—24	3
25—27	1

With reference to the table determine:

(a) The upper limit of the third class.
(b) The lower limit of the fifth class.
(c) The mid value of the seventh class.
(d) The class boundaries of the first class.
(e) The class interval size.
(f) The percentage of employees earning more than £21·5 per week.

(4) Using the frequency distribution of question (3) above, find the mid value of each class, and hence calculate:

(a) The wage bill for each class.
(b) The approximate total wage bill for the factory. Why is this only an approximate total?

(5) The lengths of one hundred sweet pea shoots were measured to an accuracy of 0·1 cm, and the frequencies recorded in the following manner:

Length		Tenths of a centimetre									
		·0	·1	·2	·3	·4	·5	·6	·7	·8	·9
Centimetres	3			1		2	2	3	5	7	6
	4	7	8	10	8	7	5	4	4	4	1
	5	3	2		2	3	1		2		2
	6	1									

Group the lengths in class intervals of 0·3 cm, starting at 3·2 cm. Complete the frequency table, including a column of mid values X, and a column fX.

How many class intervals are there? Check that $\Sigma f = 100$ and that $\Sigma fX = 435·6$. Give (a) the class limits and (b) the class boundaries for the third class and the seventh class.
Name the modal class.

3.4 Histograms and frequency polygons

The information contained in a frequency distribution is often displayed pictorially in the form of a **histogram**.

Example 1. The table below shows the distribution of goals scored per match in the English Football Leagues, Divisions I to IV, on a particular Saturday in Season 1967–68.

Number of Goals X	0	1	2	3	4	5	6	7
Frequency f	0	9	10	7	7	5	4	2

Let us represent a frequency of one by the area of the following rectangle:

☐ Represents one unit of frequency

Then we can build a picture of the distribution as follows:

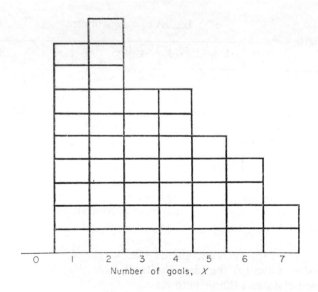

Fig. 3.1

How many values of the variable, that is how many values of X appear in the table? Into how many segments is the horizontal axis divided? Are these equal or unequal segments?

Use the diagram to count:

(a) The number of matches in which exactly four goals were scored.

(b) The number of matches in which fewer than four goals were scored.

(c) The number of matches in which more than one, but fewer than six goals were scored.

What does the total area of all the rectangles in the diagram represent?

If we now modify the diagram by omitting unnecessary cross lines, the frequencies will be represented by rectangular columns. Provided the horizontal axis is divided into **equal** segments, then the area of each column (which represents a frequency) is proportional to its height, so that a vertical axis with a scale corresponding to frequencies can be added.

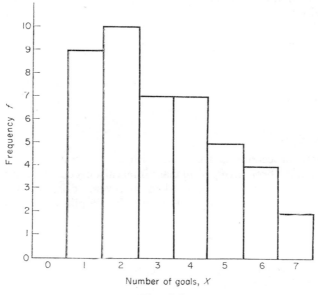

Fig. 3.2

A diagram like this is called a **histogram**. It must be emphasised again that it is **the area and not the height** of each column which represents frequency. The total area of all the rectangles represents the total frequency Σf.

Example 2. Drawing pins were sold in boxes stated to contain an average of two hundred pins per box. A sample of one hundred and seventy boxes gave the following distribution of contents per box:

Number of drawing pins X	197	198	199	200	201	202	203	204
Frequency f	7	12	32	58	38	14	6	3

Draw a histogram of the distribution using the area of a rectangle 1 cm long, 0·5 cm high, to represent a frequency of five. That is,

represents five units of frequency.

From the frequency table, what proportion of boxes contained two hundred or more pins?

From the histogram, what fraction of the total area is represented by the columns erected on the scores 200 to 204 inclusive?

Express as a percentage the number of boxes containing exactly two hundred pins.

Grouped data

The same procedure is followed with a distribution in which the variables have been grouped in class intervals, except that, in this case, the horizontal scale can be marked in several different ways. Also, the drawing of any histogram is greatly simplified using ruled or squared paper.

Example 3. The distribution of weekly wages of employees in a car assembly plant is:

Weekly wage £	5–9	10–14	15–19	20–24	25–29	30–34	35–39	40–44
Frequency f	28	92	240	147	182	87	34	18

Histogram of the distribution

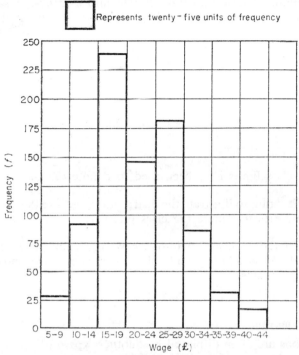

Fig. 3.3

Note that we have used the class limits to designate the segments of the horizontal axis. The axis could have been marked equally well using either:

(a) Mid values of the class intervals,

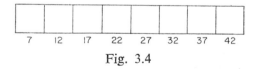

Fig. 3.4

(b) Class boundaries,

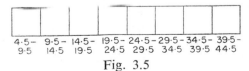

Fig. 3.5

Example 4. As part of an anti-smoking campaign, data was collected on the lengths of cigarette stubs thrown into ashtrays. A sample of one hundred and eighty stubs yielded the following distribution:

Stub length (centimetres)	1·2– 1·3	1·4– 1·5	1·6– 1·7	1·8– 1·9	2·0– 2·1	2·2– 2·3	2·4– 2·5	2·6– 2·7	2·8– 2·9	3·0– 3·1
Frequency f	5	7	12	14	20	29	43	34	10	6

Note that class limits have been used to denote the class intervals.

Make a histogram to illustrate the distribution, but use the appropriate class boundaries to denote the class intervals.

Now collect the information into a new frequency table using only **five** intervals. Make a histogram to illustrate the new table, and compare the two histograms.

Frequency polygons

Distributions are often displayed by another type of diagram called a **frequency polygon**.

Example 1. The following table shows the time taken by 34 girls to run over a measured distance:

Time (seconds)	49– 51	52– 54	55– 57	58– 60	61– 63	64– 66
Frequency f	2	3	13	9	6	1

The distribution is illustrated in Fig. 3.6 by a histogram, and in Fig. 3.7 by a frequency polygon both drawn with the same horizontal and vertical scales. Note that an extra interval has been added at each end to accommodate the end points of the polygon.

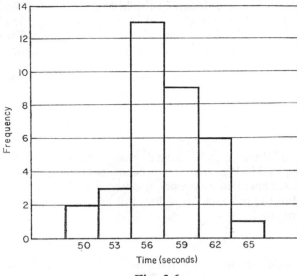

Fig. 3.6

Note that mid values have been used to denote the class intervals.

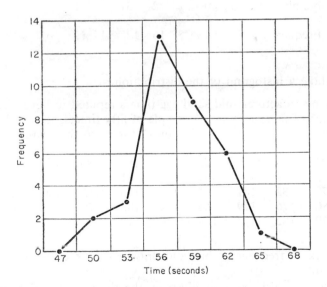

Fig. 3.7

How many columns are drawn in the histogram of Fig. 3.6?
How many **points** have been plotted in the polygon of Fig. 3.7?
Make a rough sketch of how the polygon would appear if we plotted only those points corresponding to a column of a histogram.

If you wished to draw a frequency polygon on the same diagram as the histogram, what would be the simplest method of doing so?

In the histogram, the square ☐ represents two units of frequency.

How many of these squares altogether are contained in the columns of the histogram? In Fig. 3.7, can you **count squares** (or parts of squares) to find the area enclosed by the polygon and the horizontal axis, that is the area **below** the polygon. How does this area compare with the area of the histogram?

Exercise 5

(1) The table below shows the distribution of goals scored per game in the seventy-four full soccer internationals, played between Scotland and Wales, from 1882 to 1967.

Number of goals	0	1	2	3	4	5	6	7	8	9
Frequency f	4	5	16	12	11	12	6	6	1	1

Make a histogram of the distribution.

(2) A manufacturer sold sand egg-timers reputed to have a running time of three minutes. A sample of fifty timers was checked and gave the following distribution of times (to the nearest second):

181	179	180	183	181	180	180	179	180	181
180	181	180	181	180	181	181	184	178	179
179	182	181	181	180	179	183	180	179	180
180	176	179	180	184	182	179	180	181	180
179	182	178	179	176	179	178	181	180	181

Make a frequency table, and draw a frequency polygon of the results.

(3) **Draw** a histogram to illustrate the distribution of weights of forty army recruits which was used previously.

Weight (kilogrammes)	53–55	56–58	59–61	62–64	65–67	68–70	71–73	74–76	77–79
Frequency f	1	2	4	9	9	5	4	4	2

Now make a new frequency table by grouping the weights into seven classes, each with an interval of 4 kg. Make a histogram to illustrate the new table.

(4) The diameters, in millimetres, of five hundred pellets of lead shot in a sample are recorded in the table. (The sizes were measured to an accuracy of 0·1 mm.)

Diameter (millimetres) (class limits)	0·7–0·9	1·0–1·2	1·3–1·5	1·6–1·8	1·9–2·1	2·2–2·4	2·5–2·7	2·8–3·0
Class boundaries								
Mid values								
Frequency f	12	48	115	103	83	71	54	14

Copy the table and complete the rows of class boundaries and mid values. Make a frequency polygon of the distribution.

(5) Sixty torch batteries from a consignment of seven hundred and fifty were tested by using continuously until exhausted. Their lifetimes in hours (measured to an accuracy of 0·1 hours) are recorded below:

7·8	8·3	5·4	7·1	6·6	10·4	8·4	9·2	8·3	7·9
8·5	5·0	6·2	7·8	6·2	8·5	8·6	9·0	9·8	8·1
5·9	9·2	10·2	8·7	7·9	9·6	5·9	9·4	9·2	7·2
8·5	8·6	8·0	8·0	9·0	5·8	6·9	7·0	6·9	7·5
8·9	10·0	9·2	8·4	8·2	6·4	8·0	6·2	5·4	8·9
7·7	9·5	9·5	8·4	9·9	6·4	7·4	5·5	8·6	8·0

(a) What is the range of lifetimes? Make a frequency table of the lifetimes using class intervals of an appropriate size.

(b) Add a column of mid values, X, and a final column showing the products, fX. Find ΣfX.

(c) Make a histogram, and also a frequency polygon of the distribution.

3.5 Relative frequency

Note. The reading of this section, and of section **3.6**, may be omitted at this stage, but both sections should be studied before reading Chapter 7 on probability.

Shown again is the frequency distribution of the marks of forty pupils, which was used previously in section **3.1**.

Mark	0	1	2	3	4	5	6	7	8	9	10
Frequency f	0	1	3	4	5	5	9	7	4	1	1

Total frequency $= N = \Sigma f = 40$

What proportion of pupils scored exactly four marks? Exactly eight marks? Give the answers first as common (vulgar) fractions, and then as decimal fractions to three decimal places.

What proportion of pupils scored between four marks and six marks inclusive?

These, and similar questions can, of course, be answered by referring to the table above. However, it often proves very useful to add a row, or column, to the table showing the proportion, or as it is called the **relative frequency** of occurrence of each score.

For example, five pupils scored four marks, so that the relative frequency of occurrence of the score four marks is found:

$$\text{relative frequency} = \frac{f}{\Sigma f} = \frac{5}{40} = 0 \cdot 125$$

Copy and complete the table below, showing the relative frequencies for the above distribution to three decimal places.

Mark X	Frequency f	Relative frequency $\frac{f}{\Sigma f}$
0	0	0·000
1	1	0·025
2	3	0·075
.	.	
.	.	
.	.	

From the table, what is the relative frequency of
   (a) The score of eight marks,
   (b) The scores four to six marks inclusive?
What is the **sum** of all the relative frequencies?

Exercise 6

(1) Here again is the frequency distribution of breakdowns per
    month recorded by a road haulage firm, which appeared
    previously in section **3.1,** exercise 1.

Number of breakdowns	0	1	2	3	4	5	6
Frequency f	12	13	12	6	2	2	1

   (a) Copy the table and add to it a row of relative frequencies,
       (to three decimal places).
   (b) What is the relative frequency of occurrence of no break-
       downs? Of four or more breakdowns?
   (c) What is the sum of all the relative frequencies?

(2) Here again is the frequency distribution of the weights of soap
    powder per carton, which also appeared in section **3.1,** exercise 1

Weight per carton (kilogrammes)	0·97	0·98	0 99	1·00	1·01	1·02	1·03
Frequency f	3	4	12	13	10	6	2

c

(a) Copy the table and add to it a row of relative frequencies.
(b) What proportion of cartons is
    (i) Below the advertised weight of 1·00 kg,
    (ii) Above the advertised weight?
(c) What is the sum of all the relative frequencies?

3.6 Relative frequency histograms and polygons

Note. The reading of section **3.5**, and of this section, may be omitted at this stage, but both sections should be studied before reading Chapter 7 on probability.

Previously we saw how the information contained in a frequency distribution could be displayed pictorially as a histogram. In very similar fashion, the information contained in a relative frequency distribution can be displayed as a **relative frequency histogram.**

Example 1. Let us use again the distribution of marks of forty pupils, and add to it a row of relative frequencies.

Mark	0	1	2	3	4	5	6	7	8	9	10
Frequency f	0	1	3	4	5	5	9	7	4	1	1
Relative frequency	·000	·025	·075	·100	·125	·125	·225	·175	·100	·025	·025

Total frequency $\Sigma f = 40$

If we represent a relative frequency of 0·025 by the area of a suitable rectangle, we can build a picture of the relative frequency distribution, as shown in the partially completed diagram below.

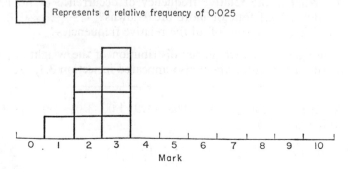

Represents a relative frequency of 0·025

Fig. 3.8

Copy and complete Fig. 3.8, by erecting on the scores four to ten inclusive the appropriate numbers of rectangles. How many rectangles will be erected on the score six marks? What does the area of these rectangles represent?

What does the total area of all the rectangles in the figure represent?

As in the case of a histogram, provided we make all horizontal intervals equal, we can attach a vertical scale of relative frequencies and omit unnecessary cross lines:

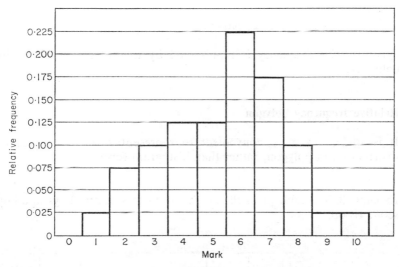

Fig. 3.9

This diagram is called a **relative frequency histogram.**

The area of any column represents the proportion, or relative frequency of occurrence, of the corresponding score. **The total area of all columns represents a relative frequency of one.**

Example 2. In a Scottish school the numbers of ordinary grade S.C.E. passes obtained by 100 pupils gave the distribution below:

Numbers of passes	0	1	2	3	4	5	6	7	8
Frequency f	3	15	20	29	16	8	5	3	1
Relative frequency $\dfrac{f}{\Sigma f}$	0·03	0·15							

Total frequency $\Sigma f =$

Copy the table and complete the row of relative frequencies. On suitable squared paper, and using the area of a one centimetre square to represent a relative frequency of 0·05, draw the relative frequency histogram of the distribution.

Use your diagram to find the proportion of pupils obtaining:

(a) Six or more passes,

(b) Fewer than three passes.

What relative frequency is represented by the total area of all the columns?

Relative frequency polygon

It is sometimes more convenient to represent a relative frequency distribution in polygon, rather than histogram form.

Example 3. The table gives the heights in metres of fifty boys in a boy scout troop.

Height (metres)	1·45– 1·49	1·50– 1·54	1·55– 1·59	1·60– 1·64	1·65– 1·69	1·70– 1·74	1·75– 1·79
Frequency f	3	4	17	12	9	3	2
Relative frequency	0·06	0·08					

Complete the row of relative frequencies. Draw the relative frequency histogram of the distribution, using a one centimetre square to represent a relative frequency of 0·05.

Draw also the relative frequency polygon of the distribution, using the same horizontal and vertical scales. How many points should be plotted to draw your polygon? Compare your polygon with Fig. 3.10.

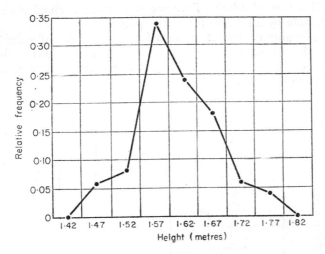

Fig. 3.10

Note that the class intervals are denoted by the mid values. What does the total area under the relative frequency polygon represent?

Exercise 7

(1) The distribution of wages in a small factory shown below was used previously in section **3.3**, exercise 4.

Weekly wage (£)	6·5– 9·5	9·5– 12·5	12·5– 15·5	15·5– 18·5	18·5– 21·5	21·5– 24·5	24·5– 27·5
Frequency f	4	5	9	16	12	3	1

Add to the table a row showing relative frequencies, and illustrate the results by a relative frequency polygon.

(2) The distribution of lifetimes of torch batteries shown below was used previously in section **3.4**, exercise 5.

Lifetime (hours)	5·0– 5·9	6·0– 6·9	7·0– 7·9	8·0– 8·9	9·0– 9·9	10·0– 10·9
Frequency f	7	8	10	21	11	3

Add a row of relative frequencies to three decimal places and illustrate by a relative frequency polygon.

(3) In a quality control check in a factory, samples of a fluid were tested, and the specific gravity measured, correct to two decimal places. The readings are illustrated by the relative frequency histogram below.

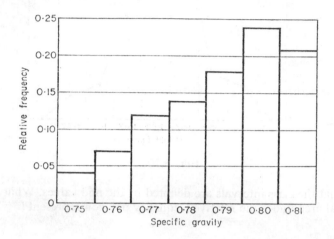

Fig. 3.11

(a) If the specific gravity of the fluid was intended to be 0·80, what proportion of the samples had this specific gravity?

(b) If a specific gravity of less than 0·79 renders the fluid unsuitable for use, what proportion of the samples should be rejected?

(c) If the relative frequency histogram was prepared from the results of two hundred readings, how many readings were recorded of specific gravity,
   (i) 0·81,
   (ii) 0·77?

(d) Calculate the frequencies of readings for the other five values of the specific gravity. Write them in the form of a frequency distribution, and hence calculate the value of ΣfX.

(4) The average weekly earnings of four hundred employees in a Birmingham factory are shown in the distribution of Table 1 below. The average weekly earnings of the two hundred and fifty employees in the factory operated by the same company in the north east of England are shown in Table 2.

Average weekly earnings (£)	10–14	15–19	20–24	25–29	30–34	35–39
Frequency f	69	104	112	60	43	12

Table 1

Average weekly earnings (£)	10–14	15–19	20–24	25–29	30–34	35–39
Frequency f	55	71	74	29	16	5

Table 2

Draw two histograms side by side, using the same horizontal and vertical scales to represent the two distributions. Are the two diagrams suitable for making comparisons of the wage distribution in the two factories? Give a reason for your answer.

To each table add a row of relative frequencies (to three decimal places) and draw, side by side, to the same scale, the relative frequency histograms for the two distributions. Are these diagrams suitable for making comparisons of the distribution of earnings?

What conclusions would you reach regarding the earnings in the two factories by comparing their relative frequency histograms?

(5) The first hundred words in a book gave the following distribution of number of letters per word:

Number of letters per word	1	2	3	4	5	6	7	8	9	10	11	12
Frequency f	2	18	21	20	9	7	7	4	8	1	1	2

Add to the table a row showing relative frequencies, and illustrate the results by a relative frequency histogram, and also a relative frequency polygon. From the histogram find the proportion of words of:

(a) Exactly five letters.

(b) Eight or more letters.

(6) In a knockout tennis tournament altogether sixty matches were played. The number of games played in each match is shown in the following array:

18	20	28	71	59	28	80	21	48	44	24	38
24	55	34	60	35	69	40	55	34	33	30	41
31	19	42	33	91	32	52	23	26	32	33	29
41	31	56	28	24	23	28	24	32	28	59	41
18	30	28	22	26	31	35	30	40	27	40	39

Make a frequency distribution from the data, using eight classes with a class interval of ten games. Add a column of mid-values X, and another column showing fX. Find ΣfX. State what the number ΣfX represents, and whether it is a precise or an approximate representation.

Add a column of relative frequencies (to three decimal places), and illustrate the distribution by a relative frequency histogram and a relative frequency polygon.

CHAPTER 4

Averages or Measures of Central Location

4.1 Mean, median and mode

Once a set of observations has been tabulated in the form of a frequency distribution, it is often convenient to find some single value to represent the distribution as a whole. In statistics such values are called **averages**. Three kinds of average are described in this section.

1. Mean

Example 1. In a rifle competition each competitor fired 10 shots at a target from a distance of 200 yards. The number of bulls scored by a group of 13 competitors was as follows:

7, 3, 8, 5, 10, 7, 8, 5, 8, 9, 2, 9, 10.

It may be considered that 5 bulls out of 10 is quite good shooting, but how does a marksman with this score compare with the group?

Can you suggest a suitable way of making this comparison? Here is one way. Find the total number of bulls scored by the 13 competitors and imagine this total shared equally by all 13. How many bulls would this give to each competitor? How does the score of 5 bulls out of 10 shots compare with this average score?

Example 2. A group of 12 other competitors took part in the competition and out of 10 shots scored bulls as follows:

4, 8, 5, 8, 6, 4, 7, 7, 2, 3, 5, 7.

How does this second group of 12 compare with the first 13?
Why would it be misleading to compare the groups by their respective total scores?
Can you suggest a suitable way of making this comparison? Here is one way. Average the 12 scores in the same way as the previous 13 were averaged.
What was the average found for the previous 13 scores?
Which group of marksmen fared better in the competition?
The number which you have just calculated in each of the above examples is called the **arithmetic mean,** or simply the **mean.**
We calculate the mean of a set of observations thus:

$$\text{mean} = \frac{\text{sum of observations}}{\text{number of observations}}$$

In example 2 above,

$$\text{mean} = \frac{66}{12}$$

$$= 5 \cdot 5$$

Notation. In all the examples on frequency distributions, presented in chapter 3, the observations or scores were denoted by the symbol X. From now on we will use one of two symbols to denote the observations. If the observations with which we are dealing form a **sample** from a larger population we will continue to use the symbol X, and we will denote the mean of the sample by $\bar{X}$. The number of observations in the sample we denote by N.

Thus for samples:

$$\text{mean} = \frac{\text{sum of observations}}{\text{number of observations}}$$

$$\text{i.e. } \bar{X} = \frac{\Sigma X}{N}$$

In example 1 above,

$$\bar{X} = \frac{\Sigma X}{N} = \frac{91}{13} = 7$$

If, however, the observations form a complete **population** then we denote the observations by x and denote the mean of the population by the Greek letter μ (mu). The number of observations in the population we denote by n. Thus, for populations:

$$\text{mean} = \frac{\text{sum of observations}}{\text{number of observations}}$$

i.e. $\mu = \dfrac{\Sigma x}{n}$

For example if the 25 marksmen in examples 1 and 2 above formed the **entire population** of competitors:

$$\mu = \frac{\Sigma x}{n} = \frac{157}{25} = 6\cdot3, \text{ to one decimal place.}$$

If at any time we are in doubt as to whether the observations form a sample or a population, we use the sample notation.

Uses of the mean

In example 1, the mean of a distribution was used as a standard with which any single observation could be compared.

In example 2, the means of two distributions were used to compare the two distributions with each other.

Exercise 1

(1) Calculate the mean of each of the following sets of observations (to 2 significant figures). Regard (a) and (c) as samples and calculate $\overline{X}$. Regard (b) as a population and calculate μ.

(a) 18, 20, 21, 17, 14, 29, 33, 31, 24.

(b) 7·6, 11·1, 4·4, 5·6, 10·0, 12·2, 9·0, 9·8, 5·8, 5·1, 7·8, 8·9.

(c) 0·031, 0·042, 0·039, 0·045, 0·034, 0·041.

(2) Fourteen girls who replied to an advertisement for a secretarial job were tested on their typing speeds. The speeds which they attained in words per minute were as follows:

36, 41, 58, 45, 47, 51, 42, 43, 41, 40, 42, 43, 48, 45.

Calculate the mean typing speed attained and state how many of the girls attained a speed greater than the mean.

(3) The numbers of runs scored by three batsmen, Green, White and Brown, in the innings which they played during the first month of a cricket season were as follows:

Green	48	13	0	60	72	24			
White	14	18	31	31	1	50	52	49	8
Brown	4	0	102	81	13	13	0	105	

Calculate the mean number of runs per innings scored by each batsman. Assuming that each innings was completed (i.e. the batsman was given out) this mean number is known as the player's batting average. Place the three batsmen in order according to their batting averages.

2. Median

Example 1. A schools' football league has 20 teams. Each team plays every other team twice, one match at home, one match away. Since it was taking too long to complete the league programme, it was decided to split the league into a first division of the 10 most successful teams and a second division of the remaining 10 teams. The numbers of points scored by the teams in the last season before dividing were:

38	32	41	30	35	51	40	34	17	55
18	46	19	48	58	34	25	40	62	37

Which 10 teams should comprise the first division?
Did you require to calculate the mean to answer this question?

Example 2. Now consider again a marksman in the group of thirteen who hit five bulls with his ten shots (example 1, page 59). Would his score of five put him in the top half or the lower half of his group? To find out arrange the thirteen scores in ascending order, and mark off the middle score:

2   3   5   5   7   7   / 8 /   8   8   9   9   10   10

When a set of observations is arranged in order like this the middle score is called the **median.** Thus the median score of the group of thirteen was eight bulls, so that the competitor with five bulls was in the lower half of the group.
Suppose you were given a list of 21 observations arranged in order. When the middle one is marked off, as in example 2, how many remain?

How many observations lie below the median, and how many above? Which observation would be the median of an ordered list containing 33 observations? 45 observations?
Describe how you would find the median of a list containing an odd number of observations (not arranged in order).

Example 3. Find the median of the scores 14, 3, 12, 17, 14, 5, 8, 9. Obviously, since this distribution contains an even number of observations, when they are arranged in order there is no middle score which can be chosen as median. However, the observations can be divided into upper and lower halves:

$$3 \quad 5 \quad 8 \quad 9 \quad / \quad 12 \quad 14 \quad 14 \quad 17$$

The median is chosen to be the mean of the **two** middle observations:

$$\text{median} = \frac{9+12}{2} = 10 \cdot 5$$

Example 4. A small knitwear factory has a staff consisting of 10 girls, 1 forewoman and a manageress, who receive the following weekly wages (in pounds):

$$10 \quad 10 \quad 10 \quad 10 \quad 10 \quad 11 \quad 11 \quad 11 \quad 13 \quad 14 \quad 20 \quad 50$$

Find the mean and median of the distribution.
Which is a better representative of the distribution as a whole, the mean or the median? Try to give reasons for your answers.

3. Mode

In some distributions one observation occurs more frequently than any other. We have already met this term when dealing with frequency distributions. When one observation in a distribution occurs more frequently than any of the others, it is called the **mode**.
For example, in the wages distribution for the knitwear factory the modal wage, or mode, is £10.
The mean, median and mode are three distinct averages or central measures, each of which can be used to represent the distribution as a whole. The mean is the most frequently used representative but is there, in fact, a need for the other two? To help answer the question let us use as an illustration the distribution of wages in the knitwear factory (example 4, above), for which you have already calculated the mean and median wages.

$$\text{Mean wage} = \frac{£180}{12} = £15$$

This is a poor representative for the distribution since no one in fact earns this amount and only two persons out of the twelve earn more than £15.

The wages arranged in order are:

10 10 10 10 10 11 / 11 11 13 14 20 50

$$\text{Median wage} = \frac{£11+£11}{2} = £11$$

This is a better representative since roughly half the personnel earn more, and roughly half earn less, than £11.

In fact in this case the modal wage of £10 is possibly the best representative since the largest group of workers, five out of twelve, actually earn this amount.

Exercise 2

(1) Find the mean, the median and the mode of each of the following lists of numbers, regarding (a), (c) and (d) as samples and (b) as a population.

(a) 19, 21, 17, 14, 12, 4, 8, 17, 16.
(b) 10, 4, 3, 2, 1, 9, 7, 2, 8, 4, 9,
    6, 5, 5, 8, 4, 3, 9, 8, 1, 2.
(c) 41, 82, 29, 49, 78, 60, 56, 65, 69, 71, 36.
(d) 7, 9, 4, 9, 3, 7, 8, 10, 11, 6, 12, 10.

(2) For each of the following distributions calculate the mean, the median and the mode, and state which of the three would best represent the distribution as a whole.

(a) Examination marks in English of a class of 15 girls. (Regard this as a population.)

58, 61, 48, 43, 62, 62, 51, 43, 54, 43, 70, 65, 42, 59, 48.

(b) Mathematics marks of the same class.

49, 53, 87, 56, 45, 38, 54, 39, 62, 70, 41, 43, 83, 49, 49.

(c) Daily noon temperatures in °C at a seaside resort over a 14 day period.

19, 20, 19, 17, 21, 18, 19, 24, 25, 25, 28, 25, 23, 18.

(3) Find the distribution of shoe sizes of the pupils in your class. Calculate the mean, median and mode of the distribution. Which of the three averages do you think a shoe manufacturer would be most interested in?

4.2 To find the mean of a frequency distribution

Example 1. The ages (in years, to the nearest year) of all the tradesmen 29 years of age and under who work in a small factory are given in the following table:

24	21	26	25	27	23	25	22	25	23
26	21	25	24	23	21	25	24	24	26
27	23	28	24	22	25	26	24	22	25

Copy and complete the frequency table. Verify that $\Sigma f = 30$, and that $\Sigma fX = 726$.

Age (years) X		f	fX
21	I I I	3	63
22			
23	I I I I	4	92
24			
25			
26			
27			
28			
		$\Sigma f = 30$	$\Sigma fX = 726$

Since the sum of the observations is given by the total ΣfX, and the number of observations by Σf,

$$\text{mean} = \frac{\text{sum of observations}}{\text{number of observations}}$$

i.e.
$$\bar{X} = \frac{\Sigma fX}{\Sigma f} = \frac{726}{30} = 24\cdot2 \text{ years}$$

As we found in chapter 3, in the case of a grouped frequency distribution, the mid-values of the class intervals are used to represent the variable X. We then calculate $\bar{X}$ exactly as above.

Example 2. In a series of experiments on silver plating the weight of silver deposited on an electrode in a fixed period was measured. The frequency distribution was as follows:

Weight of silver deposited (grammes)	0·30–0·34	0·35–0·39	0·40–0·44	0·45–0·49	0·50–0·54	0·55–0·59	0·60–0·64	0·65–0·69	0·70–0·74
Frequency f	2	5	10	20	16	9	6	3	1

Copy and complete the frequency table:

Weight of silver (grammes)	Mid-values X	Frequency f	fX
0·30—0·34	0·32	2	0·64
0·35—0·39	0·37	5	1·85
0·40—0·44	0·42	10	4·20
.	.	.	
.	.	.	
.	.	.	
		$\Sigma f = 72$	$\Sigma fX = 35\cdot99$

Verify that $\Sigma f = 72$, $\Sigma fX = 35\cdot99$ and calculate the mean weight correct to 2 decimal places.

Exercise 3

(1) In an experiment with lupin plants the number of seeds per pod was recorded. The frequency distribution is given:

Number of seeds per pod X	1	2	3	4	5	6	7	8	9	10	11	12
Frequency f	0	0	1	3	7	11	14	15	14	7	2	1

Find the mean number of seeds per pod. Find also the mode of this distribution, and compare the two measures of central location.

(2) The weekly wages distribution of the employees in a vehicle repair workshop is shown in the table:

Weekly wage (£)	Number of employees
7—9	4
10—12	5
13—15	9
16—18	16
19—21	12
22—24	3
25—27	1

Regard the total number of employees as being the entire population of the factory. Copy the table and add a column of mid-values, x. Hence calculate Σfx and find the mean wage.

$$\mu = \frac{\Sigma fx}{\Sigma f}$$

(3) Throw a die 100 times and make a frequency distribution of the 6 possible scores. Find the mean of this distribution.

(4) A sample of a tomato crop was taken and each tomato was weighed and the weights were recorded to the nearest 5 g.

60	60	55	55	60	50	60	60	65	65
65	50	65	70	70	55	65	65	50	70
65	60	55	60	50	60	55	60	65	60
55	60	60	60	60	55	65	55	55	55
60	65	50	70	55	65	55	70	60	65

Make a frequency distribution of these weights, and find the mean and the mode of the distribution.

(5) The lengths of 100 sweet pea shoots were measured to an accuracy of 0·1 cm and the frequencies were recorded in the table:

Length		Tenths of centimetres									
		·0	·1	·2	·3	·4	·5	·6	·7	·8	·9
Centimetres	3			1		2	2	3	5	7	6
	4	7	8	10	8	7	5	4	4	4	1
	5	3	2		2	3	1		2		2
	6	1									

Write this table out as a frequency distribution and find the mean length of the sweet pea shoots.

(6) The diameters (measured to 0·1 mm) of 500 pellets of lead shot are given in the table:

Diameter (millimetres)	0·7– 0·9	1·0– 1·2	1·3– 1·5	1·6– 1·8	1·9– 2·1	2·2– 2·4	2·5– 2·7	2·8– 3·0
Frequency f	12	48	115	103	83	71	54	14

Calculate the mean diameter. What is the modal class of the distribution? Compare the mean with the mid-value of the modal class.

4.3 Shorter methods for calculating the mean

1. Frequency distributions

Example 1. By adding 6 to each of the numbers in list A (19, 21, 15, 14, 12, 4, 8, 16, 17) we obtain list B (25, 27, 21, 20, 18, 10, 14, 22, 23). Calculate the means of lists A and B. How does the mean of list B compare with the mean of list A?

Example 2. By subtracting 10 from each of the numbers in list C (4, 7, 8, 10, 11, 6, 12, 10) we obtain list D (–6, –3, –2, 0, 1, –4, 2, 0). Calculate the means of lists C and D. How could you obtain the mean of list C from the mean of list D?

Example 3. Here is another list P (21·3, 20·5, 20·3, 21·1, 20·7, 20·9). Form a new list Q by subtracting 20 from each number in P. Find the mean of list Q. Using this mean, can you **write down** the mean of list P? Verify your answer by calculating the mean of list P in the usual way.

To calculate the mean of a distribution we subtract a constant A, from each observation, find the mean of the new scores and add A. The mean of the original scores is equal to the mean of the new scores plus A.

Example 4. The frequency distribution of ages of tradesmen under 30 (section **4.2**, example 1) is shown again:

Age (years) X	21	22	23	24	25	26	27	28
Frequency f	3	3	4	6	7	4	2	1

Notice that near the middle of the distribution, the two values of the variable with the largest frequencies are 24 and 25. We assume that the mean age will be around 24 years, and accordingly we choose 24 as our **assumed mean**, denoted by A. We subtract 24 from each value of the variable X, to form a new set of values $X—A$. We find the mean of $X—A$ in the usual way.

Age (years) X	Frequency f	$X—A$	$f(X—A)$
21	3	−3	−9 ⎫
22	3	−2	−6 ⎬ −19
23	4	−1	−4 ⎭
$A{\to}24$	6	0	0
25	7	1	7 ⎫
26	4	2	8 ⎬ +25
27	2	3	6 ⎪
28	1	4	4 ⎭
	$\Sigma f = 30$		$\Sigma f(X—A) = +6$

Mean of the values $(X—A)$ is given by

$$\frac{\Sigma f(X—A)}{\Sigma f} = \frac{6}{30} = 0·2$$

Mean of the values X,

$$\bar{X} = 0.2 + A = 0.2 + 24 = 24.2 \text{ years.}$$

Example 5. The temperatures at which samples of a new type of semi-conductor device failed to operate were recorded in degrees Centigrade and gave the following distribution. Use an assumed mean of 83°C. to verify that the mean failure temperature is 82·6°C.

Failure temperature (°C) X	Frequency f	X−A	f(X−A)
79	3		−12
80	9		
81	16	−2	
82	24		
A→83	28	0	
84	15		
85	11		22
86	4		
	$\Sigma f =$		$\Sigma f(X-A) =$

Mean of the values $(X-A)$ is given by

$$\frac{\Sigma f(X-A)}{\Sigma f} = \frac{\quad}{\quad} = -0.4$$

Hence $\quad \bar{X} = -0.4 + A = \quad + \quad = 82.6°C.$

Exercise 4

(1) An East of Scotland amateur golf tournament was played over 18 holes. The distribution of qualifying scores in the tournament is shown. Use the assumed mean technique to find the mean qualifying score.

Score X	69	70	71	72	73	74	75	76	77
Frequency f	2	0	3	11	13	17	13	10	11

(2) The distribution of the numbers of hours of instruction required by a flight of cadet pilots before flying solo is shown in the table. Regard the flight of cadets as a population. Use an assumed mean, $A = 15$ hours, to form a new set of values $(x-A)$.

Calculate the mean of the values $(x-A)$ and hence find the population mean, μ.

Find also the population mode and compare these two central measures.

Number of hours x	12	13	14	15	16	17	18	19	20
Frequency f	3	6	8	10	7	6	5	3	2

(3) The Ministry of Social Security checked on the retiral ages of a sample of male pensioners and found the following distribution:

Age (years) X	61	62	63	64	65	66	67	68	69	70	71	72
Frequency f	8	13	20	26	35	33	28	25	23	14	10	5

Use the assumed mean technique to find the mean retiral age.

(4) A machine designed to pack sugar in 500 g cartons was thought to be faulty. A sample of its output showed the following distribution:

Weight packed (grammes) X	492	493	494	495	496	497	498	499	500	501	502
Frequency f	2	0	3	4	12	26	38	24	17	10	4

Find the mean weight packed and compare with the modal weight.

(5) Draw a random sample of fifty pupils from your school, as described in section **2.3**, experiment 2. Find the age in years of

every pupil in your sample and make a frequency table of the ages. Use the assumed mean technique to calculate the mean age of the pupils in your sample. Can you now make an estimate of the mean age of all the pupils in the school population?

(6) A weather ship recorded the atmospheric pressure every four hours. At the end of a week the following readings (in millibars) had been obtained:

```
1005  998 1004 1008 1001 1007 1006 1000 1001 1002  998
1006 1001 1005  999 1001 1006 1002 1002  999 1005 1000
1005 1003 1000 1002 1003 1000 1000 1001 1003 1003 1002
1002  997 1003  995 1004  997  999 1004 1009 1000 1003
```

Calculate the mean atmospheric pressure.

2. Shorter methods for grouped frequencies

Example 1. Let us refer again to list C of numbers (4, 7, 8, 10, 11, 6, 12, 10) previously used on page 68. If we multiply each number in C by 3, we obtain list D (12, 21, 24, 30, 33, 18, 36, 30). Calculate the means of lists C and D. How does the mean of list C compare with the mean of list D?

Example 2. Given list F (50, 70, 25, 85, 10, 45, 70, 40, 95) divide each number by 5 to obtain list G. Calculate the means of lists F and G. How could you obtain the mean of list F from the mean of list G?

Example 3. Given list H (−12, −8, −4, 0, 4, 8, 12, 16, 20, 24) divide each number by 4 to obtain list K. From the mean of list K can you **write down** the mean of list H? Verify your answer by calculating the mean of list H in the usual way.

These examples illustrate that multiplying (or dividing) all the observations of a distribution by a constant causes the mean to be multiplied (or divided) by the same constant.

Exercise 5

(1) The mean of the list (6, 10, 12, 16, 26) is 14.
Write down the means of:

(a) (3, 5, 6, 8, 13),
(b) (9, 15, 18, 24, 39),
(c) (24, 40, 48, 64, 104),
(d) (30, 50, 60, 80, 130),
(e) (60, 100, 120, 160, 260).

(2) Calculate the mean of 0, 1, 2, 3, 4 and hence **write down** the means of:

(a)   0,   5,   10,   15,   20,
(b) 50, 55,   60,   65,   70,
(c) 10, 11,   12,   13,   14,
(d) 100, 110, 120, 130, 140,
(e)   0,   9,   18,   27,   36.

(3) Find the mean of the scores 170, 180, 190, 200, 210, 220, 230, 240. Subtract 200 from each score to give the scores in the second column of the following table, and then divide each new score by 10 to obtain the scores in the third column. Copy and complete the table.

Scores X	$X-200$	$U = \dfrac{X-200}{10}$
170	−30	−3
180	−20	−2
190		
200	0	0
210		
220		
230		
240		
		$\Sigma U = 4$

Verify that the mean of the scores U is given by,

$$\bar{U} = \frac{\Sigma U}{8} = \frac{4}{8} = 0{\cdot}5$$

Hence deduce that the mean of the scores X,
$$\bar{X} = 200 + 10 \times 0{\cdot}5$$
$$= 205$$

(4) Find the mean of the scores 1 985, 1 990, 1 995, 2 000, 2 005, 2 010, 2 015, 2 020. (**Hint.** Subtract 2 000 from each score, then divide by 5.)

(5) Find the mean of the scores 272, 280, 288, 296, 304, 312, 320, 328, 336, 344. (**Hint.** Subtract 304, then divide by 8.)

(6) Find the mean of the scores 27, 36, 45, 54, 63, 72, 81, 90, 99.

(7) Find the mean of the scores 310, 321, 332, 343, 354, 365, 376, 387, 398, 409.

We use the above properties to shorten the calculation of the means of grouped frequency distributions.

Example 4. The following frequency table shows the distribution of ages of bridegrooms (to the nearest year) whose marriages were recorded in a Registry Office in one week. Calculate the mean age of bridegrooms.

Age (years)	16–20	21–25	26–30	31–35	36–40	41–45	46–50
Frequency f	7	17	14	12	8	5	1

Following is the frequency table of the distribution. The mid-value 28 is chosen as a suitable assumed mean and a new set of values $(X—28)$ formed. Since the size of the class interval is 5, we form the set of values U, where

$$U = \frac{X—28}{5}$$

Now we find $\overline{U}$, the mean of U, in the usual way, and from $\overline{U}$ we calculate $\overline{X}$

Age of bridegroom (years)	Mid-values X	Frequency f	$X–A$	$U = \dfrac{X–A}{5}$	fU
16—20	18	7	−10	−2	−14 ⎱ −31
21—25	23	17	−5	−1	−17 ⎰
26—30	$A{\to}28$	14	0	0	0
31—35	33	12	5	1	12 ⎱
36—40	38	8	10	2	16 ⎱ +47
41—45	43	5	15	3	15 ⎰
46—50	48	1	20	4	4 ⎰
		$\Sigma f = 64$			$\Sigma fU = 16$

Then $\overline{U} = \dfrac{\Sigma fU}{\Sigma f} = \dfrac{16}{64} = 0{\cdot}25$

so that $\overline{X} = 28 + 5 \times 0{\cdot}25 = 29{\cdot}25$ years.

Example 5. In section **4.2**, example 2, the distribution of weights of silver deposited on an electrode was given and the mean weight calculated. Copy and complete the following table, and again calculate the mean weight of silver, using the assumed mean of 0·47 g. Note that the class interval is 0·05 g.

Weight of silver (grammes)	Mid-values X	Frequency f	$X-\cdot47$	$U = \dfrac{X-\cdot47}{0\cdot05}$	fU
0·30–0·34	0·32	2	—0·15	—3	—6
0·35–0·39		5			
0·40–0·44		10			
0·45–0·49	$A\to0\cdot47$	20	0	0	0
0·50–0·54		16			
0·55–0·59		9	0·10		
0·60–0·64		6			18
0·65–0·69		3			
0·70–0·74	0·72	1		5	
		$\Sigma f =$			$\Sigma fU=$

Verify that $\Sigma f = 72$ and that $\Sigma fU = 43$

Then $\qquad \bar{U} = \underline{\qquad\qquad} = 0\cdot597$

and $\qquad \bar{X} = 0\cdot47 + 0\cdot05 \times 0\cdot597$

$\qquad\qquad =$

$\qquad\qquad = 0\cdot50$ g correct to 2 decimal places.

Compare the amount of working above with that required using the longer method in example 2, page 66.

Exercise 6

(1) The table shows the winning points totals of Scottish Football League (Division I) champions between the years 1920 and 1966. (In certain war years there was no competition.) Make a frequency table using class intervals of size 5 points and by choosing a suitable assumed mean calculate the mean winning points total.

66	59	60	66	76	46	48	49	50	57
76	60	67	62	61	48	45	52	54	55
67	58	60	66	61	46	43	55	51	50
55	56	60	55	59	50	43	62	54	57

(2) The weights in kilogrammes of 55 head of cattle sold at a fatstock sale were as follows:

523	515	530	590	550	535	568	424	466	601	480
583	563	542	601	577	511	582	607	577	592	525
605	475	409	595	428	563	541	525	533	552	569
529	511	542	478	471	572	544	555	553	522	598
567	520	481	538	520	592	590	484	573	549	579

Make a grouped frequency table using class intervals of 25 kilogrammes starting with 400–424 kilogrammes. Choose a suitable assumed mean and find the mean weight to the nearest kilogramme. How many head of cattle were above the mean weight?

(3) In a survey of industrial earnings, a sample of 60 workers paid on a time basis were found to be paid at the following hourly rates (in pence):

42	38	39	36	39	56	30	54	36	58	29	34
44	46	35	47	48	66	27	45	33	37	34	45
33	30	49	72	52	44	35	47	28	41	50	53
28	41	25	50	56	48	39	42	51	45	60	62
36	56	30	54	60	38	68	44	64	42	38	66

Make a frequency table using class intervals of five pence. Choose a suitable assumed mean, and calculate the mean hourly rate to the nearest penny. Compare the mean with the mid-value of the modal class.

(4) Select a random sample of fifty pupils in your school. Question each pupil to find the average time in minutes he or she spends in travelling from home to school each morning. Make a frequency table of the times using suitable class intervals, and calculate the mean travelling time using the assumed mean technique.

(5) Choose a book and open it at any page at random. Count, and make a note of, the number of words in the first sentence on the page. Repeat the count for the second sentence, the third, and so on until you have completed 100 sentences. Make a grouped frequency distribution of the data, and use the assumed mean technique to find the mean number of words per sentence.

(6) The noise-levels (in decibels) at 150 selected locations near an airfield were recorded during the take-off of a large jet aircraft. The distribution obtained was as follows:

Noise level (decibels)	64·5– 69·5	69·5– 74·5	74·5– 79·5	79·5– 84·5	84·5– 89·5	89·5– 94·5	94·5– 99·5	99·5– 104·5	104·5– 109·5
Frequency f	3	5	8	14	40	54	22	3	1

Calculate the mean noise level. If a noise level of about 85 decibels or above is considered to make a site totally unsuitable for housing, what proportion of the locations should be considered unsuitable?

(7) The first year mathematics students at a university were divided into two sections and taught the work of the first term by two quite different methods. They sat a common examination which produced the following distributions of marks:

Section A

Mark	20–29	30–39	40–49	50–59	60–69	70–79	80–89	90–99
Frequency f	2	6	12	13	22	21	16	4

Section B

Mark	20–29	30–39	40–49	50–59	60–69	70–79	80–89	90–99
Frequency f	2	3	8	27	30	12	6	2

Calculate the mean mark for each section and use the means to compare the performances in the examination of the two sections. How would you rate the performance **in his own section** of a student in section A who scored 75 marks?
Make a similar assessment for a student in section B with the same mark.

4.4 The median of a frequency distribution

Example 1. The following table shows the average weekly wages (in pounds) of forty-nine workmen in an engineering factory. Find the median wage.

27	19	17	20	25	19	23
24	17	24	17	25	24	20
25	18	22	24	23	22	25
20	27	23	28	22	25	28
24	18	24	27	23	20	19
26	18	25	26	20	17	23
26	20	28	28	18	20	23

If the list of wages is arranged in order of magnitude the median is the middle, or twenty-fifth wage. However, to arrange the list in order is a tedious task. Instead we form a frequency distribution to which we add a column of **cumulative frequencies.** These values are obtained by adding each new frequency in turn to the total of those above, as shown:

Wage (pounds)	Frequency f		Cumulative frequency
17	I I I I	4	4
18	I I I I	4	4 + 4 = 8
19	I I I	3	8 + 3 = 11
20	++++ I I	7	11 + 7 = 18
21		0	18 + 0 = 18
22	I I I	3	18 + 3 = 21
23	++++ I	6	21 + 6 = 27
24	++++ I	6	27 + 6 = 33
25	++++ I	6	33 + 6 = 39
26	I I I	3	39 + 3 = 42
27	I I I	3	42 + 3 = 45
28	I I I I	4	45 + 4 = 49
	Σf = 49		

25th wage
←lies here
so that
the median
= £23

The twenty-fifth score is one of the group of six scores of £23, so that the median wage is £23.

Example 2. Find the median of the following scores by copying and completing the frequency table, including the column of cumulative frequencies.

18·6	18·8	19·0	18·2	18·4	18·4	19·1	18·7	18·5	18·4
18·5	18·3	19·1	18·6	18·4	18·3	18·7	18·7	19·0	19·1
18·6	18·6	18·2	18·8	18·8	18·9	18·7	18·6	18·2	18·2
18·8	18·9	18·4	18·5	18·6	18·5	19·0	18·8	18·6	18·3

Score	Frequency f		Cumulative frequency
18·2	I I I I	4	4
18·3	I I I	3	7
18·4	++++	5	12
.	.	.	.
.	.	.	.
.	.	.	.

Verify that $\Sigma f = 40$. Since there are 40 scores, the median lies between the 20th and 21st scores. Verify that the median is 18·6.

If the above method is applied to a grouped frequency distribution, it will give the class interval which contains the median score, but does not give the median itself. A more accurate method of finding the median of a grouped frequency distribution will be described in chapter 5.

Exercise 7

(1) Find the medians of the following distributions:

(a)

Score	0	1	2	3	4	5	6	7	8	9	10	11
Frequency f	4	5	8	12	14	14	18	13	12	10	9	7

(b)

Score	67	68	69	70	71	72	73	74	75	76	77
Frequency f	1	3	0	3	7	8	10	9	10	12	8

(c)

Score	0·32	0·33	0·34	0·35	0·36	0·37	0·38	0·39
Frequency f	13	18	44	61	73	80	82	59

(2) The ages in years of 50 applicants for short service commissions in the Army are shown below:

18	24	25	19	20	26	23	22	24	25
21	21	19	27	19	22	24	23	21	21
20	20	22	24	21	21	20	19	20	18
23	20	21	21	20	18	20	18	22	27
22	18	20	21	22	19	21	18	19	21

Make a frequency distribution of the data, including a column of cumulative frequencies. Find the median age of the recruits. Use the median as an **assumed mean** to calculate the mean age of the recruits. Compare the mean and median ages.

CHAPTER 5

Ogives and Frequency Curves

5.1 Cumulative frequency

Example 1. Let us look again at the distribution of lengths of cigarette stubs in the anti-smoking campaign on page 46.

Stub length (centimetres)	1·2– 1·3	1·4– 1·5	1·6– 1·7	1·8– 1·9	2·0– 2·1	2·2– 2·3	2·4– 2·5	2·6– 2·7	2·8– 2·9	3·0– 3·1
Frequency *f*	5	7	12	14	20	29	43	34	10	6

(*a*) What is the total frequency?

(*b*) Is the variable in this distribution continuous or discrete?

(*c*) What are (i) the class limits and (ii) the class boundaries of the first class?

(*d*) How many stubs were,
    (i) less than 1·55 cm,
    (ii) less than 2·15 cm,
    (iii) between 1·95 and 2·55 cm?

These and similar questions can be answered more readily if we make a **cumulative frequency** table as shown.

Stub length (centimetres)	Frequency f	Stub length less than (centimetres)	Cumulative frequency
1·2—1·3	5	1·35	5
1·4—1·5	7	1·55	12
1·6—1·7	12	1·75	
1·8—1·9	14	1·95	
2·0—2·1	20	2·15	
2·2—2·3	29	2·35	
2·4—2·5	43	2·55	
2·6—2·7	34	2·75	
2·8—2·9	10	2·95	174
3·0—3·1	6	3·15	180

(e) **Complete** the cumulative frequency column and use it to give the answers to the questions in (d) above.

Example 2. The following array shows the numbers of errors made by fifty pupils when typing a manuscript.

2	1	13	16	14	10	17	22	26	1
12	4	5	10	5	6	14	9	5	24
7	8	3	4	19	13	4	1	19	5
4	8	2	10	2	5	3	4	14	10
12	4	2	4	13	10	9	5	7	5

Copy the following table and complete the first three columns:

Number of errors	Frequency f	Cumulative frequency	
1—5	23	23	
6—10	12	35	
.	.	.	
.	.	.	
.	.	.	
.	.	.	
.	.	.	
.	.	.	

(a) In this distribution is the variable continuous or discrete?

(b) In the first column are the classes defined by class limits or class boundaries?

(c) Which of the following statements is correct?
(i) Thirty-five pupils made less than 10 errors.
(ii) Thirty-five pupils made 10 or less errors.

(d) Is it possible to tell from the table the number of pupils who made:
(i) Fewer than 14 errors,
(ii) Fewer than 15 errors?

Complete this statement: '. . . pupils made 15 errors. . . .'

Since this distribution is concerned with a discrete variable, the classes have been defined by class limits. However as was pointed out in section 3.3 and as we shall see shortly, it is sometimes useful to define the classes using class boundaries instead of class limits.

In the table above, put the heading **class boundaries** in the fourth column and complete this column.

Notice that the statement:

'Twenty-three pupils made 5 or less errors'

is equivalent to the statement

'Twenty-three pupils made less than $5\frac{1}{2}$ errors'

despite the fact that the idea of $5\frac{1}{2}$ errors is completely artificial.

The type of distribution described in examples 1 and 2 is called a **cumulative frequency distribution.** From this we can read the total number of times a value of the variable **less than the upper class boundary** has occurred.

Exercise 1

(1) The following table shows the distribution of absentees per class on a particular day in a secondary school.

Number of absentees X	0	1	2	3	4	5	6
Frequency f	1	5	7	5	3	1	0

Make a cumulative frequency table from the above data.

D

(2) The following array shows the heights of a sample of 100 young children measured to the nearest centimetre.

64	60	65	66	68	64	68	66	65	67
61	67	70	67	61	67	63	70	68	62
70	68	66	65	73	65	73	62	67	70
67	63	69	69	66	67	67	69	64	64
65	72	67	66	64	71	70	66	64	71
69	66	68	72	69	66	63	68	70	66
63	70	65	67	65	69	67	67	66	68
72	68	71	62	69	66	74	65	69	66
68	66	65	68	65	66	67	71	68	63
67	71	68	70	69	67	69	68	71	69

(a) Is the variable in this distribution continuous or discrete?

(b) Using the following headings, make a cumulative frequency distribution for the above data.

Height (centimetres) X	Frequency f	Height less than (centimetres)	Cumulative frequency
60	1	60·5	1
61	2	61·5	3
.	.	.	.
.	.	.	.
.	.	.	.
.	.	.	.
74	1	74·5	100

(c) How many children were:
  (i) Less than 64·5 cm tall,
  (ii) Less than 68·5 cm tall,
  (iii) Between 64·5 and 68·5 cm tall?

(d) How many children were:
  (i) Less than 66·5 cm tall,
  (ii) Less than 72·5 cm tall,
  (iii) Between 66·5 and 72·5 cm tall?

(3) Repeat question (2) (b) using class intervals 59·5–61·5, 61·5–63·5, etc.

(4) The following array shows the number of faulty electric light bulbs per box in 50 boxes each containing 100 bulbs:

0	0	2	5	1	2	3	1	2	0
0	1	4	0	4	1	0	2	0	2
1	1	2	0	1	0	0	0	3	0
1	0	3	3	0	1	1	0	0	2
0	0	0	0	1	0	0	1	0	1

In an investigation of this kind we might be more interested in the number of boxes having **more than** rather than having **less than** a specified number of faulty bulbs.

Complete the following table writing the X column in descending order:

Number of faulty bulbs per box X	f	Boxes with more than	Cumulative frequency
5	1	4·5	1
4	2	3·5	3
3	.	2·5	.
2	.	1·5	.
1	.	0·5	.
0	.	−0·5	.

Note that for the **more than** cumulative distribution the lower boundaries are used and that for a zero value of the variable the lower boundary is taken as −0·5.

(5) A school ordered 64 copies of a new text book. The following table shows the distribution of loose pages per book due to faulty binding:

Number of loose pages X	0	1	2	3	4	5	6	7
Frequency f	22	13	10	7	6	3	2	1

(*a*) Complete the following table:

Number of loose pages X	Frequency f	Copies with less than	Cumulative frequency
0	22	0·5	22
1	13	1·5	35
.	.	.	.
.	.	.	.
.	.	.	.
.	.	.	.

(*b*) How many copies had less than 3 loose pages?

(*c*) How many copies had less than 2½ loose pages?

(*d*) How many copies had between 3 and 6 loose pages inclusive?

(*e*) What percentage of the books was faulty?

(6) A manufacturer is mass producing a certain machine part of standard length 60 cm. The following distribution shows the actual lengths of a sample of 200, measured to the nearest 0·1 cm.

Length (centimetres)	59·2–59·3	59·4–59·5	59·6–59·7	59·8–59·9	60·0–60·1	60·2–60·3	60·4–60·5	60·6–60·7	60·8–60·9
Frequency f	3	11	27	39	43	39	26	9	3

(*a*) Is the variable in this distribution continuous or discrete?

(*b*) Does the table show class limits or class boundaries?

(*c*) Copy and complete the following cumulative frequency table:

Length (centimetres) X	Frequency f	Length less than (centimetres)	Cumulative frequency
59·2—59·3	3	59·35	3
.	.	.	.
.	.	.	.

(*d*) How many parts were:

    (i) Less than 60·15 cm,

    (ii) Less than 59·75 cm,

    (iii) Between 59·75 and 60·15 cm?

(*e*) The manufacturer claims that at least 90 per cent. are within the range 59·55—60·55 cm. Is his claim justified by the above figures?

5.2 The ogive

Example 1. The distribution of weights, measured to the nearest kilogramme, of 50 schoolboys was as follows:

Weight (kilogrammes)	Frequency f	Weight less than (kilogrammes)	Cumulative frequency
60·5—62·5	1	62·5	1
62·5—64·5	6	64·5	7
64·5—66·5	11	66·5	18
66·5—68·5	15	68·5	33
68·5—70·5	10	70·5	43
70·5—72·5	5	72·5	48
72·5—74·5	2	74·5	50

Just as the frequency distribution can be displayed pictorially as a histogram or polygon, the cumulative distribution can be expressed graphically by plotting the **upper class boundaries** against the **cumulative frequency,** i.e. plotting the points corresponding to the ordered pairs: (62·5, 1), (64·5, 7), (66·5, 18), (68·5, 33), (70·5, 43), (72·5, 48), (74·5, 50).

We shall adopt the practice of using the lower class boundary of the first class as the origin for the graph. That is, in addition to the above points we also plot the point (60·5, 0) and take it as the origin of the graph.

Plotting these points gives the following graph:

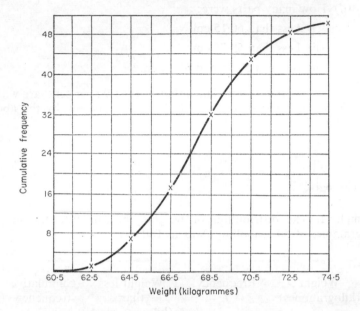

Fig. 5.1

The curve obtained by plotting cumulative frequency is called an **ogive**. The ogive is drawn as a smooth curve which can be used to obtain information not available from the table. For example, we can read from the ogive that 24 boys weighed less than 67·5 kg. Great care should be taken when interpreting results from the ogive. Corresponding to a weight of 64·5 kg is a cumulative frequency of 7. This does not imply that 7 boys weighed exactly 64·5 kg, but that 7 weighed **less than** 64·5 kg.

(a) Estimate from the ogive the number of boys who weighed:
   (i) Less than 65·5 kg,
   (ii) Less than 73·5 kg,
   (iii) Between 63·5 and 73·5 kg.

(b) Estimate the weight below which 20 of the schoolboys lie.

Example 2. One hundred people were chosen at random and each was allowed to fire 50 shots from a rifle at a target. The number of **bulls** scored by each was noted and gave the following frequency table:

Number of 'bulls'	Frequency f	Score less than	Cumulative frequency
1—5	1	5·5	1
6—10	3	10·5	4
11—15	12	.	.
16—20	16	.	.
21—25	19	.	.
26—30	18	.	.
31—35	17	.	.
36—40	11	.	.
41—45	2	.	.
46—50	1	.	.

Copy and complete the table.

Note again that although to say four scored 10 or less is equivalent to saying four scored less than 10·5, the latter, though slightly artificial, is the more statistically satisfactory.

Now draw the ogive for this distribution using upper class boundaries. Note that the horizontal scale will begin with the lower class boundary of class (1—5), that is the graph will have origin (0·5, 0).

Exercise 2

(1) Draw the ogive for the distribution of the lengths of cigarette stubs in example 1, page 81, and from it estimate,

(a) The number of stubs less than 2·25 cm long.

(b) The number of stubs less than 2·85 cm long.

(c) Copy and complete this statement: 'Half the stubs were less than . . . cm long.'

(2) Draw the ogive for example 2, page 82, and from it estimate:

(a) The number of pupils who made 18 errors or less, i.e. less than 18·5.

(b) The number of pupils who made 23 errors or less.

(c) The number of pupils who made between 18 and 23 errors. Complete this statement: '40 pupils made . . . errors or less.'

(3)—(8) Draw ogives for the questions in exercise 1, page 83.

5.3 Median, lower and upper quartiles

You may recall from chapter 4 that the **median** of a distribution was defined as the **middle score** when the scores were arranged in ascending order. You may also remember that we were able to find the median of a frequency distribution of discrete scores, but not of a grouped frequency distribution. In the latter case we were able to find only the class interval containing the median score.

Here is a method of estimating more accurately the median score of a grouped frequency distribution.

Following is the distribution of the weights of schoolboys which appeared earlier in example 1, page 87.

Weight (kilogrammes)	Frequency f	Weight less than (kilogrammes)	Cumulative frequency
60·5—62·5	1	62·5	1
62·5—64·5	6	64·5	7
64·5—66·5	11	66·5	18
66·5—68·5	15	68·5	33
68·5—70·5	10	70·5	43
70·5—72·5	5	72·5	48
72·5—74·5	2	74·5	50

Draw the ogive of the distribution. Compare your curve with Fig. 5.2.

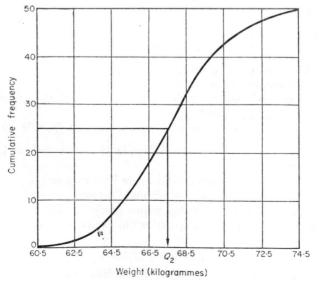

Fig. 5.2

To estimate the median weight:

    (a) Find the middle of the vertical scale.
    (In some cases, this may be done most easily using a ruler.)

    (b) Find the score on the horizontal scale corresponding to the middle of the cumulative frequency. This is denoted by Q_2 in Fig. 5.2.

    (c) Since 50% of the observations lie above Q_2 and 50% below, Q_2 must represent the middle score of the distribution. That is, Q_2 **is the median weight.** What is the value of Q_2 in Fig. 5.2?

In some branches of statistics, two other measures similar to the median are often found to be useful. These are called the **upper and lower quartiles,** and are usually denoted by Q_3 and Q_1 respectively.

Thus: Q_3 denotes the **upper quartile,**
           Q_2 denotes the **median,**
           Q_1 denotes the **lower quartile.**

The three measures are found from the ogive as follows:

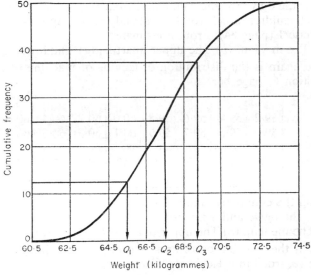

Fig. 5.3

    (a) Divide the cumulative frequency scale into **four equal parts** (hence the name quartile) as shown. (Again, using a ruler may be quicker than counting squares.)

(b) Read off the scores on the horizontal scale corresponding to Q_1, Q_2 and Q_3.

(c) Since 75% of the scores must lie below Q_3, Q_3 is the upper quartile.

Since 50% of the scores lie above and below Q_2, Q_2 is the median.

Since 25% of the scores lie below Q_1, Q_1 is the lower quartile.

Verify from Fig. 5.3 that:

(a) $Q_1 = 65.5$, (b) $Q_2 = 67.5$, (c) $Q_3 = 69.25$.

Summary

Since the upper quartile $Q_3 = 69.25$, 75% of the boys in the sample weighed less than 69.25 kg.

Since the median $Q_2 = 67.5$, 50% of the boys in the sample weighed more than 67.5 kg and 50% weighed less.

Since the lower quartile $Q_1 = 65.5$, 25% of the boys in the sample weighed less than 65.5 kg.

Exercise 3

(1) Draw the ogive for the cumulative frequency table of the heights of 100 children which you have already drawn up for question 3, exercise 1 (page 84). From it estimate:

(a) The median, (b) The upper quartile, (c) The lower quartile.

(2) Here again is the distribution of lengths of machine parts from question 6, page 86.

Length (centimetres)	59.2– 59.3	59.4– 59.5	59.6– 59.7	59.8– 59.9	60.0– 60.1	60.2– 60.3	60.4– 60.5	60.6– 60.7	60.8– 60.9
Frequency f	3	11	27	39	43	39	26	9	3

Using the cumulative table you have made for this distribution, draw the ogive and estimate:

(a) The median, (b) The upper quartile, (c) The lower quartile.

(3) Here is the distribution of ages of bridegrooms whose marriages were recorded in a Registry Office in a particular week:

Age in years	16–20	21–25	26–30	31–35	36–40	41–45	46–50
Frequency f	7	17	14	12	8	5	1

Make a cumulative frequency distribution table for **age less than upper class boundary.** Draw the ogive and find:

(*a*) The median, (*b*) The upper quartile, (*c*) The lower quartile.

Note. If you require more practice on ogives then repeat the above for the distributions from earlier sections, for example, section **3.4** on histograms.

5.4 Frequency curves

Note. The reading of this section, and of section **5.5**, may be omitted at this stage, but both sections should be studied before reading chapter 7 on probability.

Example 1. In section **3.4** you were shown how to represent a frequency distribution pictorially as a histogram or polygon. (If you find difficulty in answering the following questions then re-read section **3.4**.)

(*a*) If the square [2cm × 2cm] is used to represent one unit of

frequency, which of the following shapes will represent the **same** unit of frequency?

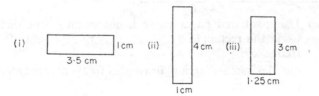

(*b*) If the rectangle [ ] represents **50 units**

of frequency, which of the following will also represent a frequency of 50?

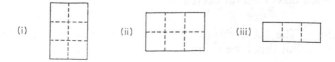

(c) If the rectangle [ ] represents one unit of frequency what will the following areas represent?

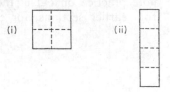

(i)   (ii)

What can be inferred about the height of a rectangle representing one unit of frequency when the base is:
(a) Halved, (b) Quartered?

Example 2. A manufacturer, over a period of time, tested 1 000 high-powered floodlamps and obtained the distribution of life-times measured to the nearest hour. The following is the distribution using class intervals of 20 hours:

Life-time in hours	0–19	20–39	40–59	60–79	80–99
Frequency f	70	450	360	111	9

(a) Using squared paper make a histogram of the distribution using the rectangle [ ] to represent 40 units of frequency.
On the same diagram draw the frequency polygon of the distribution.

(b) What frequency is represented by, (i) The total area of the histogram, (ii) The total area under the polygon?

It is useful to try to show the shape of a distribution by a smooth curve rather than by a polygon. To **smooth out** the polygon it may be necessary to increase the number of points on it. To do this the number of columns in the histogram must be increased and consequently the size of each class interval decreased.

Example 3. The table shows again the distribution of life-times of floodlamps, but this time using class intervals of 10 hours.

Life-time	0–9	10–19	20–29	30–39	40–49	50–59	60–69	70–79	80–89	90–99
Frequency	3	67	205	245	213	147	77	34	8	1

(a) Draw a histogram and polygon for this distribution keeping the width of the histogram the same as in example 2 above. This time 40 units of frequency will be represented by

the square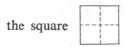

Can you explain why?

(b) Do you think the polygon now gives the best possible picture of the shape of the distribution? What do you think we can now do to improve it?

Example 4. The same distribution is shown again below, but this time using class intervals of 5 hours.

Life-time	0–4	5–9	10–14	15–19	20–24	25–29	30–34	35–39	40–44	45–49
Frequency	0	3	14	53	93	112	125	120	112	101

Life-time	50–54	55–59	60–64	65–69	70–74	75–79	80–84	85–89	90–94	95–99
Frequency	80	67	45	32	21	13	5	3	1	0

Draw the histogram for the distribution keeping the width of the histogram the same as before. This time 40 units of frequency is represented by the rectangle

On the same diagram lightly draw the frequency polygon and using this as a guide draw a reasonably smooth curve, which should look like the curve in Fig. 5.4.

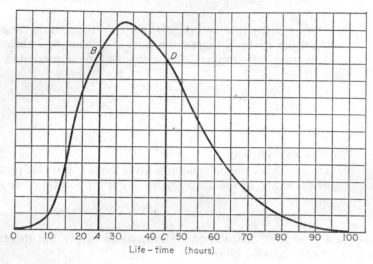

Fig. 5.4

The smooth curve you have just derived is called the **frequency curve** of the distribution. For the frequency curve, we no longer mark the horizontal scale in class intervals, but use instead a **continuous scale** as shown.

You can verify, by counting squares (4 squares represents a frequency of 40), that the total area under the curve still represents a frequency of about 1 000. The area under the curve to the left of the line CD represents the frequency of occurrence of lamps having a life-time less than 45 hours. What does the area under the curve to the left of AB represent? Between AB and CD?

By counting squares, estimate as accurately as you can the frequencies represented by the areas under the curve:

  (a) To the left of CD,
  (b) To the left of AB,
  (c) Between AB and CD.

This smoothing process obviously requires that a very large sample must be taken. This is necessary to ensure that each of the numerous class intervals contains a reasonable number of observations. In practice, provided that an adequate number of class intervals is taken initially (about 8 to 15), the general shape of the frequency distribution can be seen and a reasonable curve drawn without resorting to the rather laborious smoothing process just described.

Example 5.

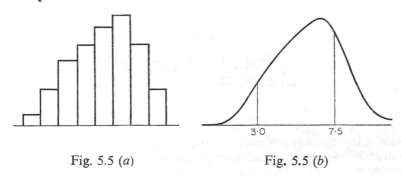

Fig. 5.5 (a)   Fig. 5.5 (b)

Fig. 5.5 (a) shows a histogram using 8 class intervals which readily leads to the frequency curve in Fig. 5.5 (b).

(a) The area to the left of the line erected at 7.5 represents the number of times a value of the variable less than 7·5 occurred. What does the area to the left of the line erected at 3·0 represent?

(b) The area to the right of 3·0 represents the number of times a value of the variable greater than 3·0 occurred. What does the area to the right of 7·5 represent? What does the area between the two lines represent?

Exercise 4

(1) Draw smooth frequency curves for some of the questions in exercise 1 of section **5.1** (page 83).

5.5 Relative frequency curves

Note. The reading of section **5.4,** and of this section, may be omitted at this stage, but both sections should be studied before reading chapter 7 on probability.

Fig. 5.6 shows the relative frequency histogram for a variable X grouped in class intervals of 5.

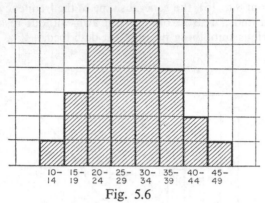

| 10–14 | 15–19 | 20–24 | 25–29 | 30–34 | 35–39 | 40–44 | 45–49 |

Fig. 5.6

How many unit squares make up the histogram?

Remembering that for a relative frequency histogram the total area represents a relative frequency of 1, what fraction of the total area is represented by the column of the histogram erected on:

    (*a*) Class 10–14,
    (*b*) Class 20–24?

The same technique that was used in section **5.4** to smooth the ordinary histogram can be used to smooth the relative frequency histogram. Again this laborious method need only be used when a very accurate curve is required. The histogram with about 8–15 columns gives a reasonable curve.

The smooth curve for the above relative histogram is given in Fig. 5.7.

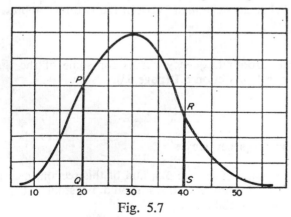

Fig. 5.7

Note, once again, that we have replaced the horizontal scale of class intervals by a continuous scale.

You can verify by counting that the total number of squares under the curve is approximately the same as the number making up the relative frequency histogram. Hence, the area under the curve still represents a relative frequency of 1.

The area under the curve to the left of *PQ* represents the relative frequency of occurrence of a variable with value less than 20.

What does the area under the curve to the right of *PQ* represent? Between *PQ* and *RS*?

By counting squares, estimate as accurately as you can the relative frequency of occurrence of a variable with value:

    (*a*) Less than 20,

    (*b*) Greater than 40,

    (*c*) Between 20 and 40.

Exercise 5

(1)

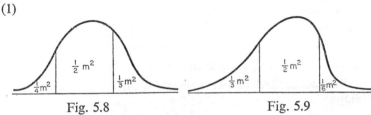

Fig. 5.8   Fig. 5.9

In Fig. 5.8 and 5.9 above the fractions represent the areas of the respective regions in square metres.

    (*a*) Find the sum of the areas of the regions in both figures.

    (*b*) In which of the two figures can the areas be taken as relative frequencies? Can you explain why?

(2) The table below shows the distribution of life-times of 1 000 floodlamps. (See example 3, page 94.)

Life-time	0–9	10–19	20–29	30–39	40–49	50–59	60–69	70–79	80–89	90–99
Frequency	3	67	205	245	213	147	77	34	8	1

Draw the relative frequency histogram and curve for the above distribution.

(3) Draw relative frequency curves for some of the examples in section **3.6**, exercise 7 (page 55).

CHAPTER 6

Dispersion

6.1 Range and semi-interquartile range

Each measure of **central location,** the mean, mode or median, gives us in its own way, some information about a distribution. None of them, however, tells us how the scores are dispersed.

Suppose ten pupils sat a chemistry examination and scored a mean mark of 55. This could have been achieved with many different sets of marks. Following are two possible sets:

Set A: 45   48   52   54   55   55   57   59   60   65
Set B: 25   32   40   45   53   60   61   71   78   85

Verify that the mean mark in each case is 55.

Let us illustrate each set of marks and the mean mark on a number line as follows:

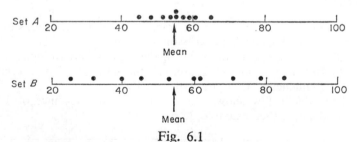

Fig. 6.1

Compare the standing of a mark of 60 (5 above the mean) in Sets A and B. What position in the class is attained, in each set, by a mark of 60? Compare the standing in each set of a mark of 45 (10 below the mean).

Compare and comment upon the **spread** of marks in the two sets as shown by the number lines. Since the marks in Set A tend to cluster close to the mean while those in Set B are scattered or dispersed more

100

widely the same marks have quite different relative values in the two sets.

In the same fashion as above compile two sets of ten marks C and D to illustrate the results of a physics examination with a mean mark of 48. Let C cluster about the mean while set D disperses widely on either side of the mean. Compare the relative standing of one or two specified marks in the two sets.

To obtain information on the pattern of the distribution we require, in addition to the mean, some measure of the amount of scatter or dispersion of the observations.

Measures of dispersion

1. Range

The range, the difference between the highest and the lowest values in a group of observations, can be used as a simple measure of dispersion.

What is the range of:

    (a) Set A,
    (b) Set B?

As you probably discovered a mark of 60 in set A with a small range represents a better performance than 60 in set B with a large range. Unfortunately the range does not always provide a good measure of dispersion. Examine the following sets of marks and the number lines which illustrate the marks.

Set E: 9 18 26 35 42 50 57 62 75 80 83 88

Set F: 9 42 43 46 50 53 56 57 59 60 62 88

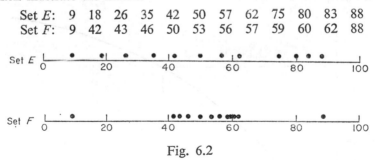

Fig. 6.2

Verify that the mean mark in each case is the same. What is the range of:

    (a) Set E,
    (b) Set F?

Compare the standing in sets E and F of a mark of (a) 62, (b) 42.

In spite of the fact that sets E and F have the same mean and range, they have quite different distributions. The scores in E are dispersed widely and fairly regularly on either side of the mean. In set F, apart from the **extreme scores** of 9 and 88, the marks cluster within 11 marks of the mean.

One disadvantage of range as a measure of dispersion is that it is based entirely on the two extreme values of the observations and takes no account of the values between. Another disadvantage is that the range can depend on the size of the sample. Generally the range of scores of 10 observations is likely to be less than the range for 50. Nevertheless range does have a use as a measure of scatter in some statistical fields such as temperature and climatic studies, medical reports, production quality control, where the number in the sample is small and constant, and so on.

2. Semi-interquartile range

A measure of dispersion which is more satisfactory because it does not depend on the extreme values of a distribution but makes use of the observations as a whole is the semi-interquartile range. As the name suggests this is half the range between the upper and lower quartiles. If as before we denote the lower and upper quartiles by Q_1 and Q_3 respectively, then Q, the semi-interquartile range is given by

$$Q = \frac{Q_3 - Q_1}{2}$$

Example. The figure shows the cumulative frequency diagram of the age distribution of workers in a factory. From the diagram find the semi-interquartile range.

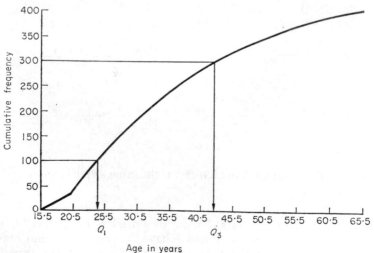

Fig. 6.3

The semi-interquartile range is

$$Q = \frac{Q_3 - Q_1}{2}$$
$$= \tfrac{1}{2}(42 \cdot 5 - 24 \cdot 5)$$
$$= 9 \cdot 0 \text{ years.}$$

Exercise 1

(1) Find the mean, median and range of the set of scores

8 18 7 16 19 8 11 18 22 9 10 14 11 15 16

(2) Here is the cumulative frequency distribution of ages of bridegrooms whose marriages were recorded in a Registry Office in a particular week:

Age in years	16–20	21–25	26–30	31–35	36–40	41–45	46–50
Cumulative Frequency	7	24	38	50	58	63	64

(a) Draw an ogive of the distribution.
(b) Calculate the semi-interquartile range.

(3) The following table gives the distribution of incomes of a selected section of the population:

Income		Frequency	Income		Frequency
Under £201	per annum	3	£1 201—£1 400	per annum	107
£201—£400	,, ,,	10	£1 401—£1 600	,, ,,	85
£401—£600	,, ,,	42	£1 601—£1 800	,, ,,	26
£601—£800	,, ,,	65	£1 801—£2 000	,, ,,	10
£801—£1 000	,, ,,	138	£2 001—£2 200	,, ,,	4
£1 001—£1 200	,, ,,	205	over £2 200	,, ,,	5

(a) Draw the cumulative frequency diagram of this distribution.
(b) From your graph, read off the median and the quartiles.
(c) Calculate the semi-interquartile range.

6.2 Standard deviation

The standard deviation is the most widely used and mathematically the most satisfactory measure of dispersion. Denoted by the Greek lower case letter σ (pronounced sigma) in the case of a population and by s in the case of a sample, standard deviation can be loosely defined as the **root mean square deviation**. The meaning of this rather difficult phrase should become clear from the examples which follow.

Example 1. Find the standard deviation of the list of numbers 30, 40, 50, 60, 70.

Let us regard the numbers as a sample and denote the standard deviation by s. The calculation is set out as follows:

Variable X	Deviation from mean $X-\bar{X}$	Square of deviation $(X-\bar{X})^2$
30	-20	400
40	-10	100
50	0	0
60	10	100
70	20	400
$\Sigma X = 250$		$\Sigma(X-\bar{X})^2 = 1\,000$

$$\bar{X} = \frac{\Sigma X}{N} \qquad \text{Mean of squared deviations} = \frac{\Sigma(X-\bar{X})^2}{N}$$

$$= \frac{250}{5} \qquad\qquad\qquad\qquad\qquad\qquad = \frac{1\,000}{5}$$

$$= 50 \qquad\qquad\qquad\qquad\qquad\qquad\qquad = 200$$

$$\text{Root of the mean of squared deviations} \qquad = \sqrt{\frac{\Sigma(X-\bar{X})^2}{N}}$$

$$s = \sqrt{200}$$

$$= 14{\cdot}1$$

The steps in the calculation, along with the corresponding notation are:

Operation	Denoted by
(1) Calculate the mean,	$\bar{X}$
(2) Find the deviation of each observation from the mean,	$X - \bar{X}$
(3) Square the deviations,	$(X - \bar{X})^2$
(4) Find the mean of the squared deviations,	$\dfrac{\Sigma(X - \bar{X})^2}{N}$
(5) Take the square root of this mean.	$\sqrt{\dfrac{\Sigma(X - \bar{X})^2}{N}} = s$

Hence we have the root of the mean of the squares of the deviations.

This should help to explain the definition **root mean square deviation**.

Example 2. Find the standard deviation of the list of numbers

41   45   47   50   51   53   56

Complete the table and perform the calculation. Verify that $\bar{X} = 49$, and that $s = 4.69$:

Variable X	Deviation from mean $(X-\bar{X})$	Deviation squared $(X-\bar{X})^2$
41	-8	64
45		16
47		
50	1	
51		
53	4	
56		
$\Sigma X =$		$\Sigma(X-\bar{X})^2 =$

$$\bar{X} = \frac{\Sigma X}{N} \qquad\qquad \frac{\Sigma(X-\bar{X})^2}{N} =$$

$$= \qquad\qquad s = \sqrt{\frac{\Sigma(X-\bar{X})^2}{N}} =$$

The standard deviation shows how the scores tend to scatter about the mean of the data. If the standard deviation is small, close clustering about the mean is indicated. A high standard deviation implies a wide scattering about the mean. Study the scatter of the scores about the mean in examples 1 and 2 and compare deviations.

Exercise 2

(1) Ten boys in a physics class each measured the length of time during which a dry Leclanché cell gave continuous, useful light. The times in minutes were recorded as follows:

126   108   115   114   122   129   123   118   120   135.

Find the mean and standard deviation of the times.

Let us regard the ten cells as a population and denote the standard deviation by σ, so that

$$\sigma = \sqrt{\frac{\Sigma(x-\mu)^2}{n}}$$

Copy and complete the table. Verify that $\sigma = 7\cdot44$ minutes.

Time (minutes) x	$(x-\mu)$	$(x-\mu)^2$
108	-13	169
114		
115		36
118		
120		
122		
123		
126		
129		
135		
$\Sigma x =$		$\Sigma(x-\mu)^2 =$

(2) Find the standard deviation of the numbers:

(a) 1, 3, 4, 4, 5, 6, 6, 6, 7, 8,

(b) 4·8, 6·2, 3·7, 3·1, 5·1, 3·4,

(c) 113, 111, 101, 117, 121, 109, 107, 123, 103, 105, 119, 115.

Regard (a) and (b) as samples and find s. Regard (c) as a population and find σ.

6.3 Shorter methods of calculating standard deviation (1)

Example. Find the mean and standard deviation of the set of marks

$$1, \quad 3, \quad 5, \quad 5, \quad 6, \quad 7, \quad 7, \quad 9.$$

Proceeding as before, complete the table and calculate s.

Mark X	$X-\bar{X}$	$(X-\bar{X})^2$
1		19·18
3	−2·38	
5		
5		
6		
7		2·62
7		2·62
9	3·62	
$\Sigma X =$		$\Sigma(X-\bar{X})^2 =$

$$\bar{X} = \frac{\Sigma X}{N} \qquad \frac{\Sigma(X-\bar{X})^2}{N} =$$

$$= \qquad s = \sqrt{\frac{\Sigma(X-\bar{X})^2}{N}} =$$

Although this is still a simple example the calculation is tiresome. When the number of observations is large and particularly when the mean is an awkward fraction it becomes impracticable to perform the calculation in this fashion. A much better method is to use the formula:

$$s = \sqrt{\frac{\Sigma X^2}{N} - \left(\frac{\Sigma X}{N}\right)^2}$$

At the end of this chapter on page 123 you will find how this formula is derived from the one used earlier.

This example is worked again using the new formula as follows:

Mark X	X^2
1	1
3	9
5	25
5	25
6	36
7	49
7	49
9	81
$\Sigma X = 43$	$\Sigma X^2 = 275$

$$\bar{X} = \frac{\Sigma X}{N} \qquad\qquad s = \sqrt{\frac{\Sigma X^2}{N} - \left(\frac{\Sigma X}{N}\right)^2}$$

$$= \frac{43}{8} \qquad\qquad = \sqrt{\frac{275}{8} - \left(\frac{43}{8}\right)^2}$$

$$= 2\cdot34$$

Not only is this formula easier to use but is normally more accurate. When the mean has to be rounded each deviation and hence its square is slightly in error.

Exercise 3

(1) Find the standard deviation of the following numbers using both methods and compare the amount of calculation involved in each case:

$$8, \quad 11, \quad 12, \quad 14, \quad 15, \quad 16.$$

(2) Use the shorter method to find the standard deviation of the numbers:

$$2, \quad 3, \quad 5, \quad 5, \quad 6, \quad 7, \quad 8, \quad 9, \quad 10, \quad 10.$$

(3) Regard the numbers 1, 3, 5, 7, 9, 11, 13, as a population and find their standard deviation using the formula for populations

$$\sigma = \sqrt{\frac{\Sigma x^2}{n} - \left(\frac{\Sigma x}{n}\right)^2}$$

(4) Below is a copy of a table made by a girl to show the number of marks she received in arithmetic tests over a period of two weeks:

Day	M	T	W	Th	F	M	T	W	Th	F
Mark	7	5	8	8	6	8	5	5	8	8

Calculate the mean and standard deviation of the marks.

Standard deviation of a frequency distribution

For a frequency distribution, the standard deviation is defined as

$$s = \sqrt{\frac{\Sigma f(X-\bar{X})^2}{\Sigma f}} \quad \text{in the case of a sample, and}$$

$$\sigma = \sqrt{\frac{\Sigma f(x-\mu)^2}{\Sigma f}} \quad \text{in the case of a population.}$$

However, calculations performed using either of these formulae prove to be too laborious, so that the formulae used in practice are:

$$s = \sqrt{\frac{\Sigma f X^2}{\Sigma f} - \left(\frac{\Sigma f X}{\Sigma f}\right)^2} \text{ and } \sigma = \sqrt{\frac{\Sigma f x^2}{\Sigma f} - \left(\frac{\Sigma f x}{\Sigma f}\right)^2}$$

Example. Find the mean and standard deviation of the marks shown in the following table:

Mark X	0	1	2	3	4	5	6	7	8	9	10
Frequency f	1	0	2	3	5	4	6	4	4	1	2

The frequency distribution is tabulated and the mean calculated, in the usual way, using columns 1, 2 and 3. Column 4 contains $f X^2$ obtained by multiplying the value of $f X$ in column 3 by the corresponding value of X in column 1.

1	2	3	4
Mark X	Frequency f	fX	fX^2
0	1	0	
1	0	0	
2	2	4	
3	3	9	
4	5	20	80
5	4		
6	6		
7	4		196
8	4		
9	1		
10	2		
	$\Sigma f =$	$\Sigma fX =$	$\Sigma fX^2 =$

$$X = \frac{\Sigma fX}{\Sigma f} \qquad\qquad s = \sqrt{\frac{\Sigma fX^2}{\Sigma f} - \left(\frac{\Sigma fX}{\Sigma f}\right)^2}$$

$$= \qquad\qquad\qquad =$$

Copy and complete the above table. Verify that $s = 2\cdot34$.

Exercise 4

(1) Throw two dice simultaneously 50 times and record, in the following table, the frequency of the total score in each throw.

Score X	2	3	4	5	6	7	8	9	10	11	12
Frequency f											

Find the mean and standard deviation of this distribution. (Regard the distribution as a sample.)

(2) The number of breakdowns per month recorded over a period of time by a road haulage firm was as follows:

```
1 0 3 1 0 2 3 2 1 4 0 0
1 3 2 5 2 1 0 2 1 1 2 0
1 6 2 0 1 3 1 2 2 0 1 2
5 1 0 3 0 1 4 1 2 3 2 1
```

Make a frequency table of the distribution and find the mean and median number of breakdowns. Calculate the standard deviation of the distribution.

(3) Use a sampling bottle containing about thirty or forty red beads and twice as many of another colour. Draw a large number of samples of ten beads and record in each case the number of red beads obtained.

Make a frequency table of the results and find the mean and standard deviation of the distribution obtained.

(4) Select a passage of prose (or poetry) from a book. Make a list of the number of letters in each of the first hundred words of the passage. Make a frequency table from the data and find the mean and standard deviation of the distribution obtained.

(5) The number of Scottish Certificate of Education Ordinary Grade passes obtained by each pupil in a class was as follows:

```
3 4 3 5 3 2 2 4 3 3
3 1 3 4 2 6 3 5 3 2
3 3 0 3 3 3 4 2 4 4
1 6 4 3 3 6 2 3 3 6
```

(a) Make a frequency distribution table of the passes obtained.
(b) Calculate the mean and standard deviation of the number of passes per person.

(6) The frequency distribution of the number of children in the families represented by the pupils of a class, is shown in the following table.
Calculate the mean and standard deviation of the number of children in a family:

Number of children X	1	2	3	4	5	6	7	8
Frequency f	0	7	14	7	6	2	3	1

(7) A Ministry of Transport examiner in two weeks awarded passes in the driving test to 48 applicants. The table shows the total number of attempts at the test each applicant had made before passing.

```
4 2 4 4 3 2 4 1 6 3 3 4
3 3 5 3 4 2 2 2 5 3 2 2
2 2 3 2 1 1 2 1 2 4 4 3
1 1 2 1 7 1 3 3 2 2 3 3
```

Calculate the mean and standard deviation of the distribution.

6.4 Shorter methods (2)

The use of the formula described above also leads to tiresome calculations where the observations themselves are large numbers. It remains, however, the best formula when calculating machines are being used.

Example 1. The winning 72 hole scores in the Open Golf Championship in the years from 1958 to 1965 were 278, 284, 278, 284, 276, 277, 279, 285. Calculate the mean and standard deviation of the scores:

Total score X	X^2
276	
277	
278	77 284
278	
279	
284	80 656
284	
285	
$\Sigma X =$	$\Sigma X^2 =$

$$\bar{X} = \frac{\Sigma X}{N} \qquad\qquad \frac{\Sigma X^2}{N} =$$

$$= \qquad\qquad s = \sqrt{\frac{\Sigma X^2}{N} - \left(\frac{\Sigma X}{N}\right)^2}$$

Complete the above table and verify that the standard deviation of the scores is 3·33.

Obviously the above method, useful enough with small numbers, is laborious with large numbers. However the assumed mean technique, which proved useful in finding the mean of the distribution, can be applied to calculations of standard deviation.

Example 2. By subtracting 4 from each of the numbers in list $R = 10, 12, 5, 8, 6, 7$ we obtain list $S = 6, 8, 1, 4, 2, 3$. Calculate the mean and standard deviation of R and S. How do the means compare? How do the standard deviations compare?

Example 3. Given list $W = 10, 13, 8, 7, 5, 14, 5, 10$, subtract 5 from each of the numbers in W to obtain list Z. Find the mean and standard deviation of Z and from these **write down** the mean and standard deviation of list W. Verify by calculating the mean and standard deviation of W in the usual way.

These examples show that subtracting a constant from all raw scores of a distribution does not change the value of the standard deviation.

Let us now apply this property to find the standard deviation of the golf scores in example 1. Assuming a mean of 278 the calculation is set down thus:

X	$X-A$	$(X-A)^2$
276	-2	4
277	-1	1
$A\rightarrow$278	0	0
278	0	0
279	1	1
284	6	36
284	6	36
285	7	49
	$\Sigma(X-A) = 17$	$\Sigma(X-A)^2 = 127$

From each score in column X we subtract 278 to obtain the set of scores $(X-A)$. The mean and standard deviation of scores $(X-A)$ are now found:

$$\text{Mean of } (X-A) = \frac{\Sigma(X-A)}{N}$$

$$= \frac{17}{8}$$

$$s \text{ of scores } (X-A) = \sqrt{\frac{\Sigma(X-A)^2}{N} - \left(\frac{\Sigma(X-A)}{N}\right)^2}$$

$$= \sqrt{\frac{127}{8} - \left(\frac{17}{8}\right)^2}$$

$$= 3\cdot33$$

$$\text{Mean of scores } X = \frac{17}{8} + A \qquad\qquad s \text{ of scores } X = 3\cdot33$$

$$= 2\cdot12 + 278$$

$$= 280\cdot1 \text{ (to one decimal place).}$$

Exercise 5

(1) Using an assumed mean of 60 kg find the mean and standard deviation of the weights in kg of the class of 12 students as follows:

57, 58, 59, 59, 60, 60, 60, 61, 61, 62, 63, 64.

(2) Find the mean and standard deviation of the ages of ten first year school pupils listed in the table. Use an assumed mean of 13 years 0 months:

Year	12	12	12	13	13	13	13	13	13	13
Month	9	11	11	0	1	1	2	3	3	4

(3) The table shows the monthly takings in pounds of a business for the year 1967. Choose a suitable assumed mean and calculate the standard deviation:

Jan.	Feb.	Mar.	April	May	June	July	Aug.	Sept.	Oct.	Nov.	Dec.
906	911	914	913	902	890	886	890	882	888	896	900

(4) Divide your class into groups each containing two pupils. Let one member of each group toss a coin while the other records the number of heads and tails obtained in 100 tosses. Tabulate the number of heads obtained by each group and calculate the mean and standard deviation of this distribution.

Using an assumed mean in a frequency distribution

Example. Matches of a certain brand are sold in boxes with average contents stated to be 52 matches. The number of matches in each of a sample of 100 boxes was as follows:

Number of matches per box X	49 50 51 52 53 54 55 56
Frequency f	2 8 15 36 20 12 6 1

Calculate the mean and standard deviation:

Number of matches X	Frequency f	$(X-A)$	$f(X-A)$	$f(X-A)^2$
49	2	−3	−6	18
50	8	−2	−16	32
51	15	−1	−15	15
$A{\rightarrow}52$	36	0	0	0
53	20	1	20	20
54	12	2	24	48
55	6	3	18	54
56	1	4	4	16
	$\Sigma f = 100$		$\Sigma f(X-A) = 29$	$\Sigma f(X-A)^2 = 203$

Standard deviation of the $(X-A)$ scores

$$= \sqrt{\frac{\Sigma f(X-A)^2}{\Sigma f} - \left(\frac{\Sigma f(X-A)}{\Sigma f}\right)^2}$$

$$= \sqrt{2 \cdot 03 - 0 \cdot 08}$$
$$= \sqrt{1 \cdot 95}$$
$$= 1 \cdot 40$$

Standard deviation of the X scores $= 1 \cdot 40$

$$\text{Mean of the } (X-A) \text{ scores} = \frac{\Sigma f(X-A)}{\Sigma f}$$

$$= 0 \cdot 29$$

$$\text{Mean of the } X \text{ scores} = 52 \cdot 29$$

$$= 52 \cdot 3 \text{ (to one decimal place)}$$

Exercise 6

(1) A machine designed to pack sugar in 500 gramme cartons was thought to be faulty. A sample of its output showed the following distribution:

Weight X (grammes)	492	493	494	495	496	497	498	499	500	501	502
Frequency f	2	0	3	4	12	26	38	24	17	10	4

Find the mean and standard deviation of the distribution.

(2) The distribution of the numbers of hours of instruction required by a flight of cadet pilots before flying solo is shown:

Number of X hours	12	13	14	15	16	17	18	19	20
Frequency f	3	6	8	10	7	6	5	3	2

Find the mean and standard deviation of the number of hours instruction required.

(3) The distribution of the attendance of members at meetings of a town council over a two year period was as follows:

E

Number of members X	46	47	48	49	50	51	52	53	54	55	56	57
Frequency f		5	4	1	4	6	10	7	2	6	4	4	2

Use the mode of the distribution as an assumed mean to find the mean and standard deviation of the distribution.

(4) The eighteen hole scores made by a professional golfer in sixteen tournaments (four rounds per tournament) showed the following distribution:

Score X	66	67	68	69	70	71	72	73	74	75	76	77	78	79
Frequency f	1	0	6	7	7	8	9	5	5	4	6	1	4	1

Find the median score of the distribution. Use the median as an assumed mean to find the mean and standard deviation of the distribution.

6.5 Shorter methods (3)

The arithmetic work involved in calculation of standard deviation can be further reduced when the scores can be multiplied or divided by a constant to form a simpler set of scores.

Example. By dividing each of the numbers of list A (3, 6, 9, 12, 15) by 3 we obtain list B (1, 2, 3, 4, 5). What are the relations between:
   (a) The means of the two lists,
   (b) The standard deviations of the two lists?

List A

X	X^2
3	9
6	36
9	81
12	144
15	225
$\Sigma X = 45$	$\Sigma X^2 = 495$

List B

X	X^2
1	1
2	4
3	9
4	16
5	25
$\Sigma X = 15$	$\Sigma X^2 = 55$

Mean of list A,

$$\frac{\Sigma X}{N} = \frac{45}{5} = 9$$

Mean of list B,

$$\frac{\Sigma X}{N} = \frac{15}{5} = 3$$

Standard deviation of list A,

$$\sqrt{\frac{\Sigma X^2}{N} - \left(\frac{\Sigma X}{N}\right)^2}$$

$$= \sqrt{99-81}$$
$$= \sqrt{18}$$
$$= 3\sqrt{2}$$

Standard deviation of list B,

$$\sqrt{\frac{\Sigma X^2}{N} - \left(\frac{\Sigma X}{N}\right)^2}$$

$$= \sqrt{11-9}$$
$$= \sqrt{2}$$

Thus mean of list A is 3 times the mean of list B and standard deviation of list A is 3 times the standard deviation of list B.

If we multiply each number of list B by 2 we obtain list C (2, 4, 6, 8, 10). Find the standard deviation of list C. How does it compare with the standard deviation of list B?

This example illustrates that multiplying (or dividing) all the raw scores of a distribution by a constant causes the standard deviation to be multiplied (or divided) by the same constant.

Exercise 7

(1) The standard deviation of 4, 10, 16, 22, 28 is 8·4. Write down the standard deviation of:

    (a) 2, 5, 8, 11, 14,

    (b) 6, 15, 24, 33, 42.

(2) Calculate the standard deviation of 0, 1, 2, 3, 4 and hence write down the standard deviation of:

    (a) 0, 5, 10, 15, 20,

    (b) 50, 55, 60, 65, 70.

(3) Subtract 130 from each number X in the list (100, 110, 120, 130, 140, 150, 160, 170) and divide the numbers so obtained by 10 to obtain the new list of numbers U, (-3, -2, -1, 0, 1, 2, 3, 4). Calculate the mean and standard deviation of U.

Verify that $\overline{U} = 0·5$ and that the standard deviation of U, denoted by $s_U = 2·29$.

Finally,

$$\overline{X} = 130 + 10\overline{U} \qquad \text{and} \quad s_X = 10s_U$$

thus $\overline{X} = 130 + 10 \times (·5)$ $s_X = 10 \times (2·29)$

        $= 135$ $= 22·9$

(4) Find the mean and standard deviation of the following list of numbers 70, 73, 76, 79, 82, 85.

Grouped frequency distributions

We use the above properties to shorten the calculation of standard deviation with grouped frequency distributions.

Example 1. Calculate the mean and standard deviation of the English marks of 40 pupils recorded below:

Mark	30–34	35–39	40–44	45–49	50–54	55–59	60–64	65–69	70–74	75–79
Frequency	1	1	5	5	6	10	3	5	2	2

The mid values of the classes form the set of variables X. The mid value 57 is chosen as a suitable assumed mean and the new set of values $X-57$ is found. Since the size of the class interval is 5 we form the set of variables U where $U = \dfrac{X-57}{5}$. Now we find the mean and standard deviation of values U in the usual way.

Mark	Frequency f	Mid-values X	$X - 57$	$U = \dfrac{X-57}{5}$	fU	fU^2
30—34	1	32	−25	−5	− 5	25
35—39	1	37	−20	−4	− 4	16
40—44	5	42	−15	−3	−15	45
45—49	5	47	−10	−2	−10	20
50—54	6	52	− 5	−1	− 6	6
55—59	10	$A\to$57	0	0	0	0
60—64	3	62	5	1	3	3
65—69	5	67	10	2	10	20
70—74	2	72	15	3	6	18
75—79	2	77	20	4	8	32
	$\Sigma f = 40$				$\Sigma fU = -13$	$\Sigma fU^2 = 185$

Then $\overline{U} = \dfrac{\Sigma fU}{\Sigma f}$ and $s_U = \sqrt{\dfrac{\Sigma fU^2}{\Sigma f} - \left(\dfrac{\Sigma fU}{\Sigma f}\right)^2}$

$$= \frac{-13}{40} \qquad = \sqrt{\frac{185}{40} - \frac{169}{1\,600}}$$

$$= \frac{85}{40}$$

Finally the mean of values X and standard deviation of values X,

$$\overline{X} = 57 + 5\left(\frac{-13}{40}\right) \qquad s_X = 5 \times \frac{85}{40}$$

$$= 55 \cdot 4 \qquad\qquad\qquad = 10 \cdot 6$$

Example 2. The frequency table below shows again the distribution of ages of bridegrooms whose marriages were recorded at a Registry Office in one week. Calculate the mean and standard deviation of the distribution.

Age of bride-groom	Frequency f	Mid-values X	$X-28$	$U = \dfrac{X-28}{5}$	fU	fU^2
16—20	7	18		-2		
21—25	17	23		-1		
26—30	14	$A\rightarrow28$		0		
31—35	12	33		1		
36—40	8			2	16	
41—45	5			3	15	
46—50	1			4	4	
	$\Sigma f = 64$				$\Sigma fU =$	$\Sigma fU^2 =$

Mean $\overline{U} = \dfrac{\Sigma fU}{\Sigma f}$ $\qquad\qquad s_U = \sqrt{\dfrac{\Sigma fU^2}{\Sigma f} - \left(\dfrac{\Sigma fU}{\Sigma f}\right)^2}$

$\overline{X} = 5\overline{U} + 28$ $\qquad\qquad s_X = 5 \times s_U$

$=$ $\qquad\qquad\qquad\qquad\qquad =$

Copy and complete the above table. Verify that $\overline{X} = 29 \cdot 25$ years and $s_X = 7 \cdot 55$ years.

Exercise 8

(1) The table shows the frequency distribution of the scores made during a shoot by a group of army recruits. Calculate the mean and standard deviation of the distribution.

Scores	60–61	62–63	64–65	66–67	68–69	70–71	72–73	74–75	76–77	78–79
Frequency f	1	2	6	13	22	26	20	8	1	1

(2) The marks obtained by second year pupils in an examination were classified as shown in the following table:

Mark	1–10	11–20	21–30	31–40	41–50
Frequency f	2	20	70	52	16

Regard the pupils as a population and find the mean (μ) and standard deviation (σ).

(3) Construct a frequency distribution of a set of class examination marks, selecting a scheme of grouping that is appropriate. Calculate the mean and standard deviation of the distribution.

(4) Make a frequency distribution of the following set of scores using class intervals of size 5, starting with the class 10–14:

```
26  18  10  25  14  56  16  42  29  23
28  23  20  34  18  46  50  47  13  16
31  33  27  44  54  34  26  28  41  36
42  45  26  52  36  41  21  17  32  53
31  50  36  18  28  25  31  37  48  28
```

Find the modal class. Use the mid-value of the modal class as an assumed mean to find the mean and standard deviation of the set of scores.

(5) The following distributions were used earlier. Calculate the mean and standard deviation for each distribution.

(a) Distribution of weights of cattle in kilogrammes:

Weight (kilogrammes)	400–424	425–449	450–474	475–499	500–524	525–549	550–574	575–599	600–624
Frequency f	2	1	2	5	7	12	11	11	4

(*b*) Distribution of lengths of cigarette stubs in centimetres:

Length of stub (centimetres)	1·2– 1·3	1·4– 1·5	1·6– 1·7	1·8– 1·9	2·0– 2·1	2·2– 2·3	2·4– 2·5	2·6– 2·7	2·8– 2·9	3·0– 3·1
Frequency *f*	5	7	12	14	20	29	43	34	10	6

(*c*) Distribution of hourly rates of workers in pence:

Hourly rate (pence)	25– 29	30– 34	35– 39	40– 44	45– 49	50– 54	55– 59	60– 64	65– 69	70– 74
Frequency *f*	5	7	12	8	9	7	4	4	3	1

6.6 Summary of methods of computing standard deviation

(1) The formulae by which standard deviation is defined are seldom used in calculations. These formulae are:

$$s = \sqrt{\frac{\Sigma(X-\bar{X})^2}{N}}$$ for distributions of single scores and

$$s = \sqrt{\frac{\Sigma f(X-\bar{X})^2}{\Sigma f}}$$ for frequency distributions, with

corresponding formulae for σ.

(2) The formula $s = \sqrt{\dfrac{\Sigma X^2}{N} - \left(\dfrac{\Sigma X}{N}\right)^2}$, and the corresponding

formula for σ, can be applied directly without an assumed mean when the data is simple and the scores are small whole numbers or when calculating machines are being used. A simple method of computing standard deviation by machine is shown in section 6.7.

(3) In practice most calculations make use of an assumed mean to obtain, from the values X, a simpler set of values. These values are:

(a) $(X-A)$ in a frequency distribution,

(b) $\dfrac{(X-A)}{\text{class interval}}$ in a grouped frequency distribution.

The standard deviation of these simpler values is found using the formula in (2) above and from this the standard deviation of the values X is calculated.

The use of calculating machines in these cases will lessen still further the amount of computation.

6.7 Computation of standard deviation using machines

Example. Find the mean and standard deviation of the numbers 46, 57, 62, 81, 85.

Procedure

(1) Set the figure 1 at the left-hand end of the setting register, and 46 at the right-hand end.

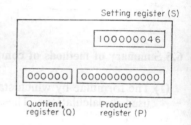

Fig. 6.4

(2) Multiply by 46.

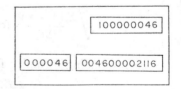

Fig. 6.5

(3) Clear the quotient register. Do not clear the setting levers but change by hand the right-hand digits from 46 to 57.

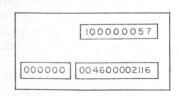

Fig. 6.6

(4) Multiply by 57.

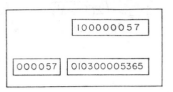

Fig. 6.7

(5) Repeat (3) and (4) changing the setting levers to 62, 81, 85 in turn.
The registers should then read:

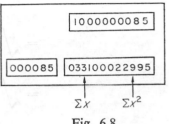

$\Sigma x \qquad \Sigma x^2$

Fig. 6.8

$$\bar{X} = \frac{\Sigma X}{N} \qquad\qquad s = \sqrt{\frac{\Sigma X^2}{N} - \left(\frac{\Sigma X}{N}\right)^2}$$

$$= \frac{331}{5} = 66{\cdot}2 \qquad\qquad = \sqrt{\frac{22995}{5} - 66{\cdot}2^2} = 14{\cdot}7$$

6.8 Proof of formulae used in computing standard deviation

(1) $\qquad \sqrt{\dfrac{\Sigma(X-\bar{X})^2}{N}} = \sqrt{\dfrac{\Sigma X^2}{N} - \left(\dfrac{\Sigma X}{N}\right)^2}$

Let $\bar{X}$ be the mean of the N observations $X_1, X_2, X_3, \ldots X_N$

Observations X	Deviation from mean $X-\bar{X}$	Square of deviations $(X-\bar{X})^2$	
X_1	$X_1-\bar{X}$	$(X_1-\bar{X})^2$ =	$X_1{}^2-2\bar{X}X_1+\bar{X}^2$
X_2	$X_2-\bar{X}$	$(X_2-\bar{X})^2$ =	$X_2{}^2-2\bar{X}X_2+\bar{X}^2$
X_3	$X_3-\bar{X}$	$(X_3-\bar{X})^2$ =	$X_3{}^2-2\bar{X}X_3+\bar{X}^2$
$\vdots$	$\vdots$	$\vdots$	$\vdots$
X_N	$X_N-\bar{X}$	$(X_N-\bar{X})^2$ =	$X_N{}^2-2\bar{X}X_N+\bar{X}^2$
		$\Sigma(X-\bar{X})^2$ =	$\Sigma X^2-2\bar{X}\Sigma X+N\bar{X}^2$

$$s = \sqrt{\frac{\Sigma(X-\bar{X})^2}{N}} = \sqrt{\frac{\Sigma X^2 - 2\bar{X}\Sigma X + N\bar{X}^2}{N}}$$

$$= \sqrt{\frac{\Sigma X^2}{N} - \frac{2\bar{X}\Sigma X}{N} + \frac{N\bar{X}^2}{N}}$$

$$= \sqrt{\frac{\Sigma X^2}{N} - 2\bar{X}.\bar{X} + \bar{X}^2}$$

$$= \sqrt{\frac{\Sigma X^2}{N} - \bar{X}^2}$$

$$= \sqrt{\frac{\Sigma X^2}{N} - \left(\frac{\Sigma X}{N}\right)^2}$$

(2) Let s_x be the standard deviation of the list of numbers $A = X_1, X_2, X_3 \ldots X_N$. Suppose a constant C is subtracted from each number of A to form the new list $B = X_1-C, X_2-C, X_3-C, \ldots, X_N-C$.

Mean of list A
$$= \frac{X_1+X_2+X_3+\ldots+X_N}{N} = \frac{\Sigma X}{N} = \bar{X}$$

Mean of list B
$$= \frac{X_1-C+X_2-C+X_3-C+\ldots+X_N-C}{N}$$

$$= \frac{\Sigma X - NC}{N} = \bar{X}-C$$

Standard deviation of A, $s_x = \sqrt{\frac{\Sigma(X-\bar{X})^2}{N}}$

Standard deviation of B, $s_{x-c} = \sqrt{\frac{\Sigma[(X-C)-(\bar{X}-C)]^2}{N}}$

$$= \sqrt{\frac{\Sigma(X-\bar{X})^2}{N}}$$

$$= s_x$$

(3) Suppose each member of list A is multiplied by constant C to form the new list $D = CX_1, CX_2, CX_3 \ldots CX_N$.

Mean of list $D = \dfrac{CX_1 + CX_2 + CX_3 + \ldots + CX_N}{N}$

$ = \dfrac{C(X_1 + X_2 + X_3 + \ldots + X_N)}{N}$

$ = \dfrac{C\Sigma X}{N}$

$ = C\bar{X}$

Standard deviation of list $D = \sqrt{\dfrac{\Sigma(CX - C\bar{X})^2}{N}}$

$ = \sqrt{\dfrac{C^2\,\Sigma(X - \bar{X})^2}{N}}$

$ = C\sqrt{\dfrac{\Sigma(X - \bar{X})^2}{N}}$

$ = C.s_X$

Revision Examples I

Set 1

(1) The table below shows the annual consumption of cigarettes per adult in the United Kingdom in certain years between 1900 and 1950. Illustrate the figures:

(a) By a compound bar graph,
(b) By a line graph.

Suggest reasons to explain the high consumption in 1945, and the fall in subsequent years.

	1900	1910	1920	1930	1940	1945	1950
Men	450	1 150	2 450	2 700	3 600	4 500	3 700
Women	0	0	0	200	650	1 150	1 350

(2) The frequency distribution of the shoe sizes for a class of boys is shown:

Shoe size	$6\frac{1}{2}$	7	$7\frac{1}{2}$	8	$8\frac{1}{2}$	9
Frequency	3	6	12	8	6	2

Make a histogram of the distribution.
What is the mode of the distribution?
If this distribution were typical of the shoe sizes for all schoolboys, how many pairs of size $7\frac{1}{2}$ should a manufacturer produce in every 1 000 pairs?

(3) The table shows the number of occasions on which a team scored a particular number of goals in the last 200 matches:

Goals	0	1	2	3	4	5	6	7
Occasions	50	69	40	24	10	4	2	1

  (a) Draw a histogram to represent the data of the table.

  (b) What is the median of this distribution?   [W.J.E.C.]

(4) Calculate the mean and standard deviation of the distribution of question (3).   [W.J.E.C.]

(5) Make a frequency distribution of the following set of scores, using suitable class intervals. Draw the ogive of the distribution, and use it to estimate the median, and the lower and upper quartiles.

6·2	7·8	7·3	7·0	4·9	4·3	5·8	5·6	4·7	7·9
4·9	5·8	6·3	6·0	6·3	5·0	7·6	5·9	7·1	5·6
5·3	5·2	6·5	4·6	7·2	6·9	8·2	5·4	5·6	5·7
7·7	5·5	3·5	6·7	4·0	8·1	6·3	7·1	4·6	5·8
3·8	4·0	6·8	5·7	7·7	5·4	3·9	6·4	6·1	4·6

Set 2

(1) (a) List the advantages and disadvantages of presenting information by means of bar charts and pie charts.

  (b) The following is a list of subjects taught in a school and the time devoted to each subject per week. Present the information in the form of a pie chart.

Subject	Time (hours)
English	3
French	3
Mathematics	4
Physics	$2\frac{1}{2}$
Chemistry	$2\frac{1}{2}$

[A.E.B.] Amended.

(2) The distributions of earnings in two companies A and B are shown below:

Annual earnings (£)	Company A Number of employees f	Company B Number of employees f
0— 999	22	32
1 000—1 999	35	25
2 000—2 999	17	16
3 000—3 999	14	11
4 000—4 999	9	8
5 000—5 999	2	1
6 000—6 999	0	2
7 000—7 999	0	2
8 000—8 999	1	3
	100	100

(a) Calculate the mean earnings for each company.

(b) What percentage of each firm's employees earn less than £1 000 per year?

(c) Comment upon the answers to (a) and (b).

(3) Three hundred competitors in a race were classified according to the minute interval in which they arrived at the finishing post, the winner arriving between 20 minutes and 21 minutes after the start.

Draw the cumulative frequency curve for the results given in the following table and estimate from your graph:

(a) The median time,

(b) The semi-interquartile range of the times,

(c) The percentage of competitors achieving a time of less than 24 min 30 sec,

(d) The range of time taken by those competitors between the third and fourth deciles.

Time in min	20–21	21–22	22–23	23–24	24–25
No. of competitors	1	5	22	47	61

Time in min	25–26	26–27	27–28	28–29	29–30
No. of competitors	64	56	33	8	3

[LOND.]

(**Note.** The third decile is the score below which three-tenths of the scores of the distribution lie, and the fourth decile, the score below which four-tenths lie.)

(4) Two dice were thrown together 200 times, and for each throw the total score was recorded. The frequencies with which the scores occurred were as follows:

Score	12	11	10	9	8	7
Frequency	7	10	20	20	30	34

Score	6	5	4	3	2
Frequency	27	21	14	11	6

By taking the score 7 as the base of your calculations, find the arithmetic mean and the standard deviation of the scores.

[LOND.]

(5) Draw the histogram for each of the distributions A and B and comment upon the way in which the two distributions:

(i) Resemble each other,
(ii) Differ from each other.

Distribution A

Score	1	2	3	4	5	6	7	8	9	10
Frequency f	0	1	2	2	12	18	12	2	2	1

Distribution *B*

Score	1	2	3	4	5	6	7	8	9	10
Frequency *f*	3	4	3	7	6	7	4	5	6	7

Calculate the means and standard deviations of the two distributions, and try to use them to verify your comments about (i) and (ii) above.

Set 3

(1) The table below shows the numbers of cars produced in 1966 by four Common Market countries, and by Britain, U.S.A. and the U.S.S.R., along with their populations to the nearest million. Make a compound bar graph to illustrate the figures.

Country	Population (millions)	Car output (millions)
Belgium	10	0·2
France	49	1·8
W. Germany	60	2·8
Italy	52	1·3
Britain	55	1·6
U.S.A.	197	8·6
U.S.S.R.	236	0·2

Which country produced the largest number of cars per head of the population?
Which country produced the smallest number per head?

(2) The table shows the intelligence quotient (I.Q.) of 90 pupils at a school:

I.Q.	65–	75–	85–	95–	105–	115–	125–	135–
Number of pupils	1	7	17	28	22	12	2	1

Each I.Q. is given correct to one decimal place. Write down the lower and upper limit for the class 95– .
Calculate the cumulative frequency table, and draw the cumulative frequency curve.
From the graph estimate:

(a) The median value of the I.Q.,

(b) The semi-interquartile range of the distribution,

(c) The percentage of children above average intelligence if an I.Q. of 100 is taken as average.   [A.E.B.] Amended

(3) The table shows the frequency distribution of the flaws in a sample of 500 metal bars of standard lengths:

Flaws per bar	0	1	2	3	4	5
Number of bars	231	172	68	18	7	4

(a) Represent the data diagrammatically,

(b) Calculate the arithmetic mean and the standard deviation of the number of flaws per bar.   [J.M.B.]

(4) The following figures show the numbers of goals scored during a season by one hundred hockey clubs:

```
 9  11  10   8  10  15  15   4  14  10
 4   5  22  15  21   3   8  27  10  14
 8  14   4  12   8  11  11   7   6   7
11  21   9   6  22   5   9   3  12  12
 9  10  11   3  16  15  23  11  21   6
 7   3   3  13  16   6   1   9  17   5
11   8   7   9   2   2   7   4  11   6
18   4   9  21  18   4  20   5  13   4
 7  14  11  12   4  14   3   6  11   9
11   4  13   8  10   8   8  10   9   2
```

Arrange these figures into an appropriate frequency distribution. Draw a diagram to illustrate the frequency distribution and comment on its shape.   [INST. OF STAT.]

(5) Find the mid-value of the modal class of the distribution shown below, and use it as an assumed mean to calculate the mean and standard deviation of the distribution.

Score X	4·50—4·74	4·75—4·99	5·00—5·24	5·25—5·49	5·50—5·74	5·75—5·99
Frequency	4	14	17	22	16	9

Set 4

(1) Write brief notes on the rules to be followed in the construction of graphs and diagrams. Explain how the public may be misled when these rules are broken.

[INST. OF STAT.]

(2) The following table gives the number of accidents in the home (row *b*) to housewives of different ages (row *a*) in a certain town in one year:

a	16–25	26–35	36–45	46–55	56–65	66–75	76–85
b	10	28	32	52	45	24	7

Construct a histogram and use it to find, to the nearest year, an estimate of the modal age for accidents to these particular housewives.

Construct also a cumulative frequency curve and find from it, to the nearest year, an estimate of the median age for their accidents.

[LOND.]

(3) The numbers of questions of equal difficulty attempted by a random sample of 1 645 pupils in a two-hour test are given in the table:

Number of questions	Number of pupils
0 —	3
3 —	22
6 —	75
9 —	194
12 —	331
15 —	402
18 —	321
21 —	192
24 —	79
27 —	22
30 —	4
	1 645

Find:
  (i) The median,
  (ii) The mode,
and calculate:
  (iii) The arithmetic mean,
  (iv) The standard deviation.

It was decided that in tests of equal difficulty about $2\frac{1}{2}\%$ of the candidates were to be given the opportunity of obtaining full marks. How many questions should the candidates be asked to answer in two hours?   [A.E.B.]

(4) Six coins were tossed and the number of heads noted. This experiment was repeated and the following frequency distribution recorded:

No. of heads	0	1	2	3	4	5	6
Frequency	1	7	13	21	15	5	2

How many times were the six coins tossed together?

Calculate the mean and the standard deviation of this distribution. ($\bar{X}$ and s.) Use the table of results to find what percentage of the total frequency:

  (i) Resulted in exactly 3 heads,
  (ii) Resulted in 5 or more heads,
  (iii) Lay between $\bar{X}-s$ and $\bar{X}+s$ heads,
  (iv) Lay between $\bar{X}-2s$ and $\bar{X}+2s$ heads,
  (v) Lay between $\bar{X}-3s$ and $\bar{X}+3s$ heads.

(5) Carry out the following experiment with a full set of twenty-eight dominoes:

  (a) Make a frequency distribution of the total number of spots on each domino. (For example, the five-four has 9, the six-three also has 9, the double blank has 0, and so on.) Find the mean and standard deviation of the distribution (which you can regard as a population).

  (b) Mix the dominoes well in a box, select one, note the number of spots and replace in the box. Mix well, draw a second domino, note the total number and replace. Repeat until two hundred have been chosen. Make a frequency distribution of the numbers obtained, and find the mean and standard deviation. (This time it is a sample distribution.)

Compare the results obtained in (a) and (b).

Set 5

(1) The expenditure of a golf club in a particular year is illustrated in the following pie chart:

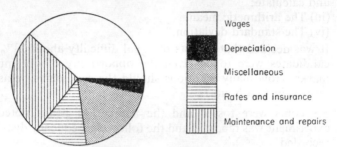

Fig. R.1

If the wages paid amounted to a total of £3 800 calculate, to the nearest £100, the cost of each of the other items of expenditure, and find the total expenditure for the year.

(2) The following table gives the distribution of marks of 1 000 candidates in an examination:

Number of candidates	Marks
15	1—10
54	11—20
112	21—30
182	31—40
240	41—50
191	51—60
133	61—70
57	71—80
16	81—100

Working from an assumed mean of $45\frac{1}{2}$, calculate the mean and standard deviation of this distribution.

[A.E.B.]

(3) Calculate a cumulative frequency table for the distribution in question (2), and draw the cumulative frequency graph.
From your graph estimate:

(*a*) The value of the median mark,

(*b*) The value of the pass mark if 40% of the candidates fail the examination,

(*c*) The semi-interquartile range.

[A.E.B.] Amended

(4) The times taken (to the nearest second) by a number of rats to find their way through a maze were recorded and gave the following distribution:

Time in seconds	Number of rats
8—12	7
13—17	15
18—22	41
23—27	19
28—32	8
33—37	6
38—42	4

Calculate the mean and standard deviation of the times taken.

[S.C.E.E.B.]

(5) In a factory a machine was set to cut rods of a certain length. A sample of rods was taken and measured correct to the nearest 0·1 cm. The frequencies with which each measurement occurred are shown in the following table:

Length—cm	89·4	89·5	89·6	89·7	89·8	89·9
Frequency	2	4	7	15	22	25
Length—cm	90·0	90·1	90·2	90·3	90·4	90·5
Frequency	20	13	7	3	1	1

Draw a cumulative frequency curve for these statistics and obtain from this curve the median value and the semi-interquartile range. Find the adjustment, to the nearest millimetre, that should have been made to the machine to obtain 85% of the sample of length 90 cm or more.

[LOND.]

Set 6

(1)
Year	1958	1959	1960	1961	1962
Profit (£000)	2 993	4 088	5 122	6 451	6 617

Year	1963	1964	1965	1966	1967
Profit (£000)	8 370	11 326	15 191	23 388	28 730

Plot these figures to show the rate of growth of profit.

[INST. OF STAT.]

(2) The following grouped frequency distribution describes the measurements of contents of 200 containers (in cc):

(a) Draw the histogram for these data and thus determine the modal volume,

(b) Draw the cumulative frequency curve and estimate from it the median value of volume.

Volumes of containers in cc	Number of containers
6 and less than 7	3
7 and less than 8	6
8 and less than 9	49
9 and less than 10	121
10 and less than 11	19
11 and less than 12	2
Total:	200

[INST. OF STAT.]

(3) In an evening at a bridge club 60 rubbers of bridge were played. The distribution of the number of hands played per rubber was as follows:

Number of hands	2	3	4	5	6	7	8	9	10	11	12	13
Frequency	1	7	7	9	11	8	5	5	3	1	1	2

Find the mean and standard deviation of the distribution and make a pictorial representation of it in the form of a frequency polygon.

(4) The table shows the weekly wage distribution in a certain factory. Determine:

(i) The median wage,

(ii) The wage limits for the middle 50% of the wage earners,

(iii) The percentage who earned more than £13 per week,

(iv) The percentage who earned £17 or less per week.

Weekly wage distribution

Wage	Number of employees
£8 and under	15
Over £8 and up to £10	20
„ £10 „ „ „ £12	48
„ £12 „ „ „ £14	76
„ £14 „ „ „ £16	112
„ £16 „ „ „ £18	64
„ £18 „ „ „ £20	32
„ £20 „ „ „ £22	10
„ £22	3
	380

[A.E.B.]

(5) Use the mid-value of the modal class of the distribution below as an assumed mean, to find the mean and standard deviation of the distribution.

Speed (metres per second)	15—19	20—24	25—29	30—34	35—39	40—44	45—49
Frequency	8	10	13	12	10	9	8

Set 7

(1) (*a*) State briefly what diagrams you would use to illustrate the following data:

    (i) The number of marriages in your town for each month of 1965,

    (ii) The proportion of the harvest yields for 1965 of the cereal crops, wheat, barley, oats and rye,

    (iii) The numbers of pairs of shoes of different sizes bought by the pupils of your school in 1965.

(*b*) The following table gives the percentage composition of meadow hay harvested at different dates:

Date of cutting	Crude protein	Fat	Soluble carbohydrates	Fibre	Ash
May 14	17·7	3·2	40·8	23·0	15·2
June 9	11·2	2·7	43·2	34·9	8·0
June 26	8·5	2·7	43·3	38·2	7·3

Illustrate the above data in one diagram. [A.E.B.]

(2) Together with three friends, you decide to spend a week investigating the proportion of lady drivers who drive each make of car. Assume that no one objects to your recordings or questions.

(a) You decide to make the survey by observation. State with reasons whether you would observe (i) at a busy road junction with traffic lights or (ii) in the town car park.
Which cars would you observe, and what observations would you record?

(b) You decide to make the survey by questioning. State with reasons whether you would put your questions (i) in a busy shopping centre or (ii) in the town car park.
What questions would you put, and to whom?

(c) If the survey were changed to determine which make of car ladies prefer to drive, would you choose method (a) or method (b)? What changes, if any, would you make in the observations or questions?

[W.J.E.C.]

(3) The following table gives the distribution of marks in a certain examination:

Mark	0–9	10–19	20–29	30–39	40–49	50–59	60–69	70–79	80–89	90–100
Frequency	5	11	32	76	88	54	43	19	10	2

Construct a cumulative frequency curve and obtain from it:
(a) The median mark, (b) The 8th decile, (c) The semi-interquartile range. [LOND.]

Note. The 8th decile is the score below which eight-tenths of the scores of the distribution lie.

(4) A market research bureau asked one hundred housewives who purchased Brand X washing powder how many packets they bought during a specified period. The purchases recorded were as follows:

1	1	3	3	3	9	9	20	2	22
10	16	1	46	11	10	24	10	13	1
22	2	14	1	7	6	1	1	6	20
15	3	2	3	23	6	15	3	15	1
7	1	1	1	1	4	1	10	2	30
6	17	5	22	2	23	10	22	3	6
1	3	2	3	1	3	23	7	24	1
3	1	1	1	1	1	14	4	11	8
4	4	9	1	6	1	6	1	13	2
10	6	10	9	4	2	16	1	3	9

Arrange these data into an appropriate frequency distribution and calculate the mean from the grouped data.

[INST. OF STAT.]

(5) The frequency distribution of the marks obtained by 400 candidates in an examination is as follows:

Marks	1–20	21–30	31–40	41–50	51–60	61–70	71–80	81–100
Frequency	9	32	89	102	78	63	21	6

(a) Calculate the arithmetic mean and the standard deviation of the distribution.

(b) The examiner decides to publish the original marks out of a total of 500, that is each candidate's mark is multiplied by 5.

Deduce the new arithmetic mean and standard deviation. Give reasons.

[A.E.B.]

Set 8

(1) The table shows the number of pupils leaving school with 2, 3, 4 or more passes in the Scottish Certificate of Education Higher Grade Examination in each year from 1962 to 1966.

	1962	1963	1964	1965	1966
2 Highers or more	8 045	8 963	10 258	12 316	12 073
3 Highers or more	5 767	6 627	7 581	9 460	9 284
4 Highers or more	3 565	4 264	5 005	6 431	6 369

(a) Draw a bar chart to illustrate the number of candidates who, in each year from 1962–1966, gained 2 or more Higher Grade passes.

On this chart indicate by different shadings

(i) The number who gained 3 Highers or more;

(ii) The number who gained 4 Highers or more.

(b) If a pupil is selected at random from the set who gained 2 Higher passes or more in 1965, what is the probability that this pupil gained exactly 3 Highers? (Leave your answer as a vulgar fraction.)

[S.C.E.E.B.]

(2) Plot a frequency polygon and ogive for the data in the frequency table below:

Scores	Frequency
95—99	2
90—94	3
85—89	9
80—84	15
75—79	28
70—74	38
65—69	45
60—64	32
55—59	20
50—54	11
45—49	6
40—44	2
35—39	1
Total	212

Estimate the upper and lower quartiles of the distribution.

[INST. OF STAT.]

(3) The marks scored by a class of 32 pupils in an English examination are given below:

49	53	58	48	54	51	54	52
56	42	51	52	50	45	59	62
53	52	50	49	55	56	53	55
51	46	50	51	53	52	54	48

Calculate the mean and standard deviation of the marks.

[S.C.E.E.B.]

(4) A machine, set to produce packets of biscuits with an advertised weight of 290 grammes, was thought to be faulty. In a check upon its output, a sample of 200 packets gave the following distribution of weights:

Weight (grammes)	281–283	284–286	287–289	290–292	293–295	296–298
Frequency f	4	18	36	82	50	10

(a) Add to the table a row of relative frequencies, and illustrate by a relative frequency histogram.

(b) If the total daily output of the machine is 4 820 packets, how many packets would you expect in a day to be:

(i) Underweight,

(ii) More than five grammes above the advertised weight?

(5) Calculate the arithmetic mean and the standard deviation of the odd numbers from 1 to 19 inclusive.

Deduce from your results the arithmetic mean and the standard deviation of:

(a) The numbers 1, 2, 3, . . ., 10,

(b) The even numbers from 10 to 28 inclusive.

[LOND.]

CHAPTER 7

Probability

7.1 Preliminary experiments

These experiments can be performed conveniently by pupils working in pairs, one performing the experiment, the other noting the results. After an experiment of about 100 trials pupils should move to a different one. At the end all results from a particular experiment can be combined, thus providing a large number of trials. It is important, however, that results so combined should refer to experiments performed with the same piece of apparatus. For example, in combining results of throwing a die, the same die should be used throughout. Also, one die thrown six times is not the same experiment as throwing six dice once.

Experiment 1. Cutting cards

Shuffle an ordinary pack of 52 playing cards. Place on the table and cut the cards. Record whether the card exposed is red (i.e. a heart or diamond) or black (i.e. a club or spade). Repeat the experiment ten times, shuffling the cards between each trial. Record in the table the number of times a black card is exposed and the number of times a red card. (These are denoted in the table by $n(B)$ and $n(R)$ respectively.) In a similar way perform the experiment a further ten times giving twenty trials in all, and record $n(B)$ and $n(R)$ for twenty trials.

Repeat until thirty, fifty and one hundred trials have been performed and recorded.

	Number of trials n				
	10	20	30	50	100
Number of times black $n(B)$					
Number of times red $n(R)$					
Relative frequency black $\dfrac{n(B)}{n}$					
Relative frequency red $\dfrac{n(R)}{n}$					

Complete the table by calculating to two decimal places the relative frequency of occurrence of black for each set of trials, thus:

$$\text{Relative frequency of occurrence of black} = \frac{\text{Number of times black}}{\text{Number of trials}}$$
$$= \frac{n(B)}{n}$$

Calculate in the same way the relative frequency of occurrence of red for each set of trials. Referring to the black suits compare the relative frequency for 10 trials, 20 trials . . . 100 trials. Can you reach any conclusion?
Can you reach any conclusion from a study of the relative frequencies of the red suits?
If possible combine your results with those of other pupils who performed the same experiment. Calculate the relative frequencies for the black and red suits using the largest possible number of trials.
What are the values of the two relative frequencies?

Experiment 2. Triangular spinner

Make a triangular spinner from stiff cardboard. An equilateral triangle of side six centimetres is a good size. Divide the triangle into three equal parts as shown in Fig. 7.1 and colour or mark the sections red, blue and green. Insert a toothpick or cocktail stick into the centre so that it protrudes about one centimetre and fix with a spot of glue.

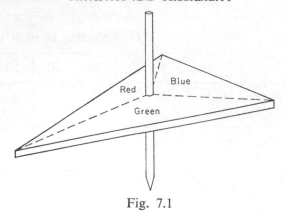

Fig. 7.1

Spin the spinner and when it comes to rest note which side lies on the table. Complete 100 trials recording $n(R)$, $n(B)$ and $n(G)$ after 10, 20, 30, 50 and 100 trials. Calculate, to two decimal places, the relative frequencies of occurrence of each of the three colours.

	Number of trials n				
	10	20	30	50	100
Number of times red $n(R)$					
Number of times blue $n(B)$					
Number of times green $n(G)$					
Relative frequency red $\dfrac{n(R)}{n}$					
Relative frequency blue $\dfrac{n(B)}{n}$					
Relative frequency green $\dfrac{n(G)}{n}$					

Can you draw any conclusion from the rows of relative frequencies? If possible combine your results with those members of the class **who used the same spinner** and calculate the relative frequencies for the largest possible number of trials.

Experiment 3. Sampling bottle with four similar beads
Use a sampling bottle containing four beads of different colours: red, blue, white, yellow. Shake the bottle well, turn it upside down, and note the colour of the bead at the bottom of the tube. Record the result and repeat. Record your results for 10, 20, 30, 50 and 100 trials in a table similar to those used in experiments 1 and 2. As before calculate the relative frequency of occurrence of each of the four colours.
Again try to combine results with other pupils to obtain the largest possible number of trials. What are the values of these four relative frequencies?

Experiment 4. Throwing a die
Throw a die 20, 30, 50, 100 and 200 times. Record in a suitable table the number of times the 1, 2, 3, 4, 5, or 6 on the die turns up in each set of trials. Calculate the relative frequency given by:

Relative frequency of $x = \dfrac{n(x)}{n}$ for $x = 1, 2, 3, 4, 5, 6$

Combine results and calculate the relative frequencies for the largest possible number of trials.
Write down these values of the six relative frequencies.

7.2 Results of experiments
The following are actual results (or a summary of results) obtained by a class of pupils performing experiments 1 to 4.

Results of experiment 1

	Number of trials n						
	10	20	30	50	100	500	5 000
Number of times black $n(B)$	3	8	13	26	48	254	2 471
Number of times red $n(R)$	7	12	17	24	52	246	2 529
Relative frequency black $\dfrac{n(B)}{n}$	0·30	0·40	0·43	0·52	0·48	0·51	0·49
Relative frequency red $\dfrac{n(R)}{n}$	0·70	0·60	0·57	0·48	0·52	0·49	0·51

Table 1

Compare your results for the first 100 trials (or 500 if you performed them) with those in table 1. In table 1 to what value does the relative frequency of occurrence seem to be tending:

    (a) For black,
    (b) For red?

Results of experiment 2

	Number of trials n						
	100	200	300	400	600	800	1 000
Number of times red $n(R)$	45	78	107	137	214	293	366
Number of times blue $n(B)$	14	37	55	83	125	164	210
Number of times green $n(G)$	41	85	138	180	261	343	424
Relative frequency red $\dfrac{n(R)}{n}$	0·45	0·39	0·36	0·34	0·36	0·37	0·37
Relative frequency blue $\dfrac{n(B)}{n}$	0·14	0·19	0·18	0·21	0·21	0·21	0·21
Relative frequency green $\dfrac{n(G)}{n}$	0·41	0·43	0·46	0·45	0·44	0·43	0·42

Table 2

If you made a spinner and performed the experiments, compare your results (for the largest possible number of trials) with those above.

In table 2 to what value does the relative frequency of occurrence seem to be tending:

    (a) For red,
    (b) For blue,
    (c) For green?

Results of experiment 3 (abridged)

		Number of trials					
		10	20	30	50	100	1 000
Relative	red	0·10	0·25	0·25	0·23	0·24	0·24
frequency of	blue	0·20	0·15	0·17	0·20	0·23	0·24
occurrence	white	0·20	0·20	0·23	0·26	0·26	0·26
of	yellow	0·50	0·40	0·35	0·31	0·27	0·26

Table 3

Compare your results as far as possible with those in table 3.
To what value does each relative frequency seem to be tending?

Results of experiment 4

Results for 1 000 trials

Score	1	2	3	4	5	6
Frequency	173	168	167	161	172	159
Relative frequency	0·17	0·17	0·17	0·16	0·17	0·16

Table 4

To what value does the relative frequency of each score seem to be tending?

7.3 Probability

Let us study again the results of the experiments of section **7.2**. The result of a single trial of an experiment we will now call the **outcome** of that trial.

F

An **event** is the occurrence of one or more outcomes of interest to us.

For example, if a single throw of a die results in a **four** appearing, the **outcome** is a **four**. If the **event** of interest is the appearance of a **six**, the event has **not** occurred.

On the other hand, if we are interested in the **event: an even number**, then the event **has** occurred.

Experiment 1. (Table 1, page 145)

Considering first the black suits, the relative frequency of occurrence shows the following successive values:

Number of trials	10	20	30	50	100	500	5 000
Relative frequency	0·30	0·40	0·43	0·52	0·48	0·51	0·49

These results indicate that the relative frequencies are tending to stabilise about 0·50 as the number of trials increases. In fact statisticians have performed this experiment a very large number of times (greatly exceeding 5 000) and have shown that the larger the number of trials the more closely does the relative frequency of occurrence of black approach 0·50.

The same results also showed that the relative frequency of occurrence of red cards approaches very closely the value 0·50 as the number of trials becomes very large.

If it is found that the relative frequency of occurrence of a particular event E tends to stabilise about a constant value as the number of trials increases, then the constant value is called the **probability** of the event occurring. Thus the probability of the event E occurring is given by

$$Pr(E) = \frac{n(E)}{n}$$

provided that the number of trials n is very large. Obviously probability will always be a number between 0 and 1 inclusive. That is:

$$0 \leqslant Pr(E) \leqslant 1$$

When $Pr(E) = 1$ the event has occurred in **every** trial.

When $Pr(E) = 0$ the event has **not** occurred during the long sequence of trials.

Using this notation, we conclude from the card cutting experiment that,

$Pr(B) = 0.50$ and $Pr(R) = 0.50$ (to two decimal places).

Experiment 2. (Table 2, page 146). On the results of 1 000 trials write down the probability that on any throw of the spinner the red side will appear. Similarly write down the probabilities that, (a) The blue side, (b) The green side will appear. Add together the three probabilities. What is their sum?

Experiment 3. (Table 3, page 147). Add together the relative frequencies of the four colours for (a) 30 trials, (b) 100 trials, (c) 1 000 trials. What is their sum in each case?
On the basis of 1 000 trials write down the probabilities of each event. Add together the four probabilities. What is their sum?

Experiment 4. (Table 4, page 147). Write down the probabilities of occurrence of each of the six faces of the die, based on 1 000 trials. Add together these probabilities. What is their sum?

This is a most important result in probability. Consider an experiment which can result in the possible outcomes, A, B, C . . . K, no two of which can occur at the same time. Then,

$$Pr(A) + Pr(B) + Pr(C) + \ldots + Pr(K) = 1$$

Outcomes or events of this kind are said to be **mutually exclusive.** For example, in tossing a die, the outcomes 1, 2, . . . 6 are mutually exclusive, since two faces cannot turn up at the same time.

Exercise 1

(1) (a) A five-sided spinner, with sides marked A, B, C, D, and E, was spun a total of 10 000 times. The frequency of occurrence of each side is shown in the following table:

Side	A	B	C	D	E
Frequency of occurrence	1 988	2 023	2 009	1 981	1 999

From the experiment, what would you conclude to be the probability of occurrence of each side (to two decimal places)?

(b) A second five-sided spinner, with sides marked P, Q, R, S and T, was spun 10 000 times, and gave the following results:

Side	P	Q	R	S	T
Frequency of occurrence	1 911	2 320	2 013	1 680	2 076

What would you conclude to be the probability of occurrence of each side (to two decimal places)?

(2) In the course of seasons 1964–65 and 1965–66 in the Scottish Football Leagues I and II and English Football Leagues I to IV, altogether 5 352 games were played, resulting in homes, aways and draws as follows:
2 812 home wins, 1 227 away wins, 1 313 draws. From these figures, write down as vulgar fractions:

(a) Pr (home win),
(b) Pr (away win),
(c) Pr (draw).

If you are able to use a calculating machine or a slide rule, calculate these probabilities to three decimal places.
Would you conclude from your results that the events, home win, away win, draw, are equally likely events?
The following table shows the results of all games played in the same leagues in the 1966–67 season. Use the figures to calculate the probabilities of home, away and draw for 1966–67 and compare the results with those obtained for the two earlier seasons.

Division	English				Scottish	
	I	II	III	IV	I	II
Home wins	232	240	298	284	142	195
Away wins	120	114	113	121	68	116
Draws	110	108	141	147	96	69

(3) (a) Over the three-year period 1965 to 1967 approximately 6·4 million driving tests were conducted. If approximately 3·0 million applicants passed the test, calculate to two decimal places, the probability that an applicant at random would succeed in passing.

(b) If 1 200 000 male applicants were taking the test for the first time and 528 000 passed, calculate the probability that a male applicant would pass the test at his first attempt.

(c) If 840 000 female applicants were taking the test for the first time and 311 000 passed, calculate the probability that a female applicant would pass the test at her first attempt.

(4) The following table shows the numbers (to the nearest thousand) of live births in Scotland for the ten year periods 1942–1951 and 1952–61, and for the four years 1962–65 (boys and girls shown separately).

Scottish births (thousands)

Years	Male	Female	Totals
1942–51	497	468	965
1952–61	493	467	960
1962–65	212	200	412

Carry out the following calculations to three decimal places:

(a) Calculate the relative frequency of a male birth for each of the three periods.

(b) Calculate the relative frequency of a female birth for each of the three periods.

(c) In 1942, 46·4 thousand male births and 44·3 thousand female births occurred. Calculate the relative frequency in 1942 of:

　(i) A male birth,
　(ii) A female birth.

(d) In 1962, 54·0 thousand male births and 50·0 thousand female births occurred. Calculate the relative frequency in 1962 of:

　(i) A male birth,
　(ii) A female birth.

Compare the results for (c) and (d) with those for (a) and (b).

(e) Calculate: (i) Pr (male birth),

               (ii) Pr (female birth),

for the whole, twenty-four year period.

(f) Would you say from these results that the birth of a boy and the birth of a girl are equally likely events?

7.4 Probability models

The probability of occurrence of an event has been defined as the long run relative frequency. We now idealise the experiments of the previous section. From symmetrical considerations backed by experience we construct probability models. The following examples illustrate the construction of three such models.

Example 1. Sampling bottle with four similar, differently coloured, beads

How many different outcomes can result from this experiment? If R, B, W and Y represent the event of obtaining red, blue, white and yellow respectively, how many outcomes give the event R? How many the events B, W, Y? Which of the four events would you expect to occur most frequently in a long sequence of trials?

In the idealised experiment we expect each event to occur in $\frac{1}{4}$ of the total number of trials. This expectation is borne out by experiment 3, page 147, in which each event was found to occur in about $\frac{1}{4}$ of the number of trials.

This suggests that a suitable model would be

$$Pr(R) = Pr(B) = Pr(W) = Pr(Y) = \tfrac{1}{4}$$

Example 2. Sampling bottle with four beads one of which is 'loaded'

Consider the last experiment with the yellow bead replaced by one of different shape and weight. Why would $Pr(R) = Pr(B) = Pr(W) = Pr(Y) = \frac{1}{4}$ not be a suitable model for this situation? Can an ideal experiment be visualised in this case? How would you find the probability of occurrence of the loaded bead?

An experiment was performed and in 1 000 trials the following results were obtained:

Event	Red	White	Blue	Yellow
Number of occurrences	199	218	201	382

In building a model we might expect the red, white and blue beads to have the same long run relative frequency of occurrence, since they are similar, while we would expect yellow to be different. This is borne out by the results of the experiment above. This leads us to set up the model:

$$Pr(Y) = \frac{n(Y)}{n} = 0.382$$

$Pr(R) = Pr(W) = Pr(B) = 0.206$ (using the mean of the three relative frequencies of red, white and blue).

Example 3. Sampling bottle with four unlike beads

Does any symmetry exist in the situation where all four beads are different in shape and weight? On what must we rely to build a probability model?

An experiment was performed and in 2 000 trials the following results were noted:

Event	Red	White	Blue	Yellow
Number of occurrences	258	532	724	486

Here we must rely on frequencies observed over a long sequence of trials and our results might lead us to set up the model:

$$Pr(\text{Red}) = \frac{n(R)}{n} = \frac{258}{2\,000} = 0.13$$
$$Pr(W) = 0.27, \quad Pr(B) = 0.36, \quad Pr(Y) = 0.24$$

These examples illustrate the methods by which probability models are built:

    (1) **By symmetry backed by experiment,**
    (2) **Long run relative frequency,**
    (3) A combination of (1) and (2).

Example 4. Triangular Spinner

Consider the home-made spinner of the previous section. With no knowledge of the experimental results what probabilities would you be inclined to assign to the events R, B and G?

Examination of the results of the experiment shows that a more suitable model for this particular spinner would be

$$Pr(R) = 0.37, \quad Pr(B) = 0.21, \quad Pr(G) = 0.42$$

Would this model fit every triangular spinner?
This example illustrates that care must be exercised when building a model from apparent symmetry. Experimental evidence should be used as the basis for all models.
Finally, the probability model must satisfy the two previous requirements:

(1) The probability of any outcome must lie between 0 and 1 inclusive.
(2) The sum of the probabilities of all possible outcomes must equal 1 (provided no two outcomes can occur at the same time, that is, the outcomes are mutually exclusive).

Exercise 2

(1) If the events A, B and C are the only possible outcomes of an experiment, which of the following are possible probability models?

(a) $Pr(A) = \frac{1}{4}$, $Pr(B) = \frac{1}{4}$, $Pr(C) = \frac{1}{4}$

(b) $Pr(A) = \frac{1}{4}$, $Pr(B) = \frac{1}{4}$, $Pr(C) = \frac{1}{2}$

(c) $Pr(A) = \frac{1}{3}$, $Pr(B) = \frac{1}{3}$, $Pr(C) = \frac{2}{3}$

(d) $Pr(A) = \frac{3}{4}$, $Pr(B) = \frac{3}{4}$, $Pr(C) = -\frac{1}{2}$

(e) $Pr(A) = \frac{3}{16}$, $Pr(B) = \frac{1}{16}$, $Pr(C) = \frac{3}{4}$.

(2) Use a sampling bottle containing the following number of beads:

10 red,   20 blue,   30 white,   40 green.

Perform the experiment of shaking the bottle, turning it upside down and noting the colour of the bead at the bottom of the tube. Perform the experiment 200 times and build a probability model for the occurrence of each of the four colours.

(3) A cuboid, square in section was accurately constructed. The four rectangular faces were marked A, B, C and D and the two square faces marked Y and Z. The cuboid was thrown in the manner of a die two thousand times and gave the following frequencies of occurrence of the six faces:

Face	A	B	C	D	Y	Z
Frequency	448	434	435	442	118	123

Build a probability model for this experiment.

(4) Make a die from a wooden cube by marking each face with one of the numbers 1 to 6. Throw the die a sufficient number of times to build a probability model.

Use a rasp or sandpaper to remove evenly from one face about 1 millimetre of wood (this task is best undertaken in the technical department). The die should now be distinctly biased. Carry out a further series of trials and build a new probability model for your asymmetric die.

7.5 Addition rule for probabilities

Let us look at two of the experiments performed at the beginning of this chapter.

Example 1. Use the results of experiment 4, page 147 (1 000 throws), to calculate the probability of throwing an even number with that particular die.

Score	1	2	3	4	5	6
Frequency	173	168	167	161	172	159
Probability	0·17	0·17	0·17	0·16	0·17	0·16

Since throwing an even number implies throwing a 2, 4 or 6:

$$Pr \text{ (even number)} = \frac{\text{number of times 2, 4 or 6 appeared}}{\text{number of trials}}$$

$$= \frac{168+161+159}{1\ 000}$$

$$= \frac{488}{1\ 000} = 0·49 \text{ to two decimal places.}$$

An alternative way of performing the calculation is:

$$Pr \text{ (even number)} = \frac{168+161+159}{1\ 000}$$

$$= \frac{168}{1\ 000} + \frac{161}{1\ 000} + \frac{159}{1\ 000}$$

$$= 0 \cdot 17 + 0 \cdot 16 + 0 \cdot 16$$

$$= 0 \cdot 49$$

This is, of course, precisely the result obtained by adding together the separate probabilities of a 2, 4 or 6. That is:

$$Pr \text{ (even number)} = Pr(2) + Pr(4) + Pr(6)$$
$$= 0 \cdot 17 + 0 \cdot 16 + 0 \cdot 16 = 0 \cdot 49$$

Example 2. Use the results of experiment 2, page 146 (1ʾ000 spins), to calculate the probability of obtaining a red or a blue with that spinner (i.e. the probability of not obtaining a green).

	Frequency	Probability
Red	366	0·37
Blue	210	0·21
Green	424	0·42

Complete the following:

$$Pr \text{ (red or blue)} = \frac{\text{number of times} \ldots}{\text{number of trials}}$$

$$= \underline{}$$

$$= 0 \cdot 58$$

Now write down the probability that neither red nor blue occurred. In general, if a trial can result in a number of outcomes (mutually exclusive) and we wish to know the probability of outcome A or B or . . . or K occurring, then

$$Pr\ (A\ \text{or}\ B\ \text{or}\ \ldots\ \text{or}\ K) = Pr(A) + Pr(B) + \ldots + Pr(K).$$

This is known as the **addition rule** for probabilities.

Finally, if p is the probability of the occurrence of an event and q the probability of its non-occurrence, then

$$p + q = 1$$

Exercise 3

(1) If the probability of an event occurring is 0·14 what is the probability of the event not occurring?

(2) An experiment can have four possible outcomes A, B, C, D. If the probabilities of the first three are $Pr(A) = 0·12$, $Pr(B) = 0·16$, $Pr(C) = 0·35$, write down the probability of the occurrence of D.

(3) Using the table of example 1, page 155, determine the probability of, in a single throw of a die, the following events occurring:

(a) An odd number,

(b) A number less than three,

(c) A number from one to six.

(4) An experiment can result in the five mutually exclusive outcomes A, B, C, D, E. If a suitable probability model for the experiment is,
$Pr(A) = Pr(B) = 0·12$, $Pr(C) = Pr(D) = 0·21$, $Pr(E) = 0·34$, determine the probability of:

(a) A or E occurring,

(b) B or C or D occurring,

(c) E not occurring.

(5) The probabilities of a marksman scoring a bull, inner and outer, are 0·23, 0·41, and 0·30 respectively. What is the probability that he will:

(a) Score an inner or better,

(b) Fail to hit the target,

(c) Fail to score a bull?

7.6 Expected frequencies

Suppose that in one thousand trials of an experiment an event A occurs 320 times. Then based upon this number of trials

$$Pr(A) = \frac{\text{number of times } A \text{ occurred}}{\text{number of trials}}$$

$$= \frac{320}{1\,000}$$

$$= 0.32$$

If we repeated the experiment a further thousand times we would expect A to occur on **about** 320 occasions. **About** how many times would you expect A to occur if the experiment were repeated:

    (a) Three thousand times,
    (b) Two hundred times?

The product of the number of trials and the probability of the event A gives us the **expected frequency** of event A, for that number of trials,

i.e. expected frequency = number of trials $\times$ $Pr(A)$.

This does not mean that A will in fact occur precisely that number of times. Expected frequency is a theoretical number which would occur in an idealised experiment. In practice, however, expected frequency tells us the number of times that A can reasonably be expected to occur.

Exercise 4

(1)

Score	1	2	3	4	5	6
Probability	0·17	0·17	0·17	0·16	0·17	0·16

Use the results of experiment 4, shown in the table above, to calculate the expected frequency of:

    (a) A six in 100 throws,
    (b) An odd number in 200 throws,
    (c) A three or a four in 300 throws.

(2) A Gallup Poll establishes that 2 out of 7 people are in favour of a certain proposal. How many people out of a total of 5 000 would you expect to vote for the proposal?

(3) If in the Scottish and English Football Leagues, the probabilities of an away win and of a draw are 0·23 and 0·25 respectively, write down the probability of a home win.
If a full programme of 64 games is played, calculate the expected frequencies of:

   (a) Home wins,
   (b) Away wins,
   (c) Draws.

7.7 The uniform probability model

As a result of experiment and experience, it has been found that many practical situations arise where each of the possible outcomes of an experiment or trial has the same probability of occurring. For example:

   (a) When throwing a fair die,

$$Pr(1) = Pr(2) = \ldots = Pr(6) = \tfrac{1}{6}$$

   (b) When tossing a fair coin,

$$Pr(H) = Pr(T) = \tfrac{1}{2}$$

   (c) If twenty-six identical counters, marked A, B, C . . . Z are shaken in a box and one counter drawn, the probability of drawing each counter is:

$$Pr(A) = Pr(B) = \ldots = Pr(Z) = \tfrac{1}{26}$$

We have already made use of this result when drawing random samples (chapter 2).

A model of the kind illustrated in (a), (b) and (c) above where each event has an equal probability of occurrence is called a **uniform probability model**. The events in this case are often called **equally likely events.**

Example 1. Assuming the uniform model, find the probability of obtaining an even number with a single throw of a die.

Since $Pr(1) = Pr(2) = \ldots = Pr(6) = \tfrac{1}{6}$

$$
\begin{aligned}
Pr(2 \text{ or } 4 \text{ or } 6) &= Pr(2)+Pr(4)+Pr(6) \\
&= \tfrac{1}{6}+\tfrac{1}{6}+\tfrac{1}{6} \\
&= \tfrac{3}{6} = \tfrac{1}{2}
\end{aligned}
$$

Observe the fraction $\frac{3}{6}$. When throwing a die, how many outcomes are possible? How many are favourable to the event (an even number)?

Example 2. A cloakroom uses thirty-six checks numbered consecutively from 1 onwards. Assuming that all checks are equally likely to be issued, find the probability that the first check issued carried a prime number.

Copy and complete the following:

Probability model: $Pr(1) = Pr(2) = \ldots = Pr(36) =$
Prime numbers less than 36: 2, 3, 5, ...
Then Pr (prime number) $= Pr(2) + Pr(3) + Pr(5) + \ldots$
$\qquad =$

Verify that the answer is $\frac{11}{36}$. How many outcomes are possible in this problem? How many are favourable to the event (prime number issued)?

From examples 1 and 2 we can deduce a simple method of calculating probabilities where the uniform model is appropriate.

In example 1, with six possible outcomes, three of which are favourable, we find,

Pr (even number) $= \frac{3}{6}$

In example 2, with thirty-six possible outcomes, eleven of which are favourable, we find,

Pr (prime number) $= \frac{11}{36}$

In general, if an event comprises one or more outcomes from a set of equally likely outcomes, the probability of the event occurring

$$= \frac{\text{number of outcomes favourable to the event}}{\text{number of possible outcomes}}$$

Example 3. Five one-centimetre cubes are made from different metals, iron, cobalt, nickel, zinc and aluminium. The first three named are magnetic metals, the remaining two, non-magnetic.

If the cubes are mixed, and two chosen at random, find the probabilities of selecting:

(a) Two non-magnetic metals,

(b) Exactly one magnetic metal,

(c) At least one magnetic metal.

Denoting the metals by their initial letters, the following partially

completed array of ordered pairs, shows the possible pairings of
metals, first choice followed by second choice:

	I	C	·N	Z	A
I		IC	IN	•	•
C .	CI		•	•	•
N	NI	•		•	•
Z	•	•	•		•
A	•	•	•	•	

Fig. 7.2

Copy and complete the array. How many pairs appear in the complete
array? How many possible outcomes of the selection are there?
How many pairings consist only of two non-magnetic metals?
What is the probability of selecting two non-magnetic metals?
In a similar manner calculate the probabilities for (b) and (c).
Verify that the required probabilities are:

(a) 0·1, (b) 0·6, (c) 0·9.

If the experiment of drawing two cubes at random is repeated fifty
times, on how many occasions would we expect to draw the two non-
magnetic metals?

Exercise 5

(1) At a church bazaar a cake is raffled. The numbers of tickets sold
from four books of different colours are:
red 154, white 104, green 141, pink 81.

(a) If a visitor to the bazaar bought five tickets find his or her
probability of winning.

(b) Find the probability that the winning ticket is white.

(2) A farmer ran two separate poultry farms on his land. On a
particular day the output of eggs from the farms was graded as
follows:

	Total number of eggs	Percentage large	Percentage standard	Percentage small
Farm *A*	450	18%	54%	28%
Farm *B*	430	30%	50%	20%

Calculate the probability that an egg chosen at random from the entire output will be graded small. Use this result to write down the probability that an egg chosen at random will be either standard or large.

(3) In the game of snooker the values of the seven colours are as follows:

Colour	red	yellow	green	brown	blue	pink	black
Points value	1	2	3	4	5	6	7

The seven balls are mixed in a bag and two balls chosen. Make an array of ordered pairs showing all possible combinations of two balls, first ball drawn followed by second ball. Calculate the probabilities of drawing:

(a) Two balls with a total value greater than ten,

(b) Two balls with a total value 4 or less.

From the answer to (b) write down the probability of drawing two balls with a total value greater than four. If the experiment is repeated 30 times, how many would we expect to result in a total of four or less?

(4) Repeat question (3) but this time assume that the balls are drawn **with replacement,** that is the first ball is drawn, colour noted and the ball replaced in the bag. The second ball is then drawn. What important difference does this method of drawing make to the ordered pairs?

(5) A signalling device consists of three lamps each of which can show no light, a red light, or a green light. For example, the sketch shows the combination red, no light, green.

| R | O | G |

Make an array of ordered triples to show all possible combinations of the three lamps. Calculate the probabilities of:

(a) All three lamps being red,
(b) All three lamps being different,
(c) Two lamps being green, one lamp red.

Out of 100 random signals, how many would we expect to show three green lamps?

7.8 Probability curves

Example 1. The distribution of pupils by age in a secondary school at the start of a new session is given in the following table. (Age 11 means having passed the eleventh birthday, but not yet reached the twelfth.)

Age in years	11	12	13	14	15	16	17	18 and over
Frequency	63	106	113	118	96	89	80	35

Total roll is 700

What is the probability that a pupil chosen at random from the school roll is fourteen years of age? Let us assume the uniform probability model, namely that each pupil has an equal chance of being chosen. Let A be the event (pupil selected at random is fourteen years old), then:

$$Pr(A) = \frac{\text{number of outcomes favourable to } A}{\text{number of possible outcomes}}$$

$$= \frac{118}{700}$$

$$= 0.17 \text{ (to two decimal places).}$$

This is, of course, precisely the relative frequency of occurrence of A. In other words:

$Pr(A)$ = relative frequency of occurrence of A.

Copy the above table and add to it a row of relative frequencies. Draw the relative frequency histogram of the distribution and verify that it is as follows:

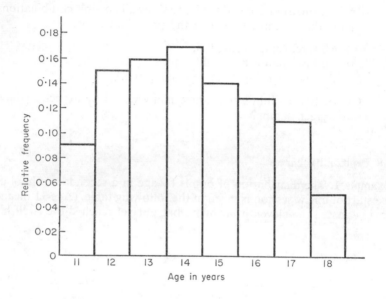

Fig. 7.3

What relative frequency does the **area** of the column erected on the age fourteen years represent? What probability does this area represent?

What relative frequency is represented by the total area of all columns on the histogram? What probability is represented by this area?

From the figure, find the probability that a pupil chosen at random is:

(a) Over school-leaving age,

(b) Between twelve and fourteen years old, inclusive.

This example illustrates that a relative frequency histogram can be used as, and in fact can equally well be called, a **probability histogram**.

Example 2. Several thousand cigarette smokers were asked the total amount which they normally spent on cigarettes in one week. The results were tabulated, and a relative frequency histogram drawn, using a large number of class intervals. From this the following **smoothed relative frequency curve** was obtained.

The area under the curve has been divided into six parts by ordinates (shown by dotted lines) at 0·8, 1·0, etc. The percentages of the whole area represented by some of these parts are:

$$B = 16\%, \quad C = 25\%, \quad D = 23\%, \quad E = 13\%$$

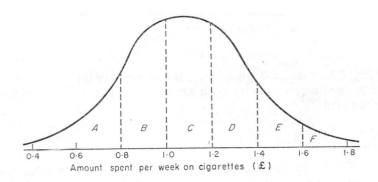

Amount spent per week on cigarettes (£)

Fig. 7.4

Since the whole area below the curve is 1, the portion C has area 0·25. That is, the relative frequency of occurrence of smokers who spend between £1·0 and £1·2 per week is 0·25.

As was demonstrated in example 1, probability is equivalent to relative frequency. Thus if a smoker is taken at random from the number who were interviewed the probability that he or she spends between £1·0 and £1·2 per week is 0·25.

Find the probability that a smoker chosen at random spends between:

(a) £1·2 and £1·4 per week,
(b) £0·8 and £1·6 per week.

If area A = area E+area F, find the probability that a smoker spends more than £1·6. Write down the probability that he or she spends less than £0·8.

When the distribution of a population (or a sample) is represented in the above manner by a smoothed relative frequency curve, we call it a **probability curve**. The total area under a probability curve represents a probability of 1.

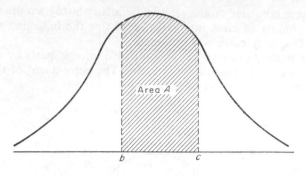

Fig. 7.5

If Fig. 7.5 represents such a curve, the probability that an element of the population (or sample) has a value lying between b and c is given by the area A.

Exercise 6

(1) Figures 7.6 and 7.7 illustrate probability curves prepared from frequency distributions of certain variables.

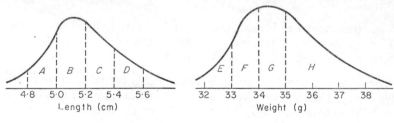

Fig. 7.6   Fig. 7.7

(a) In Fig. 7.6 the ratio of the areas A, B, C and D is $A:B:C:D = 2:4:3:1$, and these four areas represent 90% of the whole area under the curve The areas to the left of 4·8 and to the right of 5·6 centimetres are equal. Find the probability that a variable chosen at random will have length:

    (i) Between 5·0 and 5·2 cm,
    (ii) Less than 5·4 cm,
    (iii) More than 5·6 cm.

If you selected a sample of 50 of the variable, how many would you expect to find between 5·0 and 5·4 cm in length?

(b) In Fig. 7.7 areas *F* and *G* are equal and both are twice area *E*. If *E* has an area of 0·17 find the probability that a variable chosen at random will have weight:

    (i) Greater than 33 g,
    (ii) Between 33 and 35 g,
    (iii) Greater than 35 g.

In a sample of 80 variables how many would you expect to find less than 33 g?

(2) Fig. 7.8 shows the probability curve of weights (in kilogrammes) of a large number of schoolboys.

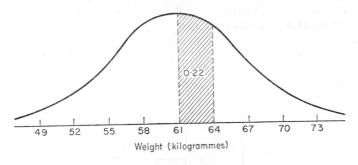

Fig. 7.8

The curve is symmetrical about the ordinate at 61 kg and the shaded area = 0·22.
Find the probability that a pupil chosen at random will have weight:

    (a) Less than 61 kg,
    (b) More than 64 kg,
    (c) Less than 58 kg.

(3) Make a probability histogram from the following distribution of breaking strengths of metal bars:

Breaking strength (kilogrammes)	64·5–69·5	69·5–74·5	74·5–79·5	79·5–84·5	84·5–89·5	89·5–94·5	94·5–99·5
Frequency	64	83	101	121	151	142	138

   (*a*) If the following standards for breaking strengths are laid
down:

        grade 1 . . . . greater than 89·5 kg,
        grade 2 . . . . between 69·5 and 89·5 kg,
        grade 3 (rejects) . . less than 69·5 kg,
        find the probabilities that a single bar selected at random will
        be classified as grade 1, grade 2, or rejected.

   (*b*) If you selected a sample of two hundred and fifty bars, about
how many would you expect to find in each of the three
grades?

(4) The probability histogram in Fig. 7.9 shows the approximate
probabilities of finding 0, 1, 2 . . . persons ahead of you in a
queue at a post-office counter.

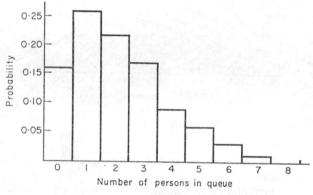

Fig. 7·9

If you enter the post office at any moment, what is the probability
of finding:

(*a*) Exactly two people in the queue?
(*b*) At least two people in the queue?
(*c*) The counter free?
In thirty visits to the post office, on how many occasions would
you expect to find:
(*d*) Three people or less in the queue?
(*e*) More than 5 people in the queue?

CHAPTER 8

The Binomial Distribution

8.1 Pascal's triangle and binomial expansions

Let us investigate the possible results obtained on tossing a number of coins. Let H denote **heads** and T denote **tails** and let HTH, for example, be written to mean obtaining a head with the first coin, a tail with the second coin, and a head with the third coin. Note that the order of the coins is important. HT, therefore, is a different result from TH.

Using this notation a table was compiled showing the possible outcomes from tossing (*a*) One coin, (*b*) Two coins, (*c*) Three coins, (*d*) Four coins. Verify that the table is correct:

No. of coins tossed	Possible results	Total no. of results
1	$H \quad T$	2
2	HT $HH \qquad TT$ TH	4
3	$HHT \quad TTH$ $HHH \quad HTH \quad THT \quad TTT$ $THH \quad HTT$	8
4	$HHTT$ $HHHT \quad HTTH \quad TTTH$ $HHTH \quad TTHH \quad TTHT$ $HHHH \qquad\qquad\qquad TTTT$ $HTHH \quad HTHT \quad THTT$ $THHH \quad THTH \quad HTTT$ $THHT$	16

From the table we observe that, in the case of one coin being tossed, there are two possible results, one of which shows 0 heads, and the other, 1 head.

169

When two coins are tossed, there are four possible results in which 0 heads appear once, 1 head appears twice. and 2 heads once. Continuing thus, another table is formed:

No. of coins tossed	No. of ways of obtaining:				
	0	1	2	3	4 heads
1	1	1			
2	1	2	1		
3	1	3	3	1	
4	1	4	6	4	1

You may have seen this number pattern before. It is called **Pascal's triangle.** Can you extend this number pattern to give another row . . ., and another?

Later in this chapter you will be required to expand expressions like $(a+b)^3$ and while you may be able to do so using the distributive law, you will find that it is rather difficult. Pascal's triangle, however, helps us to do these expansions without much difficulty.

Look at the following expansions and notice how the rows of Pascal's triangle have been used:

$$(a+b)^1 = a+b$$

$$(a+b)^2 = a^2+2ab+b^2$$

$$(a+b)^3 = a^3+3a^2b+3ab^2+b^3$$

$$(a+b)^4 = a^4+4a^3b+6a^2b^2+4ab^3+b^4$$

Note that the sum of the powers of a and b in each term is equal to the power of the original expansion. For example, in the expression of $(a+b)^4$ the sum of the powers of a and b will be 4. Check each term to verify this.

Verify that:

$$(a+b)^5 = a^5+5a^4b+10a^3b^2+10a^2b^3+5ab^4+b^5$$

$$(x+y)^3 = x^3+3x^2y+3xy^2+y^3$$

$$(q+p)^4 = q^4+4q^3p+6q^2p^2+4qp^3+p^4$$

Summary. If we are required to expand, for example, $(x+y)^3$ we look at the **third** row of Pascal's triangle and write:

$$(x+y)^3 = x^3+3x^2y+3xy^2+y^3$$

Exercise 1

(1) Using Pascal's triangle expand:

    (a) $(x+y)^2$,   (b) $(q+p)^4$,   (c) $(q+p)^3$,

    (d) $(a+b)^6$,   (e) $(q+p)^5$,   (f) $(a+\frac{1}{2})^2$,

    (g) $(\frac{1}{4}+b)^2$,   (h) $(x+\frac{1}{3})^3$,   (i) $(\frac{1}{2}+\frac{1}{2})^4$,

    (j) $(\frac{1}{4}+\frac{3}{4})^3$,   (k) $(\frac{4}{5}+\frac{1}{5})^2$,   (l) $(\frac{2}{3}+\frac{1}{3})^6$.

(2) (a) What is the second term in the expansion of $(q+p)^3$?

    (b) What is the fourth term in the expansion of $(q+p)^4$?

    (c) What is the third term in the expansion of $(\frac{1}{2}+\frac{1}{2})^3$?

    (d) What is the first term in the expansion of $(\frac{1}{5}+\frac{4}{5})^5$?

    (e) What is the third term in the expansion of $(\frac{2}{3}+\frac{1}{3})^3$?

The expansions with which you have been working are called **Binomial** expansions since they are concerned with binomial expressions like $q+p$, i.e. expressions which have **two** terms.

8.2 Success or failure situations

In this chapter we are going to be concerned with situations in which there are only two possible outcomes, and we shall perform experiments to illustrate such situations. For example, we shall toss coins. Note that the tossing of a coin has only two possible outcomes, **heads** or **tails.** It is usual in statistics to focus attention on one of these outcomes and call it a **success,** while the other is called a **failure.** We shall perform, also, experiments using a sampling bottle in which there are red and blue beads. Again we note that the colour of a bead is either red or blue. If we call a red bead a **success,** then a blue bead will be called a **failure.**

The results of experiments like these will be used to help us to deal with real life situations in which there are two possible outcomes of interest. Here are some of these situations:

(a) The goods made by a manufacturer are defective or non-defective.

(b) Television sets are able to show colour programmes or they are not.

(c) People entitled to vote in an election exercise that right or they do not.

(d) Pupils sitting an examination pass or fail.

In each case there is present the fundamental idea of **success** or **failure**. This is the basis of our work involving the Binomial distribution.

8.3 Experiments and results

Experiment 1

Toss a coin one hundred times. Note the number of times a head appears and the number of times a tail (i.e. no head) appears. Let us assume that all the coins have been tested and found to be fair, so that we can combine the results of different members of the class. Tabulate the results of your class as follows:

Score	Frequency	Relative frequency
0 heads		
1 head		

No. of trials =

Because of the result of this experiment (and many others like it) we adopt the probability model $p = \frac{1}{2}$, $q = \frac{1}{2}$ where p is the probability of a head appearing, and q is the probability of a tail appearing. We notice that $q+p = 1$.

The relative frequency distribution of heads for this model may be represented by the following diagram:

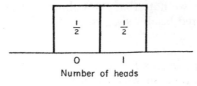

Fig. 8.1

Experiment 2

For this experiment you require to work with a partner. Each of you must toss a coin and note the result. If one obtains a head while the other obtains a tail, your combined score will be taken to be 1 head. If you both obtain heads, the score will be 2 heads, while if you both obtain tails, the score will be 0 heads. Repeat this one hundred times. Combine your results with those of the other members of your class. Tabulate the results as follows:

Score	Frequency	Relative frequency
0 heads		
1 head		
2 heads		

No. of trials =

What model would you think appropriate in this case?
It is usually found that a score of 0 heads is made on about one quarter of the trials, a score of 1 head on about a half of the trials, and a score of 2 heads on about one quarter of the trials.
The relative frequency distribution of heads for this model has the following appearance:

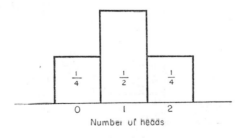

Fig. 8.2

Thus the probabilities of getting 0, 1, 2 heads when two **fair** coins are tossed appear to be $\frac{1}{4}$, $\frac{1}{2}$, $\frac{1}{4}$ respectively.

Using the results of Experiment 1 where $p = \frac{1}{2}$, $q = \frac{1}{2}$ (p = probability of a head appearing and q = probability of a tail appearing) we notice:

$$(q+p)^2 = q^2 + 2qp + q^2$$
$$= (\tfrac{1}{2})^2 + 2(\tfrac{1}{2})(\tfrac{1}{2}) + (\tfrac{1}{2})^2$$
$$= \tfrac{1}{4} + \tfrac{1}{2} + \tfrac{1}{4}$$
$$= Pr(0) + Pr(1) + Pr(2)$$

where $Pr(0)$, for example, denotes the probability of getting 0 heads. This suggests that there might be some connection between the terms of the expansion of $(q+p)^2$ and the probabilities of getting 0 heads, 1 head, and 2 heads when **two** coins are tossed.

Note. It is suggested that one group of three pupils and one group of four pupils might investigate the results from tossing three and four coins simultaneously. Experiments 3 and 4 offer alternatives to this.

Experiment 3

Place an equal number of red and blue beads in a sampling bottle. One hundred of each is suggested and the beads should be similar in size and shape.

Shake the bottle, turn it upside down and note the number of red beads in the first three in the tube.

Repeat this procedure one hundred times. Record the combined results of your class and complete the following table:

Score	Frequency	Relative frequency
0 reds		
1 red		
2 reds		
3 reds		

No. of trials =

Suggest an appropriate model for the probabilities of getting 0 red beads, 1 red bead, 2 red beads, 3 red beads in samples of three beads. The relative frequency distribution of these results usually has this appearance. Compare it with yours.

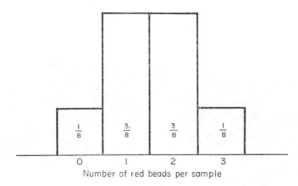

Fig. 8.3

From the results of experiments like these we adopt the model,

$$Pr(0) = \tfrac{1}{8}, \ Pr(1) = \tfrac{3}{8}, \ Pr(2) = \tfrac{3}{8}, \ Pr(3) = \tfrac{1}{8}.$$

From the results we also obtain values for p and q where
$$p = Pr(\text{red}) \ \text{and} \ q = Pr(\text{not red}).$$
For p, form the ratio:

$$\frac{\text{Total number of red beads observed}}{\text{Total number of beads observed}}$$

Using $q = \tfrac{1}{2}, \ p = \tfrac{1}{2}$, we notice:
$$\begin{aligned}
(q+p)^3 &= q^3 + 3q^2p + 3qp^2 + p^3 \\
&= (\tfrac{1}{2})^3 + 3(\tfrac{1}{2})^2(\tfrac{1}{2}) + 3(\tfrac{1}{2})(\tfrac{1}{2})^2 + (\tfrac{1}{2})^3 \\
&= \tfrac{1}{8} + \tfrac{3}{8} + \tfrac{3}{8} + \tfrac{1}{8} \\
&= Pr(0) + Pr(1) + Pr(2) + Pr(3)
\end{aligned}$$

Thus the probabilities of getting 0, 1, 2, 3 red beads, when samples of three beads are observed, appear to be obtained by evaluating the terms of the expansion of $(q+p)^3$.

Experiment 4

Carry out a similar experiment to the previous one. Shake the sampling bottle and note the number of red beads in the first four in the tube. Repeat this procedure as before, record your results and complete the following table.

Score	Frequency	Relative frequency
0 reds		
1 red		
2 reds		
3 reds		
4 reds		

No. of trials =

The relative frequency distribution of these results usually tends to have the following appearance. Compare it with the one compiled from your own results.

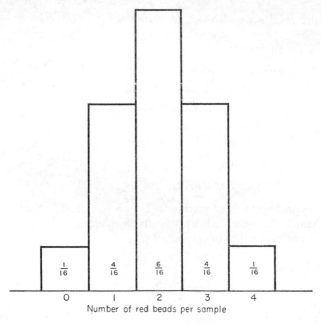

Fig. 8.4

From the results of experiments like this one it would appear that a reasonable model for the probabilities of obtaining 0, 1, 2, 3, 4 red beads in samples of four would be $\frac{1}{16}$, $\frac{4}{16}$, $\frac{6}{16}$, $\frac{4}{16}$, $\frac{1}{16}$.
Expand $(q+p)^4$ and using $q = \frac{1}{2}$, $p = \frac{1}{2}$ find the value for each term.

Thus the probabilities of getting 0, 1, 2, 3, 4 red beads in samples of four beads appear to be obtained by evaluating the terms of $(q+p)^4$ where p = probability of getting a red bead when equal numbers of red and blue beads are tossed and q = probability of getting a blue bead.

Experiment 5

In the experiments in this chapter so far we have been concerned with equal values of p and q. Let us now consider a situation where p and q will have **unequal** values.

Fill a sampling bottle with a large number of red beads and twice as many blue ones. Shake the bottle, turn it upside down, and note the colours of the first two beads.

The following are results obtained by pupils carrying out this experiment:

Score	Frequency	Relative frequency
0 reds	134	$\frac{134}{300} = \frac{402}{900}$
1 red	131	$\frac{131}{300} = \frac{393}{900}$
2 reds	35	$\frac{35}{300} = \frac{105}{900}$

No. of trials = 300.

From these results a reasonable probability model can be formed. The probability of a red bead appearing no times in a single trial is $\frac{4}{9}$, appearing once is $\frac{4}{9}$, and appearing twice is $\frac{1}{9}$.

i.e. $Pr(0) = \frac{4}{9}$, $Pr(1) = \frac{4}{9}$, $Pr(2) = \frac{1}{9}$

The relative frequency distribution of the results has this appearance:

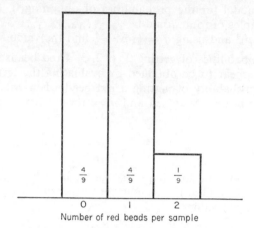

Fig. 8.5

Notice that this time the distribution is not symmetrical.

In the experiment, 600 beads in all were observed. Of these 201 were red (from the table 1 red had a frequency of 131 and 2 reds a frequency of 35). This leads us to state that Pr(red) is $\frac{1}{3}$ or $p = \frac{1}{3}$ and Pr(not red)$= 1-\frac{1}{3}$ or $q = \frac{2}{3}$.

The results were compared with those obtained by expanding $(q+p)^2$ and putting $q = \frac{2}{3}$ and $p = \frac{1}{3}$,

$$(q+p)^2 = \quad q^2 \quad + 2qp \quad +p^2$$
$$= \quad (\tfrac{2}{3})^2 \quad +2(\tfrac{2}{3})(\tfrac{1}{3})+(\tfrac{1}{3})^2$$
$$= \quad \tfrac{4}{9} \quad + \quad \tfrac{4}{9} \quad + \tfrac{1}{9}$$
$$= Pr(0) + Pr(1) + Pr(2)$$

It seems reasonable to conclude that the probabilities of a red bead appearing no times, once, twice when two beads are observed will be obtained by evaluating the terms of $(q+p)^2$ with appropriate values for q and p.

8.4 Probability model

Mathematicians do, in fact, use binomial expansions as a mathematical model for working out probabilities in situations similar to those in the experiments you have just completed.

There are certain requirements which must be fulfilled.

(a) Each trial must have only two possible outcomes—either a particular result happens or it does not happen. When the result occurs we call the outcome a **success** and when it does not occur we call the outcome a **failure.**

(b) It is usual to assign p to the probability of a success and q to the probability of a failure. We note that $q = 1-p$.

(c) The number (n) of trials must be known. This gives the **power** of the binomial expansion.

(d) The probability of obtaining a certain number of successes in n trials will be given by the appropriate term in the expansion of $(q+p)^n$.

$$(q+p)^n = Pr(0) + Pr(1) + Pr(2) + \ldots + Pr(n)$$

Worked examples

(1) One person in six in a city prefers coffee to tea in the morning. If three people are interviewed, what is the probability that one of them prefers coffee?

Let **preferring coffee** be a success and **preferring tea** be a failure.

$$p = \tfrac{1}{6}, q = 1 - \tfrac{1}{6} = \tfrac{5}{6}, n = 3$$

Number of successes required is one.

$$(q+p)^3 = q^3 + 3q^2p + 3qp^2 + p^3$$

$$= Pr(0) + Pr(1) + Pr(2) + Pr(3)$$

Therefore
$$Pr(1) = 3q^2p$$

$$= 3(\tfrac{5}{6})^2(\tfrac{1}{6})$$

$$= 3 \times \tfrac{25}{36} \times \tfrac{1}{6}$$

$$= \tfrac{25}{72}$$

Probability that one prefers coffee $= \tfrac{25}{72}$.

Note that $Pr(1)$ is given by the term in the expansion with p to the power 1, i.e. $3q^2p$.

(2) Five people in seven voted at a certain election. If four of those on the voters' roll are interviewed, what is the probability that **at least** three voted?

Note. At least three means that we must include the probability that four people voted as well as three.

Let **voting** be a success and **not voting** be a failure.

$$p = \tfrac{5}{7}, q = 1 - \tfrac{5}{7} = \tfrac{2}{7}, n = 4$$

Number of successes required is at least three, i.e. required probability is $Pr(3) + Pr(4)$.

$$(q+p)^4 = q^4 + 4q^3p + 6q^2p^2 + 4qp^3 + p^4$$
$$= Pr(0) + Pr(1) + Pr(2) + \boxed{Pr(3) + Pr(4)}$$
$$Pr(3) + Pr(4) = 4qp^3 + p^4$$
$$= 4(\tfrac{2}{7})(\tfrac{5}{7})^3 + (\tfrac{5}{7})^4$$
$$= (4 \times \tfrac{2}{7} \times \tfrac{125}{343}) + \tfrac{625}{2401}$$
$$= \tfrac{1000}{2401} + \tfrac{625}{2401}$$
$$= \tfrac{1625}{2401}$$

Probability that at least three voted $= \tfrac{1625}{2401}$.

(3) If 20% of the bolts produced by a certain machine are defective, what is the probability that, from a group of five chosen at random, **at most** two will be defective?

Note. At most two means that we must include the probabilities of no bolts being defective and of one bolt being defective as well as two.

Let **a defective bolt** be a success and **a non-defective bolt** be a failure.

$$p = \tfrac{1}{5}, q = 1 - \tfrac{1}{5} = \tfrac{4}{5}, n = 5$$

Number of successes required is at most two, i.e. required probability is $Pr(0) + Pr(1) + Pr(2)$.

$$(q+p)^5 = q^5 + 5q^4p + 10q^3p^2 + 10q^2p^3 + 5qp^4 + p^5$$
$$= \boxed{Pr(0) + Pr(1) + Pr(2)} + Pr(3) + Pr(4) + Pr(5)$$
$$Pr(0) + Pr(1) + Pr(2) = q^5 + 5q^4p + 10q^3p^2$$
$$= (\tfrac{4}{5})^5 + 5(\tfrac{4}{5})^4(\tfrac{1}{5}) + 10(\tfrac{4}{5})^3(\tfrac{1}{5})^2$$
$$= \tfrac{1024}{3125} + \tfrac{1280}{3125} + \tfrac{640}{3125}$$
$$= \tfrac{2944}{3125}$$

Probability of **at most** two defective bolts $= \tfrac{2944}{3125}$

(4) A drug cures two persons in every five suffering from a certain disease. What is the probability that when the drug is given to five patients who have the disease, at least two will be cured? Let a cure be a **success** and no cure a **failure**.

$$p = \tfrac{2}{5}, q = 1-\tfrac{2}{5} = \tfrac{3}{5}, n = 5$$

Number of successes is at least two, i.e. required probability is

$Pr(2)+Pr(3)+Pr(4)+Pr(5)$

Verify that $Pr(2)+Pr(3)+Pr(4)$ $Pr(5) = \tfrac{2072}{3125}$

You will have completed rather a cumbersome calculation to find this result.
The calculation is made easier by noticing that since:

$Pr(0)+Pr(1)+Pr(2)+Pr(3)+Pr(4)+Pr(5) = 1$

$Pr(2)+Pr(3)+Pr(4)+Pr(5) = 1-[Pr(0)+Pr(1)]$

Show that $1-[Pr(0)+Pr(1)] = \tfrac{2072}{3125}$

In the examples following, watch out for questions in which the calculation will be made easier by using the above method.

Exercise 2

(1) A drug cures three out of five people suffering from a disease. What is the probability that when the drug is given to four patients, three of them will be cured?

(2) 80% of those who sit a certain examination pass. What is the probability that out of a group of four examinees (*a*) Three, (*b*) Two, (*c*) At least three pass?

(3) One man in three is 1·80 m or more in height. What is the probability that two out of five men chosen at random are in this category?

(4) At a certain school, seven out of ten pupils have Saturday morning employment. What is the probability that three out of four pupils asked at random will be employed on Saturday mornings?

(5) Two people in seven will catch a cold this winter. In a group of three, what is the probability that at most two will catch a cold this winter?

(6) Two men in five attend football matches on a Saturday afternoon. Four men are interviewed at random. What is the probability that at least two of them watch football on Saturday afternoons?

8.5 Expected frequencies

Example. One person in six in a city prefers coffee to tea in the morning. Sixty interviewers each choose three people at random, and question them about their preference. What is the number of interviewers who may be expected to report that only one of the three people interviewed prefers coffee to tea?

We proceed as before and find the probability that an interviewer reports that only one prefers coffee to tea in the morning.

$$p = \tfrac{1}{6}, q = \tfrac{5}{6}, n = 3$$
$$(q+p)^3 = q^3 + 3q^2p + 3qp^2 + p^3$$
$$= Pr(0) + Pr(1) + Pr(2) + Pr(3)$$
$$Pr(1) = 3q^2p$$
$$= 3(\tfrac{5}{6})^2(\tfrac{1}{6})$$
$$= \tfrac{25}{72}$$

The **expected** number of interviewers is obtained from $N \times Pr(1)$, where N is the number of interviewers.

The expected number of interviewers $= 60 \times \tfrac{25}{72}$
$$\doteqdot 21$$

Common sense tells us that we must have a whole number of interviewers! We, therefore, give an estimate by **rounding off** our answer in the usual way.

Exercise 3

(1) In a city three motorists in eight are members of a certain motoring organisation Thirty pupils are asked to stand at different points in the city and to note how many of the first three cars to pass them display the badge of the organisation. How many of the pupils can be expected to report that two of their groups of three cars displayed the badge?

(2) Two thousand dozen eggs are delivered to a large supermarket in boxes of six. If one egg in ten is cracked, estimate how many boxes will contain three cracked eggs?

(3) One television set in four has a B.B.C. 2 Channel. One hundred investigators each interviewed five owners of television sets taken at random. Find approximately how many of the investigators will report that two of those interviewed by them owned a television set with a B.B.C. 2 Channel.

(4) One in eight new models of a car is fitted with automatic transmission. Twenty car showrooms each receive four new models.

Find approximately how many of these showrooms have two new cars fitted with automatic transmission delivered to them.

(5) On a certain road, the police stop cars in groups of three taken at random and check the condition of the tyres. If one car in ten has faulty tyres, estimate how often they will find that none of the cars in a group has faulty tyres when thirty groups (i.e. ninety cars in all) have been stopped.

(6) A plumber calls at every house in a street containing fifty houses to inspect the water taps. If every house has four taps and one tap in ten is faulty, how often can he expect to find a house with two faulty taps?

(7) In a town one car in four is garaged in the owner's private garage. In a district of this town forty interviewers each select five car owners at random. Approximately how many of these interviewers find that three of the five car owners have private garages?

8.6 Binomial distribution

Consider what happens when four coins are tossed. The probabilities of the various numbers of heads occurring will be obtained from the expansion of $(q+p)^n$ where $q = \frac{1}{2}$, $p = \frac{1}{2}$, $n = 4$.

$$(\tfrac{1}{2}+\tfrac{1}{2})^4 = (\tfrac{1}{2})^4 + 4(\tfrac{1}{2})^3(\tfrac{1}{2}) + 6(\tfrac{1}{2})^2(\tfrac{1}{2})^2 + 4(\tfrac{1}{2})(\tfrac{1}{2})^3 + (\tfrac{1}{2})^4$$

$$= \tfrac{1}{16} + 4\times\tfrac{1}{16} + 6\times\tfrac{1}{16} + 4\times\tfrac{1}{16} + \tfrac{1}{16}$$

$$= Pr(0) + Pr(1) + Pr(2) + Pr(3) + Pr(4)$$

If we wish an ideal frequency distribution of the number of heads obtained in 16 tosses of four coins we multiply the probabilities by 16. We can complete the following table:

Number of heads x	Frequency f	fx	fx^2
0	1 _2_	0 _0_	0 _0_
1	4 _8_	4 _8_	4 _8_
2	6 _12_	12 _24_	24 _48_
3	4 _8_	12 _24_	36 _72_
4	1 _2_	4 _8_	16 _32_
	$\Sigma f = 16$ _32_	$\Sigma fx = 32$ _64_	$\Sigma fx^2 = 80$ _160_

for $N = 32$ $\sigma^2 = \dfrac{160}{32} - \left(\dfrac{64}{32}\right)^2 = 5 - 4 = 1$

$$\text{Mean} = \frac{\Sigma fx}{\Sigma f} \qquad\qquad \text{Standard deviation} = \sqrt{\frac{\Sigma fx^2}{\Sigma f} - \left(\frac{\Sigma fx}{\Sigma f}\right)^2}$$

$$= \frac{32}{16} \qquad\qquad\qquad\qquad = \sqrt{\frac{80}{16} - 4}$$

$$= 2 \qquad\qquad\qquad\qquad\qquad = 1$$

Compare these results with the formulae

(i) $\mu = np$, (ii) $\sigma = \sqrt{npq}$.

Here $n = 4$ (number in the sample)

$p = \frac{1}{2}$

$q = \frac{1}{2}$

Thus the mean $= 4 \times \frac{1}{2} = 2$.

And standard deviation $= \sqrt{4 \times \frac{1}{2} \times \frac{1}{2}} = 1$.

The results are the same as those obtained by the usual method shown in the table above.

$\mu = np$ and $\sigma = \sqrt{npq}$ are the formulae which mathematicians use when they wish to calculate the mean and standard deviation of a binomial distribution. We are not yet able to prove these formulae. We merely compare the results of using them with the results we find by other means, and note the agreement.

Example. In the same way, verify that when tossing five coins 32 times we get

$$\mu = \frac{5}{2} \text{ and } \sigma = \frac{\sqrt{5}}{2}$$

$$(\tfrac{1}{2}+\tfrac{1}{2})^5 = (\tfrac{1}{2})^5 + 5(\tfrac{1}{2})^4(\tfrac{1}{2}) + 10(\tfrac{1}{2})^3(\tfrac{1}{2})^2 + 10(\tfrac{1}{2})^2(\tfrac{1}{2})^3 + 5(\tfrac{1}{2})(\tfrac{1}{2})^4 + (\tfrac{1}{2})^5$$

$$= \frac{1}{32} + 5 \times \frac{1}{32} + 10 \times \frac{1}{32} + 10 \times \frac{1}{32} + 5 \times \frac{1}{32} + \frac{1}{32}$$

$$= Pr(0) + Pr(1) + Pr(2) + Pr(3) + Pr(4) + Pr(5)$$

Multiplying the probabilities by 32 we obtain what we may think of as an ideal frequency distribution of the number of heads obtained when five coins are tossed 32 times.

Copy and complete the following:

Number of heads x	Frequency f	fx	fx^2
0	1		0
1		5	
2	10	20	40
3			90
4	5	20	
5	1	5	
	$\Sigma f = 32$	$\Sigma fx =$	$\Sigma fx^2 = 240$

Mean =   Standard deviation =

$\mu = np$ $\sigma = \sqrt{npq}$

=   =

Let us recall the results of Experiment 5, page 177. The following table of results was formed:

Score x	Frequency f
0 reds	134
1 red	131
2 reds	35

Verify that the mean and standard deviation of this distribution are both approximately equal to $\frac{2}{3}$.
Calculate μ and σ using the formulae when $n = 2$, $p = \frac{1}{3}$, $q = \frac{2}{3}$.

Worked example

Nine housewives in ten buy tinned soup. Find the mean and standard deviation for the number of housewives who buy tinned soup when random samples, in groups of 100, are interviewed at a large number of supermarkets.

$$\mu = np \qquad\qquad \sigma = \sqrt{npq}$$
$$= 100 \times \frac{9}{10} \qquad\qquad = \sqrt{100 \times \frac{9}{10} \times \frac{1}{10}}$$
$$= 90 \qquad\qquad\qquad = \sqrt{9}$$
$$\qquad\qquad\qquad\qquad = 3$$

The mean number of housewives is 90 and the standard deviation of the distribution is 3.

Exercise 4

(1) Of those housewives who own washing-machines two in five own machines which are fully automatic. Find the mean and standard deviation for the distribution of housewives who have fully automatic washing-machines when random samples of two hundred are interviewed.

(2) Three houses in five have refrigerators. Find the mean and standard deviation for the distribution of houses with refrigerators when samples of one hundred houses are visited.

(3) One car in four is three years old or less. Find the mean and standard deviation for the distribution of the number of cars which are three years old or less when samples of 100 cars are inspected.

(4) One in seven people holiday by caravan. Samples of thirty-five people are interviewed. Find the mean and standard deviation for the number who holiday by caravan.

(5) Two houses in seven use tea-bags rather than loose tea. If samples of forty-nine householders are interviewed at random, find the mean and standard deviation for the number of homes using tea-bags.

CHAPTER 9

Normal Distribution

9.1 Normal distribution

In the earlier part of this course on statistics you collected data and displayed the data in tables (e.g. frequency distribution tables) or in charts, graphs and histograms. We now recall what some of these distributions looked like.

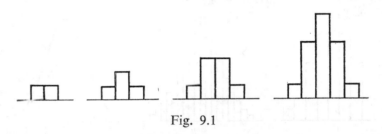

Fig. 9.1

Each of the diagrams in Fig. 9.1 arose from coin-tossing experiments and illustrates the frequency with which 0, 1, 2, . . . heads appear when 1, 2, 3, . . . coins are tossed together.

Look again at another distribution you have met before.

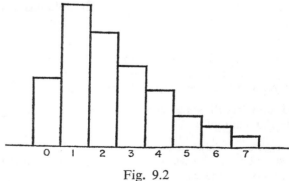

Fig. 9.2

This histogram arose from the **experiment** of playing a large number of football matches on a certain Saturday afternoon (e.g. the Scottish Football League games). The number of teams scoring 0, 1, 2, 3, . . . goals was recorded and the histogram drawn.

Does this histogram (Fig. 9.2) differ in some way from the histograms obtained from coin-tossing experiments? The following statements may help you to answer this question.

Some histograms:

    (a) Are symmetrical,
    (b) Have most of their values located near the centre,
    (c) **Tail-off** at one end,
    (d) **Tail-off** at both ends.

Now recall some of the examples in which you collected data about the heights (or weights) of all the pupils in your year at school, or of the individuals in some other large group.

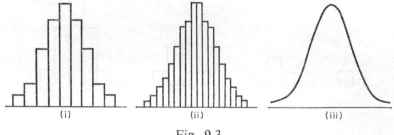

Fig. 9.3

The histogram had a shape not unlike the one shown in Fig. 9.3 (i). When this investigation of height distribution was extended to include a larger population and when smaller class intervals were used the histogram had the shape shown in Fig. 9.3 (ii). The outline of the histogram became smoother and the tops of the columns of the histogram had approximately the shape of the smooth curve shown in Fig. 9.3 (iii).

An examination of the shapes shown in Fig. 9.3 shows that the histograms are approximately symmetrical, that most values are located near the centre, and that the shape **tails-off** at each end.

You should now recall some other distributions which you have investigated. For example:

    (a) The weights of pupils in your year at school,
    (b) The estimates for the width of your classroom, made by all the pupils who use the classroom.

(c) The times taken by all the pupils in your year at school to travel to school on one particular morning.

(d) The marks scored by every pupil who sat a certain examination.

(e) Any other distributions which had histograms shaped like those shown in Fig. 9.3.

We now have a number of such histograms and we wish to find out if they have any special properties other than those discussed on page 188.

Example 1. The following table shows a frequency distribution of the speeds (to the nearest one kilometre per hour) of 400 vehicles found by a radar check on a stretch of road.

Speed (km/h)	$24\frac{1}{2}$ $-29\frac{1}{2}$	$29\frac{1}{2}$ $-34\frac{1}{2}$	$34\frac{1}{2}$ $-39\frac{1}{2}$	$39\frac{1}{2}$ $-44\frac{1}{2}$	$44\frac{1}{2}$ $-49\frac{1}{2}$	$49\frac{1}{2}$ $-54\frac{1}{2}$
Number of cars	4	8	11	37	60	79

Speed (km/h)	$54\frac{1}{2}$ $-59\frac{1}{2}$	$59\frac{1}{2}$ $-64\frac{1}{2}$	$64\frac{1}{2}$ $-69\frac{1}{2}$	$69\frac{1}{2}$ $-74\frac{1}{2}$	$74\frac{1}{2}$ $-79\frac{1}{2}$	$79\frac{1}{2}$ $-84\frac{1}{2}$
Number of cars	81	61	35	13	7	4

(a) (i) Draw a histogram.

(ii) Is it reasonably symmetrical?

(iii) Are most values located near the centre?

(iv) Does the shape of the histogram **tail-off** at each end?

(b) Verify by calculation that:

(i) The mean speed is 54·5 km/h.

(ii) The standard deviation is 10·0 km/h (correct to one decimal place).

(c) State the speed of a vehicle which is travelling at a speed which is:

(i) One standard deviation below the mean speed,

(ii) One standard deviation above the mean speed,

(iii) Two standard deviations below the mean speed,

    (iv) Two standard deviations above the mean speed,
     (v) Three standard deviations below the mean speed,
    (vi) Three standard deviations above the mean speed.

(*d*) Use the frequency distribution table to estimate the percentage number of vehicles travelling at speeds between:

    (i) One standard deviation below and one above the mean speed,
    (ii) Two standard deviations below and two above the mean speed,
    (iii) Three standard deviations below and three above the mean speed.

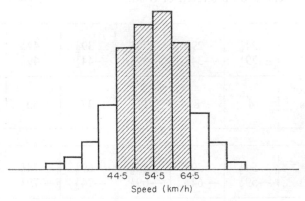

Fig. 9.4

(*e*) Fig. 9.4 shows a shaded area which represents the percentage of vehicles travelling at speeds between 44·5 and 64·5 km/h. Draw a histogram with shaded areas showing the answers to questions (*d*) (ii) and (*d*) (iii).

Example 2. The following table shows the frequency distribution of the times (to the nearest whole minute) taken by 300 pupils to get to school in the morning.

Time (minutes)	0·5 —2·5	2·5 —4·5	4·5 —6·5	6·5 —8·5	8·5 —10·5	10·5 —12·5
Number of pupils	2	7	10	26	45	58

Time (minutes)	12·5 —14·5	14·5 —16·5	16·5 —18·5	18·5 —20·5	20·5 —22·5	22·5 —24·5
Number of pupils	62	46	27	8	6	3

(a) (i) Draw a histogram,
   (ii) Is it reasonably symmetrical?
   (iii) Are most values located near the centre?
   (iv) Does the shape of the histogram **tail-off** at each end?

(b) Verify by calculation that:

   (i) The mean time to get to school is 12·5 minutes,
   (ii) The standard deviation is 4·0 minutes (correct to one decimal place).

(c) State the time taken to get to school by a pupil if the time taken is:

   (i) One standard deviation below the mean time,
   (ii) One standard deviation above the mean time,
   (iii) Two standard deviations below the mean time,
   (iv) Two standard deviations above the mean time,
   (v) Three standard deviations below the mean time,
   (vi) Three standard deviations above the mean time.

(d) Use the frequency distribution table to estimate the percentage number of pupils whose time of travel to school lies between:

   (i) One standard deviation below and one above the mean time,
   (ii) Two standard deviations below and two above the mean time,
   (iii) Three standard deviations below and three above the mean time.

(e) Display your answers to questions (d) (i), (ii), (iii) by shaded regions in a histogram.

(f) Now compare your answers to Example 1 (d) and Example (2) (d) and comment.

The agreement just found between these two sets of results is not just a coincidence. Many of the populations which are studied in statistics are distributed in much the same way as those just studied in Examples 1 and 2. Such populations are said to be **normally distributed** and their histograms have the appearance of the one shown in Fig. 9.3 (ii).

In a previous chapter you came across examples where experiments carried out on a large scale indicated certain results. For example, there was experimental evidence to suggest that if a coin is tossed the probability (p) that it will show a head is $\frac{1}{2}$. The mathematician set up a mathematical model for this experiment of tossing a coin and it was agreed that the model answer would be $p = \frac{1}{2}$. Similarly the mathematical model for the probability of throwing a six with one throw of a die is $p = \frac{1}{6}$. Mathematicians also produced a model for finding the number of heads when a number of coins were tossed. In this case they used the terms of the binomial expansion $(q+p)^n$ where $p = \frac{1}{2}$, $q = \frac{1}{2}$ and n is the number of coins tossed.

In the same way mathematicians have produced a mathematical model for populations which are normally distributed. This model is a curve having the shape shown in Fig. 9.3 (iii), which is a **smoothed** version of the histogram shown in Fig. 9.3 (ii). The smooth curve of Fig. 9.3 (iii) is called a **normal curve** and has certain important properties which have already been hinted at and discussed in Examples 1 and 2:

(a) The curve is symmetrical about the mean of the distribution. (See the histograms in Examples 1 and 2.)

(b) About 68% of its area lies within one standard deviation of the mean. (See Fig. 9.4 and Fig. 9.5 (i).)

(c) About 95% of its area lies within two standard deviations of the mean. (See Fig. 9.5 (ii).)

(d) About 99·8% of its area lies within three standard deviations of the mean. (See Fig. 9.5 (iii).)

(e) The curve tails off at both ends.

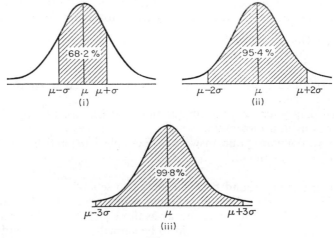

Fig. 9.5

Example 3. The speeds of 400 vehicles were dealt with in Example 1. The mean speed was 54·5 km/h and the standard deviation was 10·0 km/h. The mathematical model for this problem is shown in Fig. 9.6. The percentages are the theoretical values calculated by mathematicians when they set up their model for the kind of population which is normally distributed.

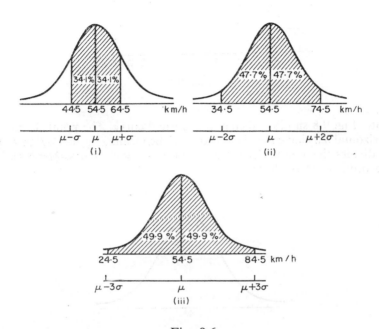

Fig. 9.6

(a) Compare the percentages which you found in Example 1 (d) with those shown in Fig. 9.6.

Note in particular that **all** the speeds in Example 1 (d) fell within the range $\mu-3\sigma$ to $\mu+3\sigma$. The theoretical model gives 99·8% as the answer. In practice this discrepancy is too small to worry about.

(b) Sketch the corresponding normal distribution curves for Example 2, and verify that your answers look like those in Fig. 9.6 except that the scale in km/h is replaced by a scale in minutes as shown in Fig. 9.7.

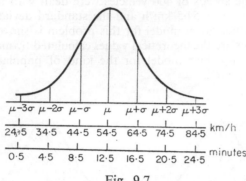

Fig. 9.7

Note. Fig. 9.8 shows a sketch of a normal curve. The point M on the horizontal axis indicates the position of the mean. The line MP through M divides the area under the curve into two equal parts. MP is called the ordinate through M.

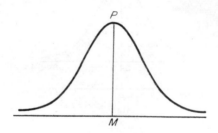

Fig. 9.8

Exercise 1

(1) For a certain frequency distribution the mean score μ is 40 and the standard deviation σ is 6. Find the score which is:

    (a) One standard deviation above the mean,
    (b) One standard deviation below the mean,
    (c) Two standard deviations above the mean,
    (d) Two standard deviations below the mean,
    (e) Three standard deviations above the mean,
    (f) Three standard deviations below the mean.

If the size of the population is 1 000 and the population is normally distributed about the mean how many scores would you expect to find in the range:

(g) 34 to 46?
(h) 28 to 52?
(i) 22 to 58?

(2) For a certain frequency distribution the mean score μ is 38 and the standard deviation σ is 5. Copy and complete the following table:

Score	28		38	43	
Deviation from mean		$-\sigma$	0		2σ

(3) The total area under a normal curve is 100% or 1. Express the area:

(a) To the left,
(b) To the right,

of the ordinate drawn through the mean in percentage and in decimal form.

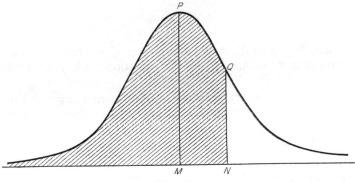

Fig. 9.9

(4) In Fig. 9.9 MP is the ordinate through the mean and NQ is the ordinate drawn through the score which is one standard deviation above the mean.

(a) Find the area under the curve to the left of NQ.
     (**Hint.** 50% of the area under a normal curve lies to the left of MP.)

(b) Find the area under the curve to the right of the ordinate NQ.
(**Hint.** Either, subtract the area to the left of NQ from the
whole area under the curve, *or*, subtract the area between
MP and NQ from . . .?)

(5) Find the area under the normal curve to the left of the ordinate
drawn at $\mu - \sigma$.

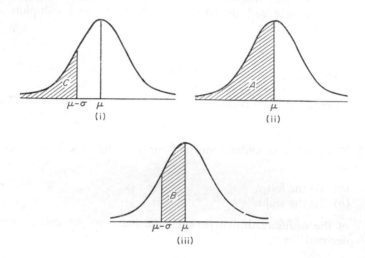

Fig. 9.10

(**Hint.** Fig. 9.10 illustrates that: Area C = area A − area B.)
Compare your answer to this question with your answer to
question (4) (b).

(6) Using the symmetry properties of the normal curve and the fact
that 95·4% of the area under the curve lies between the ordinates
at $\mu - 2\sigma$ and $\mu + 2\sigma$ find:

(a) The area between the ordinates at μ and $\mu + 2\sigma$,
(b) The area to the left of the ordinate at $\mu + 2\sigma$,
(c) The area to the right of the ordinate at $\mu + 2\sigma$.

(7) Find the area under the normal curve between the ordinates
at $\mu + \sigma$ and $\mu + 2\sigma$.

(8) Find the area between the ordinates at $\mu - 2\sigma$ and $\mu - \sigma$.

(9) Find the following areas under the normal curve

(a) Between the ordinates at μ and $\mu + 3\sigma$,
(b) To the left of the ordinate at $\mu + 3\sigma$,
(c) To the right of the ordinate at $\mu + 3\sigma$,

(d) Between the ordinates at $\mu-3\sigma$ and μ,
(e) To the left of the ordinate at $\mu-3\sigma$,
(f) To the right of the ordinate at $\mu-3\sigma$.

(10) Find the area under the normal curve between the ordinates at:

(a) $\mu+2\sigma$ and $\mu+3\sigma$,
(b) $\mu-3\sigma$ and $\mu-2\sigma$.

(11) A group of boys has a mean weight of 50 kg with a standard deviation of 2·5 kg. Assuming that the weights are distributed normally about the mean find the probability that a boy chosen at random from this group will weigh

(a) Less than 52·5 kg,
(b) More than 52·5 kg.

Note. (52·5—50) kg = 2·5 kg which is a deviation of one standard deviation above the mean,

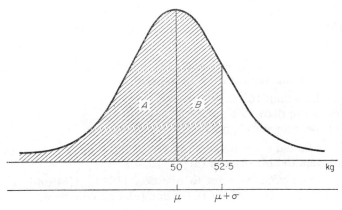

Fig. 9.11

Area A+area B = 0·500+0·341
                = 0·841

Hence the probability of the weight of a boy chosen at random from the group being less than 52·5 kg is approximately 0·84.
To answer part (b) find the area to the right of the ordinate at 52·5.

(12) Use the data for question (11) to find the probability that a boy chosen at random from the group has a weight of:

(a) Less than 47·5 kg,
(b) More than 47·5 kg,
(c) Between 47·5 and 52·5 kg.

Why should your answers to questions (12) (*a*) and (*b*) be the same as your answers to (11) (*b*) and (*a*) respectively?

(13) Use the data for question (11) to find the probability that a boy chosen at random from this group will weigh:

(*a*) Less than 57·5 kg,
(*b*) More than 57·5 kg,
(*c*) Less than 42·5 kg,
(*d*) More than 42·5 kg,
(*e*) Between 42·5 kg and 57·5 kg.

(14) It has been found that over a long period of time the maximum temperatures for June form a distribution which is approximately normal. If the mean maximum temperature was found to be 20°C with a standard deviation of 4°C, find the probability of having a maximum temperature in June of:

(*a*) Less than 24°,
(*b*) More than 24°.

Compare your answers with those of question (11) (*a*) and (*b*), and comment.

(15) Use the data of question (14) to find the probability of having a maximum temperature in June of:

(*a*) Less than 16°C,
(*b*) More than 16°C,
(*c*) Between 16°C and 24°C.

Why should your answers to (15) (*a*) and (*b*) be the same as your answers to (14) (*b*) and (*a*)?

Compare your answers to question (15) (*a*), (*b*) and (*c*) with those of question (12) (*a*), (*b*) and (*c*), and comment.

(16) Use the data for question (14) to find the probability of having a maximum temperature in June of:

(*a*) Less than 32°C,
(*b*) More than 32°C,
(*c*) Less than 8°C,
(*d*) More than 8°C,
(*e*) Between 8°C and 32°C.

Compare your answers with those of question (13), and comment.

(17) In a certain school the times taken by pupils to travel to school are normally distributed with mean time $\mu = 41$ minutes and standard deviation $\sigma = 9$ minutes. Out of 1 000 pupils how many take:

(a) Less than 50 minutes to reach school,

(b) Between 50 and 59 minutes,

(c) Longer than 68 minutes,

(d) Less than 14 minutes?

9·2 Standard scores

The weights in kilogrammes of seven people are:

$$62, \quad 64, \quad 66, \quad 68, \quad 70, \quad 72, \quad 74.$$

Verify that the mean of the weights μ is 68 kg, and that their standard deviation is 4 kg.

A weight of 72 kg can be expressed as a weight of 4 kg above the mean weight of 68 kg.

A weight of 62 kg can be expressed as a weight of 6 kg below the mean weight of 68 kg.

These weights can be expressed in other ways.

For example:

Since the mean weight is 68 kg, and the standard deviation is 4 kg, then

$$(72-68) \text{ kg} = 4 \text{ kg}$$
$$= 1 \text{ standard deviation above the mean weight.}$$

Thus a weight of 72 kg can be expressed as a weight of one standard deviation above the mean weight. Similarly since $(68-62)$ kg

$$= 6 \text{ kg}$$
$$= 1\tfrac{1}{2} \text{ standard deviations,}$$

a weight of 62 kg can be expressed as a weight of $1\tfrac{1}{2}$ standard deviations below the mean weight.

Copy and complete the following table:

Weight in kilogrammes x	Deviation from mean weight in kilogrammes $x-\mu$	Number of standard deviations from mean weight $\dfrac{x-\mu}{\sigma}$
62	-6	$-1\frac{1}{2}$
64		
66		
68		
70		
72	$+4$	$+1$
74		

Note that the three columns each supply the same information about a person's weight, for example, a person can be described as having a weight of:

(a) 62 kg,
(b) 6 kg below the mean weight of 68 kg,
(c) $1\frac{1}{2}$ standard deviations below the mean weight of 68 kg.

Example. The times in minutes taken by seven workmen to finish a job are: 104, 108, 112, 116, 120, 124, 128. Show that $\mu = 116$ minutes and $\sigma = 8$ minutes.

Copy and complete the following table:

Time in minutes x	Deviation from mean time in minutes $x-\mu$	Number of standard deviations from mean time $\dfrac{x-\mu}{\sigma}$
104	-12	$-1\frac{1}{2}$
108		
112		
116	0	0
120		
124	$+8$	
128		

Note that the three columns each supply the same information about the time taken to complete the work.

In each of these examples the raw scores (x) have first of all been changed into deviations from the mean ($x-\mu$), and have then been expressed as a number of standard deviations from the mean.

The raw scores have been transformed into new scores which are called **standard scores**. These are sometimes called z-scores where

$$z = \frac{x-\mu}{\sigma}.$$

Exercise 2

(1) If $\mu = 36$ and $\sigma = 5$, express the score $x = 44$ as a number of standard deviations above the mean (i.e. express $x = 44$ as a z-score).

(2) If $\mu = 50$ and $\sigma = 8$, find z when $x = 60$.

(3) If $\mu = 31$ and $\sigma = 8$, find z when $x = 39$.

(4) If $\mu = 69$ and $\sigma = 9$, find z when $x = 60$.

(5) If $\mu = 50$ and $\sigma = 8$, find x when:

(a) $z = 1$,   (b) $z = 2$,   (c) $z = 1\cdot5$,
(d) $z = -1$,   (e) $z = -2$,   (f) $z = -1\cdot5$.

(6) In an earlier example when dealing with the weights of seven people we used the following table of results:

Raw scores x	z scores $z = \dfrac{x-\mu}{\sigma}$
62	$-1\frac{1}{2}$
64	-1
66	$-\frac{1}{2}$
68	0
70	$+\frac{1}{2}$
72	$+1$
74	$1\frac{1}{2}$

It was found that for the raw scores the mean was 68 and the standard deviation was 4. Calculate the mean and standard deviation for the corresponding z-scores.

(7) Show that the set of raw scores 102, 106, 110, 114, 118, 122, 126 has a mean equal to 114 and a standard deviation equal to 8. Convert the raw scores into z-scores and find the mean and standard deviation for these z-scores.

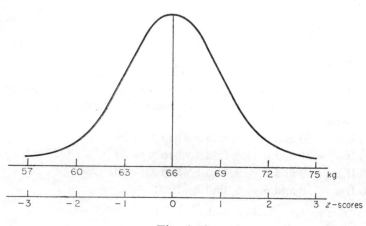

Fig. 9.12

Suppose that the weights of a large number of schoolboys were measured and that these weights were normally distributed about a mean weight of 66 kg with a standard deviation of 3 kg .The mathematical model for the distribution would look like Fig. 9.12. Immediately underneath the scale of weights in kg is shown the scale of corresponding z-scores. Thus a weight of 69 kg corresponds to a weight of 3 kg above the mean weight of 66 kg, which in turn corresponds to a z-score of $+1$. Verify that a weight of 57 kg corresponds to $z = -3$.

When the raw scores are changed to z-scores, then the curve of normal distribution still has the same appearance as before except that the mean is now zero and the standard deviation is now unity. (See **exercise 2,** examples 6 and 7.)

The area A between the ordinates at $z = 0$ and $z = 1$ is 34·1% or 0·341. The area B between the ordinates at $z = 0$ and $z = 2$ is 47·7% or 0·477. The area C between the ordinates at $z = 0$ and $z = 3$ is 49·9% or 0·499. (See Fig. 9.13.)

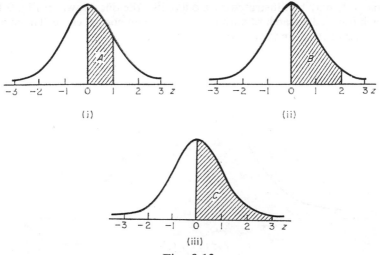

Fig. 9.13

9.3 Use of simplified tables

In many real life problems z does not have simple values like ±1, ±2, ±3 but may have fractional values. In order to make better use of the normal curve mathematicians have calculated not only the areas A, B, C shown in Fig. 9.13, but have calculated the corresponding areas for fractional values of z. The area which has been calculated is the area to the right of the ordinate at $z = 0$. This area is usually written as $A(z)$. (See Fig. 9.14.) For example $A(1\frac{1}{2})$ means the area under the curve between the ordinates at $z = 0$ and $z = 1\frac{1}{2}$. Mathematicians have shown that

$$A(1\tfrac{1}{2}) = 43 \cdot 3\% = 0 \cdot 433$$

This result, and others like it, have been tabulated in a table like the following one:

z	$A(z)$
0·00	0·000
0·50	0·191
1·00	0·341
1·50	0·433
2·00	0·477
2·50	0·494
3·00	0·499

This table may be illustrated by a curve like the one shown in Fig. 9.14 which is called a **standard normal curve** or a **unit normal curve**. The mean is zero and the standard deviation is unity.

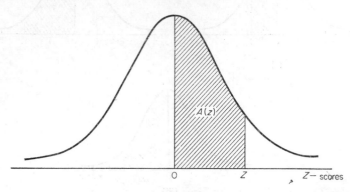

Fig. 9.14

The table is simple to use. For example, to find the area between $z = 0$ and $z = 2.50$ go down the z-column until you find $z = 2.50$. Opposite this, in the $A(z)$ column, you will find the value 0·494 which is the required area.

To find the value of z such that the area $A(z)$ is 0·433 go down the $A(z)$ column until you find 0·433. Opposite this, in the z-column, you will find the value 1·50 which is the required z-value.

Exercise 3

(Use the table of areas shown above to answer the following questions.)

(1) Find the area under the standard normal curve:

   (a) To the left of the ordinate at $z = 1.50$,
   (b) To the right of the ordinate at $z = 1.50$,
   (c) To the left of the ordinate at $z = -1.50$,
   (d) To the right of the ordinate at $z = -1.50$,
   (e) Between the ordinates at $z = 0.50$ and $z = 1.50$,
   (f) Between the ordinates at $z = -0.50$ and $z = -1.50$,
   (g) Between the ordinates at $z = 1.50$ and $z = 2.50$,
   (h) Between the ordinates at $z = -1.50$ and $z = -2.50$.

(2) A certain manufacturer's television tubes have a mean life of 3 000 hours and a standard deviation of 600 hours.

   (a) Assuming the distribution to be normal calculate the probability that a tube chosen at random from the manu-

facturer's output of 10 000 tubes will burn out in the first
2 100 hours of continuous testing.
Calculate also how many of the 10 000 tubes are likely
to burn out within this period of testing.

(b) How many tubes are likely to last twice as long as this before
burning out?

(c) What is the probability that a tube will last between 2 700
and 3 300 hours? How many tubes are likely to burn out
during this period of time?

(d) After how many hours would you expect to find still working:
(i) Only 31% of the tubes,
(ii) Only 16%?

(e) After how many hours of working life would you expect
to find only 60 of the original batch of 10 000 tubes still
working?
(**Hint.** Express 60 as a percentage of 10 000 and consider the
right hand tail of the curve.)

(3) (a) A boy scored 68 marks in a Mathematics test. The average
mark was 62 with a standard deviation of 6 marks. In a later
test he managed to score only 60 marks. This time the average
mark was 45 with a standard deviation of 10 marks. How
could the boy convince his parents that his work had
improved?
(You may assume that the marks in each test are normally
distributed. Convert the raw scores of 68 and 60 into z-scores.)

(b) In the same two tests a girl scored 55 and 45 marks
respectively. In which test did she do better?

(c) A boy scored 74 marks in the first test. Express this in
standard deviations above the mean.
What mark should he score in the second test in order to do
as well as he did in the first test?

(4) The marks in an examination were investigated and the following
information noted:

		Mathematics	Latin
Mean	μ	47	83
Standard deviation	σ	6	8

One boy scored 56 marks in Mathematics and 87 marks in
Latin. Compare this boy's performance in Mathematics and in
Latin with the class results, and decide whether he is better at

Mathematics or at Latin. Assume that the marks are normally distributed about the mean.

(**Hint.** Show that a raw score of 56 in Mathematics gives a z-score of $1\frac{1}{2}$. That is, 56 is $1\frac{1}{2}$ standard deviations above the mean. Show also that a raw score of 87 in Latin gives a z-score of $\frac{1}{2}$. That is, 87 is $\frac{1}{2}$ standard deviation above the mean.

Conclusion: Compared with the class as a whole, a mark of 56 in Mathematics is better than a mark of 87 in Latin.)

(5) Use the data of question (4) to answer the following questions:
  (*a*) Compare a mark of 41 in Mathematics with a mark of 71 in Latin.
  (*b*) What mark in Latin corresponds to a mark of 53 in Mathematics?
  (*c*) What mark in Mathematics corresponds to a mark of 59 in Latin?

(6) In an examination the average mark was 56 and the standard deviation was 12. Assuming the marks to be approximately normally distributed about the mean, within what limits would you expect the following percentage of the candidates to lie:
  (*a*) About 34% on either side of the mean,
  (*b*) About 19% on either side of the mean,
  (*c*) About 47·5% on either side of the mean,
  (*d*) Nearly all the candidates?
  Express your answers
      (i) In terms of the corresponding z-scores,
      (ii) In terms of raw scores.

(7) Assuming that the heights of a large number of senior pupils in school are distributed normally and that just over 95% of these lie between 160 cm and 190 cm, estimate the mean and standard deviation of this distribution of heights.

9.4 Use of tables

In all the examples so far we have been solving problems in which the z-scores had values like $\pm\frac{1}{2}$, ±1, $\pm1\frac{1}{2}$. . . . This enabled us to use a simplified set of tables. But most real life problems involve awkward fractional values for z and problems to be solved now will require the use of a more complete table.

Verify from the tables in this book that areas under the normal distribution curve are given for values of z from $z = 0\cdot00$ to $z = 3\cdot39$ in steps of $0\cdot01$.

Verify also that the values given in our simplified table agree with those given in the more complete **table of area.**

Example 1. The mean weight of 500 schoolboys is 55 kg and the standard deviation is 4 kg. Assuming that the weights are normally distributed, find the number of schoolboys who would be expected to weigh:

(a) More than 58 kg,
(b) Between 58 and 60 kg,
(c) 60 kg.

(a) Since we assume that the weights are recorded to the nearest kilogramme, any weight recorded as being **greater** than 58 kg will have a value **greater than 58·5 kg.**

$$x = 58\cdot5 \text{ corresponds to } z = \frac{x-\mu}{\sigma}$$

$$= \frac{58\cdot5-55}{4}$$

$$= \frac{3\cdot5}{4}$$

$$= 0\cdot88 \text{ (to two decimal places).}$$

Verify that $\qquad\qquad A(z) = 0\cdot311$
$Pr\,(x{>}58) = 0\cdot500{-}0\cdot311 \qquad = 0\cdot189$
Expected number of schoolboys $= 500 \times 0\cdot189$
$$\doteqdot 94.$$

(b) In this case the weight can have any value **from 57·5 to 60·5 kg.**

$$x = 60\cdot5 \text{ corresponds to } z = \frac{60\cdot5-55}{4}$$

$$= 1\cdot38 \text{ (to two decimal places).}$$

Verify that $A(z) \qquad = 0\cdot416$

$$x = 57\cdot5 \text{ corresponds to } z = \frac{57\cdot5-55}{4}$$

$$= 0\cdot62 \text{ (to two decimal places).}$$

Verify that $\qquad\qquad A(z) = 0\cdot232$
$Pr\,(58{\leqslant}x{\leqslant}60) = 0\cdot416{-}0\cdot232 = 0\cdot184$
Expected number of schoolboys $= 500 \times 0\cdot184$
$$= 92$$

(c) A weight recorded as 60 kg can have any value **from 59·5 to 60·5 kg**

$x = 59·5$ corresponds to $z = \dfrac{59·5-55}{4}$

$= 1·12$ (to two decimal places).

Verify that $A(z) = 0·369$

From (b), when $x = 60·5$, $z = 1·38$, $A(z) = 0·416$

$Pr(x = 60) = 0·416-0·369 = 0·047$

Expected number of schoolboys $= 500 \times 0·047$

$\doteqdot 24$

Example 2. Eight hundred candidates sat an examination the results of which were normally distributed with a mean score of 60 marks and a standard deviation of 10 marks. How many candidates would be expected to score:

(a) Less than 50 marks,
(b) Between 50 and 75 marks,
(c) 60 marks exactly?

Note. Although examination marks are **discrete** data we treat the data as **continuous** and apply the method of example 1.

(a) We regard a mark of **less** than 50 as having any value **less than 49·5.**
Verify that $x = 49·5$ gives $z = -1·05$ and $A(z) = 0·353$.
Verify also that $Pr(x<50) = 0·147$ and that expected number of candidates $\doteqdot 118$.

(b) We consider marks **from 49·5 to 60 and from 60 to 75·5.**
Verify that $x = 75·5$ gives $z = 1·55$ and $A(z) = 0·439$.
Use this result along with (a) above to verify:
$Pr(50 \leqslant x \leqslant 75) = 0·792$ and that expected number of candidates $\doteqdot 634$.

(c) We regard a mark of 60 exactly as having any value **from 59·5 to 60·5.**
Verify that $x = 60·5$ gives $z = 0·05$ and $A(z) = 0·020$,
$x = 59·5$ gives $z = -0·05$ and $A(z) = 0·020$,
$Pr(x = 60) = 0·040$, and that
expected number of candidates $= 32$.

Exercise 4

(1) Verify from your tables that if $z = 0·40$ then $A(z) = 0·155$ and read off the values of $A(z)$ corresponding to the following values of z:

(a) 0·41,   (b) 0·69,   (c) 1·05,   (d) 1·68,
(e) 2·24,   (f) 3·28,   (g) 3·00,   (h) 2·38.

(2) Verify from your tables that if $A(z) = 0.446$ then $z = 1.61$ and read off the values of z corresponding to the following values of $A(z)$:

(a) 0.300, (b) 0.465, (c) 0.485, (d) 0.163,
(e) 0.075, (f) 0.493, (g) 0.480, (h) 0.048.

(3) Assuming that scores are normally distributed about a mean μ with standard deviation σ calculate the percentage area under the normal curve between the ordinates at:

(a) $\mu-\sigma$ and $\mu+2\sigma$,
(b) $\mu-\frac{1}{2}\sigma$ and $\mu+\frac{1}{2}\sigma$,
(c) $\mu-2\sigma$ and $\mu+\sigma$,
(d) μ and $\mu+1.75\sigma$,
(e) $\mu-1.75\sigma$ and μ,
(f) $\mu-0.6\sigma$ and $\mu+0.6\sigma$.

(4) A set of scores (x) is normally distributed about a mean of 20 with a standard deviation of 2. Convert to standard scores and find the area under the normal curve:

(a) From $x = 20$ to $x = 22$,
(b) From $x = 18$ to $x = 21.6$,
(c) From $x = 15$ to $x = 22.2$,
(d) From $x = 16.4$ to $x = 17.6$,
(e) From $x = 19.1$ to $x = 23.7$.

(5) Tennis balls were tested by dropping each ball from a given height and measuring the height to which it rebounded. It was decided that a ball bounded too high if it rose above a height of 147 cm. Assume that the heights of rebound were normally distributed about a mean height of 140 cm with standard deviation 3 cm. What is the probability that a ball taken at random from this batch of tennis balls will bounce too high?

(6) 1 000 candidates sat an examination, the results of which were normally distributed with a mean score of 50 marks and a standard deviation of 10 marks. How many candidates would be expected to score:

(a) 75 marks or less,
(b) 25 marks or less,
(c) 60 marks exactly?

(7) Intelligence tests are designed to produce a normal frequency distribution of scores with mean 100 and standard deviation 15. What percentage of the scores are expected to lie between:

(a) 70 and 140,
(b) 100 and 120,
(c) 120 and 140?

Within what range, placed symmetrically about the mean, would you expect to find:

(d) 50% of the scores,

(e) 75% of the scores?

9.5 Normal approximation to the binomial probability distribution

In section **9.1** we looked at various frequency histograms and used them to investigate the properties of the normal frequency distribution and the standard normal curve. We now look more closely at the histogram of a binomial distribution. Recall the well-known experiment of tossing four coins a large number of times and noting the frequency of occurrence of 0, 1, 2, 3, 4 heads. The mathematical model for calculating the probabilities of obtaining 0, 1, 2, 3, 4 heads is the binomial distribution $(q+p)^n$ where $n = 4$, $p = \frac{1}{2}$, $q = \frac{1}{2}$.

$$(\tfrac{1}{2}+\tfrac{1}{2})^4 = (\tfrac{1}{2})^4+4(\tfrac{1}{2})^3(\tfrac{1}{2})+6(\tfrac{1}{2})^2(\tfrac{1}{2})^2+4(\tfrac{1}{2})(\tfrac{1}{2})^3+(\tfrac{1}{2})^4$$
$$= \tfrac{1}{16}+\tfrac{4}{16}+\tfrac{6}{16}+\tfrac{4}{16}+\tfrac{1}{16}$$

Number of heads x	0	1	2	3	4
Probability of x heads $Pr(x)$	$\frac{1}{16}$	$\frac{4}{16}$	$\frac{6}{16}$	$\frac{4}{16}$	$\frac{1}{16}$

Note that $\Sigma Pr(x) = \frac{16}{16} = 1$

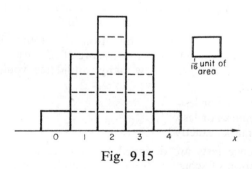

Fig. 9.15

Fig. 9.15 shows the histogram for the probability distribution when four coins are tossed, using the rectangle shown to represent $\frac{1}{16}$ unit of area. Note that the histogram contains 16 such rectangles in order that the total area of the histogram should be unity.

Use the formulae $\mu = np$ and $\sigma = \sqrt{npq}$ to verify that the mean number of heads is 2, with standard deviation 1 head.

Now consider the experiment of tossing 9 coins. The mathematical model for calculating the probabilities of obtaining 0, 1, 2, ..., 9 heads is the binomial distribution $(q+p)^n$ where $n = 9$, $p = \frac{1}{2}$, $q = \frac{1}{2}$.

$$(\tfrac{1}{2}+\tfrac{1}{2})^9 = (\tfrac{1}{2})^9 + 9(\tfrac{1}{2})^8(\tfrac{1}{2}) + 36(\tfrac{1}{2})^7(\tfrac{1}{2})^2 + \ldots$$

Use the ninth row of Pascal's Triangle to complete the expansion of $(\tfrac{1}{2}+\tfrac{1}{2})^9$ and verify that the following table gives the probabilities of obtaining x heads when 9 coins are tossed together.

Number of heads x	0	1	2	3	4	5	6	7	8	9
Probability of x heads $Pr(x)$	$\frac{1}{512}$	$\frac{9}{512}$	$\frac{36}{512}$	$\frac{84}{512}$	$\frac{126}{512}$	$\frac{126}{512}$	$\frac{84}{512}$	$\frac{36}{512}$	$\frac{9}{512}$	$\frac{1}{512}$

Note that $\Sigma Pr(x) = \frac{512}{512} = 1$.

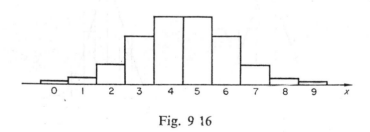

Fig. 9 16

Fig. 9.16 shows the histogram for the probability distribution of the number of heads when 9 coins are tossed. **This histogram has the same column width and the same unit area as the histogram in Fig. 9.15.** Verify that the mean number of heads is $4\frac{1}{2}$ with standard deviation $1\frac{1}{2}$ heads.

We now re-draw the histogram in Fig. 9.16 making the column widths narrower. Since the histogram must still enclose the same unit area the heights of the columns must be increased suitably. For example,

H

if the column widths were halved the column heights would require
to be doubled in order to keep the area unchanged. Let us assume that
the width of column in Fig. 9.15 and Fig. 9.16 is $1\frac{1}{2}$ cm. If we now make
the column width 1 cm, we must make each column height $1\frac{1}{2}$ times
as tall as it is in Fig. 9.16.

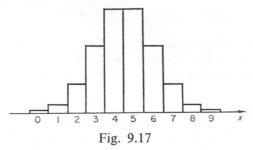

Fig. 9.17

Fig. 9.17 gives the same information as Fig. 9.16 (namely, the probabilities of obtaining 0, 1, 2, . . ., 9 heads when 9 coins are tossed together).
In each case the area of the histogram is unity.

Why have we chosen the scale in Fig. 9.15 to be $1\frac{1}{2}$ cm per column
width, and in Fig. 9.17 to be 1 cm per column width? Remember that
for $n = 4$, $\sigma = 1$, while for $n = 9$, $\sigma = 1\frac{1}{2}$. **Our scales have been
chosen so that the length on the x-axis representing σ is the same length
in each histogram.**

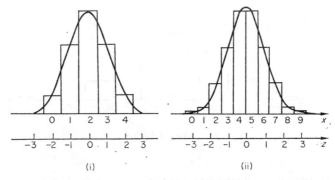

Fig. 9.18

Fig. 9.18 shows the histograms of the binomial probability distributions
for $n = 4$ and $n = 9$ side by side with smooth curves drawn through
the mid-point of the tops of each column.

In Fig. 9.18 (i), $\mu = 2$ and $\sigma = 1$. Use the formula $z = \dfrac{x-\mu}{\sigma}$ to

verify the entries in the following table:

x	0	1	2	3	4
z	-2	-1	0	1	2

In Fig. 9.18 (ii), $\mu = 4\frac{1}{2}$ and $\sigma = 1\frac{1}{2}$.

Copy and complete the following table:

x	0	1·5	3·0	4·5	6·0	7·5	9·0
z	-3			0		2	

Verify that in Fig. 9.18 (i) and 9.18 (ii) the z-scores agree with the corresponding x- scores. The tops of the columns fit a curve which has certain properties:

(a) The curve is symmetrical,
(b) Most scores are located near the centre,
(c) The curve tails off at both ends,
(d) In terms of z- scores, $\mu = 0$ and $\sigma = 1$,
(e) The area under the curve is unity, since it is equal to the area of the histogram.

These are properties of the standard normal curve. It can be shown that when $p = \frac{1}{2}$ and when n is reasonably large ($n > 10$) the standard normal curve becomes a good approximation to the binomial probability distribution. It can also be shown that even when $p \neq \frac{1}{2}$ (for example, in dice experiments where $p = \frac{1}{6}$) the standard normal curve is still a good approximation to the binomial probability histogram. In every case n must be reasonably large. If $p = \frac{1}{2}$ then n should be greater than 10. If $p = \frac{1}{6}$ then n should be greater than 30. This is best remembered by noting that the normal approximation to the binomial probability distribution can be used when np and nq are both greater than 5. This is difficult to prove, but the following examples, worked by both methods, should convince you of the usefulness of the approximation.

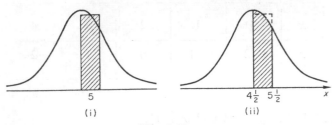

Fig. 9.19

Example 1. If 9 coins are tossed find the probability of obtaining 5 heads:

    (a) **Using the histogram** (table on page 211. See also Fig. 9.19 (i))
    Pr (5 heads) $= \frac{126}{512} = 0{\cdot}246 = 0{\cdot}25$ (to two decimal places).

    (b) **Using the area under the standard normal curve**
    We find the area under the curve between the ordinates at $x = 4\frac{1}{2}$ and $x = 5\frac{1}{2}$. (See Fig. 9.19 (ii).)
    Verify that the corresponding z- scores are 0 and 0·67.
    From a table of areas we find that when

$$z = 0{\cdot}67, A(z) = 0{\cdot}249.$$

    Hence Pr (5 heads) $= 0{\cdot}249 = 0{\cdot}25$ (to two decimal places).
    This answer agrees quite closely with that found in (a).

Example 2. Find the probability of obtaining 5 or 6 heads when 9 coins are tossed.

    (a) **Using the histogram** (table on page 211)
    Pr (5 or 6 heads) $= \frac{126}{512} + \frac{84}{512} = \frac{210}{512}$
                                   $= 0{\cdot}410$
                                     $= 0{\cdot}41$ (to two decimal places).

    (b) **Using the area under the standard normal curve**
    We find the area under the curve between the ordinates at $x = 4\frac{1}{2}$ and $x = 6\frac{1}{2}$.
    Verify that this corresponds to the area between $z = 0$ and $z = 1{\cdot}33$.
    From a table of area verify that when
    $z = 1{\cdot}33, A(z) = 0{\cdot}408$.
    Hence Pr (5 or 6 heads) $= 0{\cdot}408 = 0{\cdot}41$ (to two decimal places).
    Once again there is close agreement between the two answers.

Example 3. Find the probability of obtaining 6 or 7 heads when 9 coins are tossed.

(a) **Using the histogram** (table on page 211).

Pr (6 or 7 heads) $= \frac{84}{512}+\frac{36}{512} = \frac{120}{512}$

$= 0\cdot234$

$= 0\cdot23$ (to two decimal places).

(b) **Using the area under the standard normal curve**

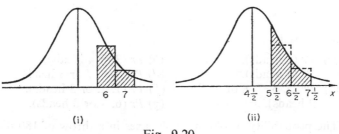

(i)   (ii)

Fig. 9.20

Verify that the required area lies between the ordinates at $x = 5\frac{1}{2}$ and $x = 7\frac{1}{2}$, i.e. between $z = 0\cdot67$ and $z = 2\cdot00$.

Verify also from a table of areas that

when $z = 0\cdot67$, $A(z) = 0\cdot249$ and

when $z = 2\cdot00$, $A(z) = 0\cdot477$.

Required area $= 0\cdot477-0\cdot249 = 0\cdot228$.

Hence Pr (6 or 7 heads) $= 0\cdot228 = 0\cdot23$ (to two decimal places).

Once again there is close agreement between the two answers.

Note. In each of the examples 1, 2 and 3, $n = 9$, $p = \frac{1}{2}$, $q = \frac{1}{2}$, so that $np = nq = 4\frac{1}{2}$. That is, neither np nor nq is greater than 5. **In spite of this there is close agreement** between the results obtained using the binomial distribution and those obtained using the normal approximation to the distribution. Even closer agreement is achieved when np and nq are both greater than 5.

Example 4. When 180 dice are thrown together the probabilities of obtaining 0, 1, 2, . . ., 180 sixes are given by the binomial expansion $(q+p)^n$

where $n = 180$, $p = \frac{1}{6}$, $q = \frac{5}{6}$.

Verify that $\mu = 30$ and $\sigma = 5$.

The probability of obtaining 30 sixes has been calculated from the binomial expansion $(\frac{5}{6}+\frac{1}{6})^{180}$ to be 0·080.

Verify that np and nq are both greater than 5 so that the area under the standard normal curve can be used to find an approximate value for this probability. Note that this means finding the area between the ordinates at $x = 29\frac{1}{2}$ and $x = 30\frac{1}{2}$.

Verify that when $x = 29\frac{1}{2}$, $z = -0.10$ and $A(z) = 0.040$. Consider also the solution for the case when $x = 30\frac{1}{2}$.
Explain why the required probability is 2×0.040.

Exercise 5

(1) Use the methods shown in Examples 1, 2 and 3 to compare the pairs of answers for the following probabilities when nine coins are tossed:

(a) Pr (4 heads),   (b) Pr (3 or 4 heads),
(c) Pr (3 heads),   (d) Pr (5, 6, 7 or 8 heads),
(e) Pr (5, 6, 7, 8 or   (f) Pr (1, 2, or 3 heads),
9 heads),   (g) Pr (6, 7 or 8 heads).

(2) The probability of obtaining 40 sixes in a throw of 180 dice has been calculated from the binomial expansion $(\frac{5}{6}+\frac{1}{6})^{180}$ to be 0.011. Compare this answer with the value obtained by using the normal approximation to the binomial distribution.

(3) Sixteen coins are tossed together. The probabilities of obtaining x heads are shown in the following table, for values of x from $x = 6$ to $x = 12$:

x	6	7	8	9	10	11	12
$Pr(x)$	0.122	0.175	0.196	0.175	0.122	0.067	0.028

Use the normal approximation to the binomial distribution to calculate the following probabilities, and in each case compare your answers with those obtained from the given table:

(a) Pr (8 heads),   (b) Pr (10 heads),   (c) Pr (6 heads),
(d) Pr (7, 8 or 9   (e) Pr (9, 10 or 11   (f) Pr (6 or 7
heads),   heads),   heads).

(4) The probability of obtaining 45 even scores in a throw of 100 dice has been found from the binomial expansion of $(\frac{1}{2}+\frac{1}{2})^{100}$ to be 0.049. Compare this answer with the value found by using the normal approximation to the binomial distribution.

(5) If 100 dice are thrown together, find the probability that:

(a) Exactly 55,
(b) Not more than 55,
(c) Not less than 55,
of the dice show an even score.

Find the sum of the two probabilities in (b) and (c). Comment on this sum and explain how it is related to the probability found in (a).

(6) Thirty-six coins are tossed together. The probabilities of obtaining x heads are shown in the following table, for values of x from x = 16 to x = 20.

x	16	17	18	19	20
Pr(x)	0·106	0·125	0·132	0·125	0·106

Use the normal approximation to the binomial distribution to calculate the following probabilities, and in each case compare your answers with those obtained from the given table:

(a) Pr (18 heads), (b) Pr (20 heads),
(c) Pr (16 heads), (d) Pr (17, 18 or 19 heads),
(e) Pr (18, 19 or 20 heads), (f) Pr (19 or 20 heads).

(7) If 180 dice are thrown together find the probability that:

(a) Exactly 40,
(b) Not more than 40,
(c) Not less than 40,
of the dice show a six.
Find the sum of the two probabilities in (b) and (c).
Comment on this sum and explain how it is related to the probability found in (a).

(8) It is known that 25% of the plums in an orchard have been damaged by wasps. What is the probability that in a sample of 100 plums the number damaged will be:

(a) Exactly 20,
(b) 20 or less,
(c) 20 or more,
(d) Less than 20,
(e) More than 30,
(f) Between 20 and 30.

CHAPTER 10

Elementary Sampling

10.1 Introduction

In chapter 2 we investigated some methods of drawing samples from a population and tried to demonstrate how, by correct sampling, valid conclusions can be drawn about a population.

In this chapter, our investigation will be from a more mathematical standpoint and we shall look at the mechanics of elementary sampling.

10.2 Sampling from a normal population

Experiment 1. The following set of results was obtained using 640 identical cards. The cards were numbered as follows:

10 cards marked 1,
60 cards marked 2,
150 cards marked 3,
200 cards marked 4,
150 cards marked 5,
60 cards marked 6,
10 cards marked 7.

$B(n, p)$ $n = 6$ $p = \frac{1}{2}$

$X = $ number on a card drawn at random

$P(X = 3) = \frac{15}{64}$. If Binom, $P(X = 2) = \binom{6}{2}\left(\frac{1}{2}\right)^2\left(\frac{1}{2}\right)^4$

$\therefore Y$ is binom. where $Y = X - 1$ $= \frac{15}{64}$

This population of numbers, which is approximately normal, is illustrated in Fig. 10.1.

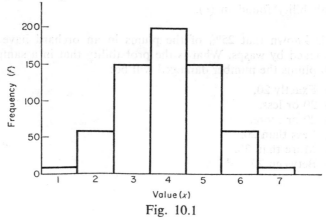

Fig. 10.1

For this population, verify that the mean, $\mu = 4$ and that the standard deviation, $\sigma = 1\cdot22$.

The cards were placed in a large box and various samples drawn, every card being replaced before a new one was drawn. The results are displayed in the following frequency distributions and histograms:

(*a*) Sample of 5 cards:

x	1	4	5	
f	1	1	3	$\Sigma f = 5$

$\overline{X} = 3\cdot8$

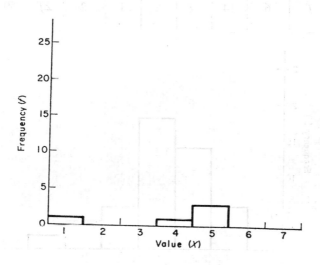

Fig. 10.2

(*b*) Sample of 10 cards:

x	3	4	5	6	
f	2	4	2	2	$\Sigma f = 10$

$\overline{X} = 4\cdot4$

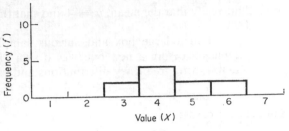

Fig. 10.3

(c) Sample of 50 cards:

x	2	3	4	5	6	7	
f	6	14	18	6	4	2	$\Sigma f = 50$

12   42   72   30   24   14 $\bar{x} = \dfrac{194}{50} = 3.88$

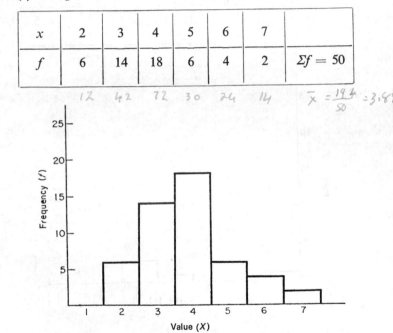

Fig. 10·4

(d) Sample of 100 cards:

x	1	2	3	4	5	6	7	
f	7	9	31	29	15	5	4	$\Sigma f = 100$

7   18   93   116   75   30   28 $\bar{x} = 3.67$

$\doteqdot 4 - 2.7\sigma_{\bar{x}}$

unlikely

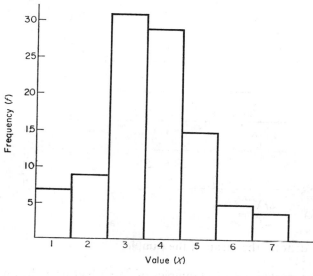

Fig. 10.5

What do you notice about the shape of the distributions as the sample size increases?

Experiment 2 A sample of size 5 was drawn and gave the following distribution. The mean was calculated as shown.

X	f	fX
1	1	1
4	1	4
5	3	15
	$\Sigma f = 5$	$\Sigma fX = 20$

$$\bar{X} = \frac{\Sigma fX}{\Sigma f} = \frac{20}{5} = 4$$

A second sample of five cards was drawn. Copy and complete the table for this distribution and verify that the mean is 3·8:

X	f	fX
2	1	
3	2	
5	1	
6	1	
	$\Sigma f = 5$	

$$\overline{X} = \frac{\Sigma fX}{\Sigma f} =$$

where $\overline{X}$ denotes the mean of the sample.

This was repeated until 100 samples of size 5 had been drawn and the means calculated for all samples. Copy and complete the following table:

Distribution of means $\overline{X}$

Class boundaries	Mid-values ($\overline{X}$)	Frequency (f)	$f\overline{X}$
2·3—2·7	2·5	1	
2·7—3·1	2·9	4	
3·1—3·5	3·3	11	
	3·7	24	
	4·1	30	
4·3—4·7	4·5	20	
	4·9	8	
5·1—5·5	5·3	2	

402

mean = 4·02

Verify that the mean of this distribution is 4·02 and the standard deviation is 0·55.

This distribution is illustrated in Fig. 10.6:

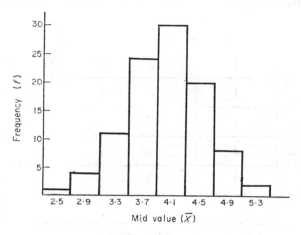

Fig. 10.6

Because it is obtained from the means of samples, it is called the **sampling distribution of means.**

Experiment 3. A sample of size 10 was drawn and the mean calculated as shown:

X	f	fX
2	1	2
3	3	9
4	4	16
5	2	10
	$\Sigma f = 10$	$\Sigma fX = 37$

$$\bar{X} = \frac{\Sigma f X}{\Sigma f} = \frac{37}{10} = 3{\cdot}7$$

A second sample of ten cards was drawn and gave the following distribution. Copy and complete the table and verify that the mean is 3·2.

X	f	fX
1	1	
2	2	
3	3	
4	3	
6	1	
	$\Sigma f = 10$	

$$\bar{X} = \frac{\Sigma f X}{\Sigma f} =$$

One hundred such samples were drawn and gave the following **distribution of means:**

Mid value $\bar{X}$	3·1	3·3	3·5	3·7	3·9	4·1	4·3	4·5	4·7	4·9
Frequency f	2	4	8	13	16	24	15	10	6	2

Since this is a distribution of means, $\bar{X}$, the mean of the distribution is denoted by $\mu_{\bar{X}}$ and the standard deviation by $\sigma_{\bar{X}}$.

This standard deviation, $\sigma_{\bar{X}}$, is sometimes referred to as the **standard error of the mean.**

For these results verify that $\mu_{\bar{X}} = 4{\cdot}04$ and $\sigma_{\bar{X}} = 0{\cdot}39$.

Fig. 10.7 shows the frequency distribution of this distribution of means.

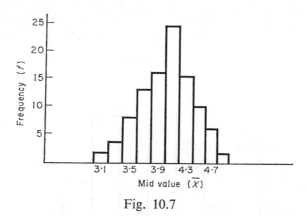

Fig. 10.7

Experiment 4.

One hundred samples of size 25 were now drawn. The means were calculated and gave the following distribution of means:

Mid value $\overline{X}$	3·46	3·58	3·70	3·82	3·94	4·06	4·18	4·30	4·42	4·54
Frequency f	2	5	10	15	20	16	13	10	6	3

For these results, verify that $\mu_{\overline{X}} = 4$ and $\sigma_{\overline{X}} = 0.25$.

Fig. 10.8 shows the frequency distribution of this distribution of means:

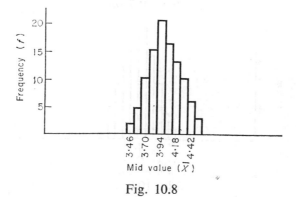

Fig. 10.8

Let us take a closer look at the sampling distribution of means for samples of size 5, 10 and 25. Following are the histograms of Figs. 10.6, 10.7 and 10.8 drawn with the same scales.

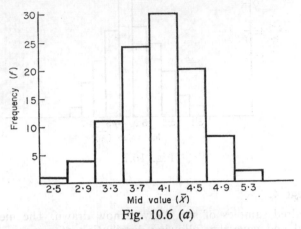

Fig. 10.6 (*a*)

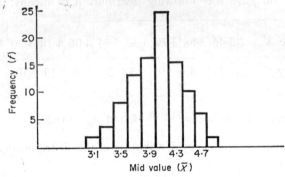

Fig. 10.7 (*a*)

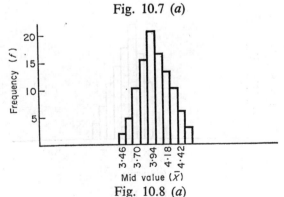

Fig. 10.8 (*a*)

In all cases, the **mean value** for these distributions stays almost constant, nearly 4 in this case, but the **spread** of the distributions alters.
For samples of size 5, the values ranged from 2·5 to 5·3.
For samples of size 10, the values ranged from 3·1 to 4·9 and for samples of size 25, the range is from 3·46 to 4·54.
Consequently, we would expect the standard deviation to decrease. This is in accordance with the results obtained above. The corresponding standing deviations are:

For samples of size 5, $\sigma_{\bar{X}} = 0·55$,
For samples of size 10, $\sigma_{\bar{X}} = 0·39$,
For samples of size 25, $\sigma_{\bar{X}} = 0·25$.

Bearing in mind that samples are generally taken to determine information about a background population we can verify two important formulae connecting a population and sample sizes:

(1) For a normally distributed background population, the **mean** of the **sampling distribution of means** resulting from a large number of samples is equal to the mean of the population.

That is $\mu_{\bar{X}} = \mu$

For example in experiment I the mean of the 640 scores of the parent population was calculated to be 4.
The results of experiments 2, 3 and 4 were as follows:

Sample size	$\mu_{\bar{X}}$
5	4·02
10	4·04
25	4·00

(2) When a large number of samples is drawn from a normal population, the **standard deviation of the sampling distribution of means (i.e. the standard error of the mean)** decreases as the sample size increases.
Mathematicians have shown that the exact relationship is given by the formula:

$$\sigma_{\bar{X}} = \frac{\sigma}{\sqrt{N}}$$

where N is the sample size, σ is the standard deviation of the population, and $\sigma_{\bar{X}}$ is the standard error of the mean. The following table summarises the results of experiments 2, 3 and 4. (Remember that on page 219, we calculated: $\sigma = 1 \cdot 22$.)

N	$\sigma_{\bar{X}}$	$\dfrac{\sigma}{\sqrt{N}}$
5	0·55	0·55
10	0·39	0·39
25	0·25	0·24

These results verify the formula for $\sigma_{\bar{X}}$.

Summary

For a normal population:
(a) If the means of many samples are calculated, they give rise to a **sampling distribution of means;**
(b) This sampling distribution of means is **normally distributed** with
   (i) $\mu_{\bar{X}} = \mu$,

   (ii) $\sigma_{\bar{X}} = \dfrac{\sigma}{\sqrt{N}}$.

10.3 Sampling from distributions other than normal

Six hundred cards, numbered as shown in the frequency distribution, were put in a box.

Value (x)	Frequency (f)
1	250
2	150
3	100
4	75
5	25
	$\Sigma f = 600$

The histogram of the distribution is shown in Fig. 10.9:

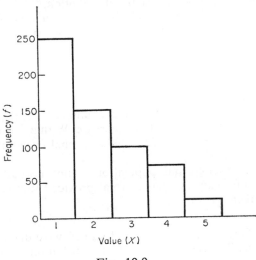

Fig. 10.9

Verify that for this background population the mean $\mu = 2.12$ and the standard deviation $\sigma = 1.20$.

Example 1. One hundred samples of size 5 were taken and the resulting sampling distribution of means was as follows:

Mid value $\bar{X}$	0·9	1·3	1·7	2·1	2·5	2·9	3·3	3·7
Frequency f	1	16	25	29	18	8	2	1

Verify that the mean $\mu_{\bar{X}}$ is 2·04 and the standard deviation $\sigma_{\bar{X}}$ is 0·54. Construct a histogram to show the sampling distribution of means.

Example 2. Samples of 25 were taken and the following sampling distribution of means obtained:

Mid value $\bar{X}$	1·76	1·88	2·00	2·12	2·24	2·36	2·48	2·60	2·72
Frequency f	4	6	13	19	23	16	9	6	4

Verify that the mean $\mu_{\bar{X}} = 2.23$, and standard deviation $\sigma_{\bar{X}} = 0.23$, and construct a histogram for the distribution.

For the samples of size 5, and size 25, the shapes of the sampling distributions of means resemble that of a normal distribution but **not** that of the original population.

Test the formula $\sigma_{\bar{X}} = \dfrac{\sigma}{\sqrt{N}}$ for both sets of samples and verify that there is a fairly good agreement.

In fact, the conclusions stated in the summary on page 228 are true for most populations, normal or otherwise. With a normal population, the sampling distribution of means is normal even for small sample sizes.

Although the background population is not normal, the sampling distribution of means is again normal provided samples of size 30 or more are taken.

Example 3. One hundred samples of size 50 were drawn from the 600 marked cards. The resulting sampling distribution of means is shown below:

Mid value $\bar{X}$	1·79	1·86	1·93	2·00	2·07	2·14	2·21	2·28	2·35	2·42
Frequency f	5	6	7	10	16	14	13	12	10	7

For this distribution verify that the mean, $\mu_{\bar{X}}$ is 2·13, and standard deviation, $\sigma_{\bar{X}}$ is 0·17.

Construct a histogram to show the sampling distribution of means. Since the population is not normal, the sample size (N) chosen was greater than 30, in this case 50.

There is close agreement between:

(a) $\mu_{\bar{X}} = 2.13$ and $\mu = 2.12$,

(b) $\sigma_{\bar{X}} = 0.17$ and $\dfrac{\sigma}{\sqrt{N}} = \dfrac{1.20}{\sqrt{50}} = 0.17$

10.4 Sampling model

So far in this chapter, the sampling results quoted were obtained from actual experiments. Consequently, results do not agree perfectly with theoretical expectations.

Consider now an **ideal** experiment with ideal results. Three balls of equal size, numbered 1, 4, 7 respectively, are placed in a bag. This is our **ideal** population.

Verify that its mean μ is 4 and its standard deviation σ is $\sqrt{6}$.

A sample of size 2 is drawn. This is done by drawing one ball, noting its number and replacing it in the bag before drawing the second ball of the sample. What are the possible combinations of two numbers from the population 1, 4 and 7?

Copy and complete the following table to show these nine samples, with their respective means:

First draw	1	1	1	4	4	4	7	7	7
Second draw	1	4	7						
Mean ($\overline{X}$)	1	2·5							

Copy and complete the following table for the sampling distribution of means:

$\overline{X}$	1	2·5	4	5·5	7
f	1			2	

For this sampling distribution of means, verify that the mean

$$\mu_X = \frac{\Sigma f \overline{X}}{\Sigma f} = 4$$

This is precisely the value calculated for the mean of the distribution. That is, $\mu_X = \mu$.

Verify that the standard deviation of the sampling distribution of means, σ_X is $\sqrt{3}$.

$$\text{Thus } \frac{\sigma}{\sqrt{N}} = \frac{\sqrt{6}}{\sqrt{2}} = \sqrt{3} = \sigma_X$$

If every possible combination of a given sample size is taken, then the relationships:

(a) $\mu_X = \mu$,

(b) $\sigma_X = \dfrac{\sigma}{\sqrt{N}}$ are true.

Exercise 1

(1) If $\mu_{\bar{X}}$ is 3, find μ.

(2) If the mean of a population is 10, find the mean of the sampling distribution of means.

(3) If σ is $\sqrt{3}$, find $\sigma_{\bar{X}}$ where each sample taken consists of 3 elements.

(4) If $\sigma_{\bar{X}}$ is 3, find σ where each sample is of size 16.

(5) If the standard deviation of a population is 16, find the standard deviation of the sampling distribution of means when each sample has 36 elements.

(6) The standard deviation of a population is $2\sqrt{3}$. Find the standard error of the mean when the number of elements in each sample is 3.

(7) A certain make of valve is found to have a mean life of 960 hours with a standard deviation of 30 hours. What will be the mean and standard deviation of the sampling distribution of means when samples of 25 are taken?

(8) The distribution of the weights of 2 000 college students is normal and it is found that the mean and standard deviation are 64 kg and 3 kg respectively. If a large number of samples of size 16 is chosen from this population, find the mean and standard error of the mean, of the resulting distribution of means.

(9) To find the mean life and standard deviation of certain electric light bulbs manufactured by a company, a large number of samples of 36 bulbs was tested. The mean and standard deviation of the resulting sampling distribution of means are found to be 960 hours and 10 hours respectively. Calculate the mean life and standard deviation of the light bulbs.

Exercise 2

(1) To find the mean life and standard deviation of motor-car tyres manufactured by a company, a large number of samples of 100 tyres was tested. The mean and standard deviation of the resulting distribution of means were found to be 20 000 km and 200 km respectively. Find the mean life and standard deviation of the tyres manufactured by this company.

(2) The weights of a certain population are normally distributed with mean 180 kg and standard deviation 20 kg. A large number of samples of size 16 is taken. Find the mean and standard error of the mean of the resulting distribution of means.

(3) To find the mean and standard deviation of money spent by holidaymakers abroad, a large number of interviewers each questioned 50 people. The mean and standard deviation of the sampling distribution of means were £60 and £1 respectively. Find the mean and standard deviation of the money spent by holiday-makers abroad.

(4) A certain firm manufactures car batteries. A large number of samples of 16 batteries had their voltages tested. The resulting sampling distribution of means had a mean of 12 volts and standard deviation 0·05 volts. Calculate the mean voltage and standard deviation of all the car batteries manufactured by the firm.

CHAPTER 11

Significance Testing

11.1 Confidence

Example 1. Many new articles are advertised with a guarantee. For example, manufacturers may guarantee:

(a) Car batteries for two years,

(b) Television tubes for six months,

(c) Parts of a new car for one year.

Can you think of other examples? Why are guarantees like these offered? Would a television tube be guaranteed for six months if a large percentage lasted less than that period?

Suggest a way by which a manufacturer could decide what period of time the guarantee should cover. What would be the result if the period of guarantee was (a) Too short, (b) Too long compared with the mean life of the product?

Example 2. Food is sold in packets which indicate that the contents weigh 2 kg. By law, these contents should weigh not less than 2 kg, and the manufacturer finds that it is uneconomical for the weight to exceed 2·1 kg. If you tested the contents of a large number of these packets, would you expect:

(a) 50%, (b) 75% (c) 95%, (d) a **very high** percentage to have weight between these limits?

Example 3. The international specification for the height of bounce of tennis balls is as follows: When dropped from a certain height on to a concrete base, a ball should bounce to a height greater than 135 cm, and less than 147 cm (to the nearest cm).

Would you buy a type of ball knowing that:
(a) 50%, (b) 75%, (c) 95%, (d) 99%, (e) 99·9% satisfied these conditions?

Example 4. Suppose a coin is tossed 5 times. The probabilities of obtaining 0, 1, 2, 3, 4 or 5 heads are given by the expansion of $(q+p)^n$ where $n = 5$, $q = \frac{1}{2}$ and $p = \frac{1}{2}$.

$$(\tfrac{1}{2}+\tfrac{1}{2})^5 = (\tfrac{1}{2})^5 \quad +5(\tfrac{1}{2})^4(\tfrac{1}{2})+10(\tfrac{1}{2})^3(\tfrac{1}{2})^2+10(\tfrac{1}{2})^2(\tfrac{1}{2})^3+5(\tfrac{1}{2})(\tfrac{1}{2})^4+(\tfrac{1}{2})^5$$
$$= \tfrac{1}{32} \quad + \quad \tfrac{5}{32} \quad + \quad \tfrac{10}{32} \quad + \quad \tfrac{10}{32} \quad + \quad \tfrac{5}{32} \quad + \quad \tfrac{1}{32}$$
$$= Pr(0) \quad + \quad Pr(1) \quad + \quad Pr(2) \quad + \quad Pr(3) \quad + \quad Pr(4) \quad + \quad Pr(5)$$

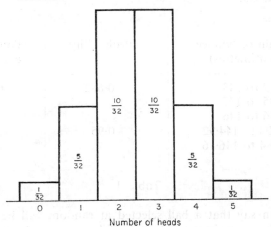

Represents a probability of $\frac{1}{32}$

Number of heads

Fig. 11.1

If we wished to forecast the outcome of such an experiment, the prediction that 2 or 3 heads would occur could be made fairly confidently, since the probability of 2 or 3 heads occurring is $\frac{20}{32}$. That is, we expect 2 or 3 heads to occur about 20 times in 32 trials. The prediction that 1, 2, 3 or 4 heads would occur could be made very confidently since the probability of 1, 2, 3 or 4 heads occurring is $\frac{30}{32}$. That is, we expect 1, 2, 3 or 4 heads to occur about 30 times in 32 trials.

Could a fair coin give 0 heads or 5 heads in 5 tosses?

Would you regard such an outcome as: (a) Probable, (b) Improbable, (c) Highly improbable?

11.2 Confidence intervals

Example. A manufacturer makes tennis balls which, when tested in accordance with regulations, have height of bounce normally distributed with mean 141 cm and standard deviation 2 cm. Since height of bounce is normally distributed, the probability is 0·682 that a ball selected at random will bounce to a height between one standard deviation below and one standard deviation above the mean, that is, between 139 and 143 cm.

In statistics, we say that **we can be 68·2% confident** that a ball selected at random will bounce to a height between these two limits.

Copy and complete the following table, which refers to the height of bounce of tennis balls selected at random and tested in accordance with regulations:

Height of bounce (centimetres)	Probability	Percentage confidence
139 to 143	0·682	68·2
135 to 147		
136 to 146		
137·08 to 144·92	0·95	
135·84 to 146·16		99

Table 1

Since we can say that a ball selected at random will lie in a given interval with a certain percentage confidence, we call the interval a **confidence interval.** Thus, the interval from 139 cm to 143 cm (from one standard deviation below to one standard deviation above the mean) is called the **68·2% confidence interval.** The end points, 139 cm and 143 cm, are called the **68·2% confidence limits.**

Describe in a similar way the confidence intervals and limits in table 1.

In general, for a set of scores normally distributed with mean μ and standard deviation σ, we would refer to the interval from:

(a) $\mu - \sigma$ to $\mu + \sigma$ as the 68·2% confidence interval,
(b) $\mu - 2\sigma$ to $\mu + 2\sigma$,, ,, 95·4% ,, ,, ,
(c) $\mu - 3\sigma$ to $\mu + 3\sigma$,, ,, 99·8% ,, ,, ,
(d) $\mu - 1·96\sigma$ to $\mu + 1·96\sigma$,, ,, 95% ,, ,, ,
(e) $\mu - 2·58\sigma$ to $\mu + 2·58\sigma$,, ,, 99% ,, ,, .

Clearly both manufacturer and consumer wish a high degree of confidence, and, for this reason, the 95% and 99% confidence intervals and limits are most often used. Note that the confidence intervals we shall use will nearly always be symmetrical about the mean.

95% Confidence

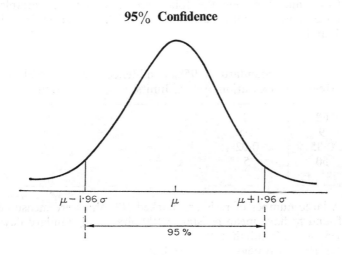

Fig. 11.2

99% Confidence

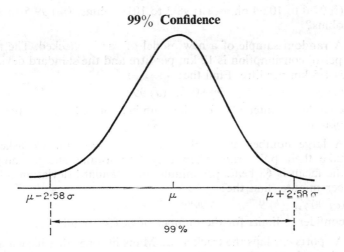

Fig. 11.3

Exercise 1

In the following questions, assume that the variables are normally distributed.

(1) Copy and complete the following table for the variables the mean and standard deviation of which are given in columns 1 and 2:

Mean	Standard Deviation	95% confidence limits	99% confidence limits
62	8		
9	1·5		
0·85	0·02		
50	5		

(2) A large number of resistors marked 100 ohms are measured and found to have mean resistance 100 ohms and standard deviation 1·5 ohms. Find the:

(a) 95%,   (b) 99%

confidence limits for the resistance.

How would you refer to the following intervals:

(i) 97·6 to 102·4 ohms, (ii) 98·2 to 101·8 ohms, (iii) 99·5 to 100·5 ohms?

(3) A random sample of a new model of car is checked. The mean petrol consumption is 12 km per litre and the standard deviation is 1·5 km per litre. Find the:

(a) 50%,   (b) 75%,   (c) 90%,   (d) 99%

confidence intervals for the number of kilometres per litre obtained.

(4) A large number of people, selected at random, are asked to take their pulse rate when they first awake one morning. If the mean is 68 beats per minute and standard deviation 5 beats per minute, find the:

(a) 90%,   (b) 95%,   (c) 99%

confidence limits for the number of beats per minute.

(5) A sports car laps the track at Le Mans in times that have a mean of 4 minutes 27 seconds and standard deviation 5·4 seconds. Find the:

(a) 75%, (b) 85%, (c) 95%

confidence intervals for the time per circuit.

(6) 95% of a certain type of light bulb have a life between 853 and 1 147 hours. Assuming that the scores are symmetrical about the mean, calculate:

(a) The mean,
(b) The standard deviation,
(c) The 99% confidence limits,

for these light bulbs.

(7) Copy and complete the following table for scores symmetrically distributed about the mean:

Mean	Standard deviation	95% confidence limits	99% confidence limits
		5·04 and 8·96	
		4·8 and 5·6	
			82 and 87
			7 and 15
		26·8 and 25·2	

11.3 Confidence intervals for the distribution of means

Example. Reference was made in section **11.2** to a type of tennis ball which had height of bounce normally distributed with mean 141 cm and standard deviation 2 cm. Suppose a large number of samples of 100 were taken and the mean height of bounce for each sample calculated. Then we would expect the distribution of means to be normal with mean $\mu_{\bar{X}}$ and standard deviation $\sigma_{\bar{X}}$, where

$$\mu_{\bar{X}} = \mu \qquad \text{and } \sigma_{\bar{X}} = \frac{\sigma}{\sqrt{N}} \quad (N = \text{sample size})$$

$$= 141 \text{ cm} \qquad\qquad = \frac{2}{\sqrt{100}}$$

$$= 0 \cdot 2 \text{ cm}$$

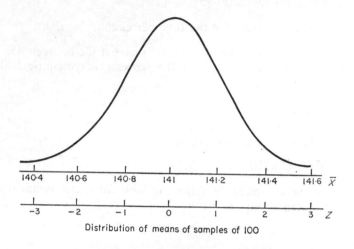

Distribution of means of samples of 100

Fig. 11.4

Verify that the mean height of bounce of 68·2% of these samples would lie between 140·8 cm and 141·2 cm. We refer to this interval as the 68·2% confidence interval for the means of samples of 100 balls.

Copy and complete the following table, which refers to the mean height of bounce of samples of 100:

Sample mean (centimetres)	Probability	Percentage confidence
140·8 to 141·2	0·682	68·2
140·6 to 141·4		
140·5 to 141·5		
140·608 to 141·392		
140·484 to 141·516		

Table 2

If the sample size is changed to 25 what will now be the values of $\mu_{\bar{X}}$ and $\sigma_{\bar{X}}$? Copy and complete the following table which refers to samples of this size:

Sample mean (centimetres)	Probability	Percentage confidence
	0·682	95·5
	0·95	99

Table 3

Exercise 2

(1) A population has mean 12 and standard deviation 4. Find the 95% and 99% confidence intervals for the means of samples of size
(a) 100, (b) 64, (c) 400, (d) 144.

(2) Electrical components manufactured by a company have a mean life 1 200 hours and standard deviation 150 hours. Find the: (a) 90%, (b) 95%, (c) 99% confidence intervals for the means of samples of 100.

(3) A manufacturer makes ropes which have mean breaking strength 2 000 kg and standard deviation 50 kg. For samples of size 64 find the:
(a) 90%, (b) 95%, (c) 99%
confidence limits for the mean breaking strength. Repeat for samples of size 144 and for samples of size 400.

(4) Electric light bulbs have a mean life of 1 000 hours and standard deviation 75 hours. Between what limits would you expect to find 95% of the means of samples of:
(a) 100, (b) 400, (c) 36?

(5) Tins of food leaving a factory have mean weight 2 kg and standard deviation 0·10 kg. The factory distributes the food in two sizes of container, one of which takes 16 tins, the other 25. Find (to two decimal places):
(a) 95%, (b) 99%
confidence limits for the mean weight of the tins in each container.

(6) When a random sample of 100 is taken from a population, the sample is found to have mean 82·0 and standard deviation 12·0.

Using the standard deviation of the sample as an estimate of the standard deviation of the population, find:

(*a*) 90%,   (*b*) 95%,   (*c*) 99%

confidence limits for the mean of the population.

(7) A machine produces bags of flour, and to estimate the mean weight of the bags, a random sample of 144 is taken. The sample mean and standard deviation are found to be 230·0 g and 2·4 g respectively. Using 2·4 g as an estimate of the population standard deviation, find:

(*a*) 90%,   (*b*) 95%,   (*c*) 99%

confidence limits for the mean weight of bags produced by the machine.

11.4 Decision rules

Example 1. Suppose that before a game we wanted to make sure that our team had an even chance of winning the toss. We could make 5 practice tosses of the coin to test its fairness, and reject that it was fair if we obtained 0 heads or 5 heads.

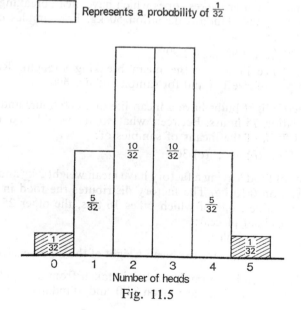

Fig. 11.5

Such a decision could be justified by arguing that in 5 tosses of a **fair** coin, the occurrence of 0 heads or 5 heads is highly unlikely, since:

Pr (0 or 5 heads) $= \frac{2}{32} = \frac{1}{16}$, while

Pr (1, 2, 3 or 4 heads) $= \frac{30}{32} = \frac{15}{16}$

The probability of obtaining 0 heads or 5 heads is shown in Fig. 11.5 by the shaded areas.

Definition. A rule which enables us to decide whether or not to reject a claim is called a **decision rule.**

For example, our decision rule in example 1 was:

   (a) Reject the fairness of the coin if we obtain 0 or 5 heads, and

   (b) Accept the fairness of the coin otherwise, that is, if we obtain 1, 2, 3 or 4 heads.

Notice that a decision rule could give us a **wrong decision.** It **is possible** to obtain 0 or 5 heads in 5 tosses of a fair coin, although the probability of such a result is only $\frac{1}{16}$. We would, therefore, expect to make a wrong decision only one time in sixteen.

Example 2. A die is thrown 180 times to test whether or not the **correct** number of sixes is occurring. For a fair die, we would expect to obtain approximately 30 sixes in 180 throws, since:

$$np = 180 \times \tfrac{1}{6} = 30$$

Outside certain limits above and below 30, we would reject a claim that this die was fair.

Since

$$np = 30 \text{ and } nq = 180 \times \tfrac{5}{6} = 150$$

both np and nq are greater than 5. Using the normal approximation to the binomial distribution,

$$\mu = np \quad \text{and} \quad \sigma - \sqrt{npq}$$
$$= 30 \qquad\qquad = \sqrt{180 \times \tfrac{1}{6} \times \tfrac{5}{6}}$$
$$= 5$$

(1) Verify that the 95% confidence limits are 20·2 and 39·8.

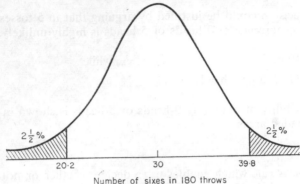

Number of sixes in 180 throws

Fig. 11.6

Suppose that, in 180 throws, we obtained less than 21 or more than 39 sixes. This is such an unexpected outcome for a fair die that we would reject a claim that this die was fair. That is, such an outcome is obtained so seldom by chance from a fair die (5 times in 100) that we reject this outcome as being a chance occurrence and conclude that the die is unfair.

Note that we would expect such a decision to be **wrong** about 5% of the time, and this is indicated by saying that we reject the fairness of the die **at the 0·05 level of significance,** or that the result is **significant at the 0·05 level.**

Hence our decision rule in this case is:

(a) Reject the fairness of the die at the 0·05 level of significance if less than 21 or more than 39 sixes are obtained, and

(b) Accept the fairness of the coin otherwise.
Would we reject the fairness of the die at the 0·05 level if, in the 180 throws, we obtained the following number of sixes?
(i) 25, (ii) 17, (iii) 16, (iv) 44, (v) 43, (vi) 19, (vii) 42.

(2) Verify that the 99% confidence limits are 17·1 and 42·9.

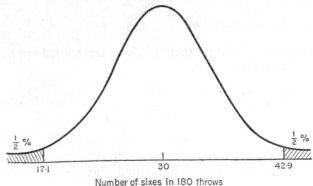

Number of sixes in 180 throws

Fig. 11.7

Suppose that, in 180 throws, we obtained less than 18 or more than 42 sixes. Such an outcome would be **even more unexpected** for a fair die than that discussed in (1). We would again conclude, even more confidently, that the die was unfair. That is, such an outcome is obtained so very seldom by chance from a fair die (1 in 100 times) that we would strongly reject this outcome as being a chance occurrence and reject the claim that the die was fair.

Note that, in this case, we would expect our decision to be **wrong** only 1% of the time, and we say that the fairness of the die has been rejected **at the 0·01 level of significance,** or that the result is **significant at the 0·01 level.**

What is our decision rule for the 0·01 level of significance?

Would we reject the fairness of the coin at this level if in 180 throws we obtained the following number of sixes?

(a) 25, (b) 17, (c) 16, (d) 44, (e) 43, (f) 19, (g) 42.

Note. (1) Many other levels of significance are possible, although the 0·05 and 0·01 levels are most often used.

(2) **The level of significance to be used should be decided before the experiment is carried out.**

We can sum up like this:

0·05 level of significance

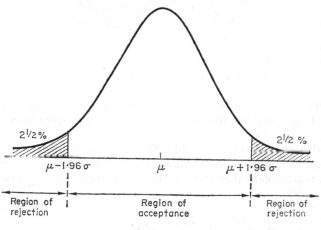

Fig. 11.8

Our decision rule for the 0·05 level of significance is: $|X-\mu|>1.96\sigma$

(a) Reject at the 0·05 level of significance if a random sample score is more than 1·96σ from the mean, and

(b) Accept at the 0·05 level of significance otherwise.

$f\ |X-\mu|<1.96\sigma$

0·01 level of significance

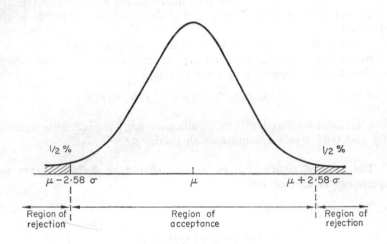

Fig. 11.9

Our decision rule for the 0·01 level of significance is: $|X-\mu|>2.58\sigma$

(a) Reject at the 0·01 level of significance if a random sample score is more than 2·58σ from the mean, and

(b) Accept at the 0·01 level of significance otherwise. $|X-\mu|<2.58\sigma$

In practice, if the random sample score falls on the boundary of a region of rejection, the test is inconclusive and no decision is reached.

Alternative method. Problems like that illustrated in example 2 may also be answered by converting the raw scores to z-scores. For example, if 18 sixes are obtained in 180 tosses of a die, we convert 18 to a z-score thus:

$$\frac{x-\mu}{\sigma} = \frac{18-30}{5} = -\frac{12}{5} = -2.4$$

Since 2·4>1·96, we reject that the die is fair at the 0·05 level.
Since 2·4<2·58, we accept that the die is fair at the 0·01 level.
By referring to Figs. 11.8 and 11.9, answer the following:

$|x - \mu| < 1.96$

(i) If you accept at the 0·05 level of significance, is it necessary to test at the 0·01 level?
(ii) If you reject at the 0·05 level of significance, is it necessary to test at the 0·01 level?

(The answer to (i) is no, and the answer to (ii) is yes. Can you give reasons?)

11.5 Two-tail tests: binomial distribution

Let us now examine further the ideas introduced in the previous section.

Example. In studying the relative breeding rate of two types of fish A and B, a lake is stocked with the two types in the ratio 2 : 5. Some time later, a random sample of 150 is taken to find whether or not the ratio remains at 2 : 5.

If the two types remain in the ratio 2 : 5 then

$$np = 150 \times \tfrac{2}{5} = 60$$

This is, approximately 60 of the fish from the sample should be of type A. Outside certain limits above and below 60, we decide that the proportion of type A has changed significantly.

Since

$$nq = 150 \times \tfrac{3}{5} = 90$$

both np and nq are greater than 5, so we can use the normal approximation to the binomial distribution with

$$\mu = np = 60 \quad \text{and} \quad \sigma = \sqrt{npq}$$
$$= \sqrt{150 \times \tfrac{2}{5} \times \tfrac{3}{5}}$$
$$= 6$$

The test is performed in the following order:

(a) **Claim.** We must first be clear as to what we are testing. In this case we are testing the claim that the ratio is still 2 : 5,

(b) **Decision rule.** We must next decide what level of significance we are going to use for the decision rule. Since

$$\mu = 60 \quad \text{and} \quad \sigma = 6$$

the 95% confidence limits are:

$$\mu - 1 \cdot 96\sigma = 60 - (1 \cdot 96 \times 6) = 48 \cdot 24$$
$$\text{and} \quad \mu + 1 \cdot 96\sigma = 60 + (1 \cdot 96 \times 6) = 71 \cdot 76.$$

Hence the decision rule for the 0·05 level is:

(i) Reject that the ratio is 2 : 5 if less than 49 or more than 71 fish are of type A, and

(ii) Accept that the ratio is 2 : 5 otherwise.

Also, since the 99% confidence limits are:

$$\mu - 2 \cdot 58\sigma = 60 - (2 \cdot 58 \times 6) = 44 \cdot 52$$
$$\text{and} \quad \mu + 2 \cdot 58\sigma = 60 + (2 \cdot 58 \times 6) = 75 \cdot 48$$

the decision rule for the 0·01 level is:

(i) Reject that the ratio is 2 : 5 if less than 45 or more than 75 fish are of type A, and

(ii) Accept that the ratio is 2 : 5 otherwise.

(c) **Experiment.** The random sample of 150 fish is now taken and the number of fish of type A noted.

(d) **Conclusion.** From the number of fish of type A in the sample, the claim is either rejected or accepted using our decision rule.

Would we reject or accept the claim at the (a) 0·05, (b) 0·01 level if our random sample of 150 gave (i) 49, (ii) 74, (iii) 45, (iv) 43, (v) 69, (vi) 76, (vii) 47, (viii) 77, (ix) 48, (x) 72 fish of type A?

Exercise 3

In the following questions, draw diagrams and shade the areas corresponding to the regions of rejection.

(1) In studying the relative breeding rate of two types of fish A and B, a lake was stocked with the two types in the ratio 2 : 1. Some time later, a random sample of 72 was drawn to find whether or not the ratio remained at 2 : 1.

If the two types of fish were still in the ratio 2 : 1, how many of type A would you expect to find in the sample of 72?

(a) $48; \sigma = \sqrt{\left(72 \cdot \frac{2}{9}\right)} = 4; 40 - 56; 38 - 58$

What is the standard deviation of the number of type A in samples of this size?

Outside what limits would you reject the 2 : 1 ratio at the

(a) 0·05, (b) 0·01 level of significance?

(2) In a certain district, it was found that one car in five sold in one year was made by a certain manufacturer. The following year, a random sample of 100 cars was taken to find if the manufacturer's share of the market was unchanged.

Would you reject that his share had remained the same if the sample revealed that the following number were made by him:

(a) 9, (b) 20, (c) 21, (d) 12, (e) 29, (f) 31, (g) 27, (h) 11, (i) 10, (j) 28?

Consider both 0·05 and 0·01 levels of significance.

(3) In another district the same manufacturer's share one year was one in four. Outside what limits would you decide that his share of the market had changed if, in the following year, a random sample of 48 was taken?
Consider both 0·05 and 0·01 levels of significance.

(4) It is stated that one person in six is left-handed. Make decision rules to test this statement, using both levels of significance, if a random sample of 180 is to be taken.

Would you reject the statement if the sample revealed the following number of left-handers:

(a) 25, (b) 20, (c) 40, (d) 17, (e) 43, (f) 41, (g) 18, (h) 19, (i) 38, (j) 16?

(5) A coin is tossed 100 times. Make decision rules to test the fairness of the coin using both a 0·05 and a 0·01 level of significance.

(6) A die is tossed 500 times and the number of sixes recorded. Would you reject the fairness of the die at the (a) 0·05, (b) 0·01 level of significance if the following number of sixes occurred:

(i) 65, (ii) 81, (iii) 103, (iv) 106, (v) 100, (vi) 61, (vii) 62, (viii) 93, (ix) 67, (x) 59?

Note. Study the part of the diagram you have shaded in the above examples. Since we were testing, in each case, to find whether or not a random sample score lay in one or other of the **tails** of the distribution, we call this a **two-tail test**.

Notice that the tails of the normal curve most often used are those outside either the 95% or 99% confidence limits.

11.6 Two-tail tests: distribution of means

We can often test statements and claims using the distribution of means of samples. Consider the following example:

Example 1. When an intelligence test is applied on a nation-wide scale, pupils of a certain age score a mean of 100 with standard deviation 15. An experimenter takes a sample of 225 pupils and claims that the sample is random. When the pupils sit the test, however, they score a mean of 98. Should we reject the claim?

Notice that, since the **mean** score of the 225 pupils is in question, we must compare this mean with the sampling distribution of means. We calculate:

$$\mu_{\bar{X}} = \mu \quad \text{and} \quad \sigma_{\bar{X}} = \frac{\sigma}{\sqrt{N}} \quad (N = \text{sample size})$$

$$= 100 \qquad\qquad = \frac{15}{\sqrt{225}}$$

$$= 1$$

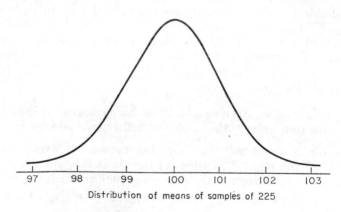

Distribution of means of samples of 225

Fig. 11.10

The various stages of the test would be carried out in the following order:

    (*a*) **Claim.** The claim is that the sample is random and so has mean approximately 100.

(b) **Decision rule.** If we use a 0·05 level of significance, the 95% confidence limits are:

$$\mu_{\bar{X}} - 1·96\sigma_{\bar{X}} = 100 - (1·96 \times 1) = 98·04$$

and $\mu_{\bar{X}} + 1·96\sigma_{\bar{X}} = 100 + (1·96 \times 1) = 101·96$

Hence our decision rule for the 0·05 level is

(i) Reject that the sample is random if the sample mean is less than 98·04 or more than 101·96, and

(ii) Accept that the sample is random otherwise.

Since

$$\mu_{\bar{X}} - 2·58\sigma_{\bar{X}} = 100 - (2·58 \times 1) = 97·42$$

and $\mu_{\bar{X}} + 2·58\sigma_{\bar{X}} = 100 + (2·58 \times 1) = 102·58$

the decision rule for the 0·01 level is:

(i) Reject that the sample is random if the sample mean is less than 97·42 or more than 102·58, and

(ii) Accept that the sample is random otherwise.

(c) **Experiment.** Once it is clear what the claim and decision rule are, the experiment is carried out. In this case, the result is that the 225 pupils score a mean of 98.

(d) **Conclusion.** Using our decision rule for the 0·05 level, we **reject** that the sample is random.
Using the decision rule for the 0·01 level, we **accept** that the sample is random.

Alternative method. The above test may be performed throughout using z-scores. We convert 98 to a z-score:

$$\frac{\bar{X} - \mu_{\bar{X}}}{\sigma_{\bar{X}}} = \frac{98 - 100}{1} = -2$$

Since $2 > 1·96$, we use the decision rule to reject the sample at the 0·05 level.

Since $2 < 2·58$, we accept the sample at the 0·01 level (using the other decision rule).

Handwritten annotation top right: $H_0:$ $\mu = 56$

Exercise 4

(1) A variable with standard deviation 5 is thought to have mean 56. Would you reject this mean at the 0·05 level of significance if

    (a) A random sample of 64 had a mean of: *(handwritten: $\sigma_{\bar{x}} = \cdot625$ $\mu \pm 1\cdot225$)*
       (i) 57, (ii) 54·8, (iii) 54·3, (iv) 57·6. *(handwritten: $54\cdot39 \leqslant \mu \leqslant 57\cdot61$)*
    (b) A random sample of 36 had a mean of: *(handwritten: $\sigma_{\bar{x}} = \cdot833 \Rightarrow 54\cdot37 \leqslant \mu \leqslant 5?$)*
       (i) 57·5, (ii) 54, (iii) 58·2, (iv) 58·1? *(handwritten: $53\cdot85 \leqslant \mu \leqslant 58\cdot15$)*

Answer the same questions for the 0.01 level of significance.

(2) A variable with standard deviation 6 is thought to have mean 65. Would you reject the mean at the (a) 0·05, (b) 0·01 level of significance if a random sample of 36 gave a mean score of:

    (i) 63·3, (ii) 63, (iii) 67, (iv) 66·9, (v) 68, (vi) 67·7, (vii) 62·3, (viii) 64·9?

(3) A firm manufactures ropes with mean breaking strength 200 kg and standard deviation 12 kg. Another manufacturing process gives ropes with the same standard deviation, and the mean is also claimed to be the same. Comment on the claim at both levels of significance if a random sample of 100 of the second type gave mean breaking strength:

    (a) 197·4 kg, (b) 195·6 kg, (c) 202·9 kg, (d) 203·4 kg, (e) 201·7 kg, (f) 198·9 kg.

(4) A manufacturer claims that all resistors manufactured by him which are marked 100 ohms actually have mean 100 ohms and standard deviation 1·5 ohms. Having selected 64 resistors at random and calculated their mean resistance, an experimenter rejected the manufacturer's mean at the 0·05 level. Outside what range of values must the mean of the 64 resistors have been? What is the possible range of values for the mean resistance of 64 resistors if the manufacturer's mean is to be rejected at the 0·05 level but accepted at the 0·01 level?

11.7 One-tail tests: binomial distribution

Let us consider again sampling from a binomial population.

Example 1. Two friends A and B have played each other at table-tennis over a long period and each has won the same number of games. That is, we assume they are of equal ability. A goes on a coaching course. On his return, B claims that there is no improvement in A's play. In the next 36 games between the two players, however, A wins 24.

Should we reject B's claim and conclude that A has improved significantly? Before A went on the coaching course, we would have expected each player to win about 18 games out of 36, since:

$$np = 36 \times \tfrac{1}{2} = 18$$

Also, since both np and nq are greater than 5, we can use the normal approximation to the binomial distribution with:

$$\mu = np \quad \text{and} \quad \sigma = \sqrt{npq}$$
$$= 18 \qquad\qquad = \sqrt{36 \times \tfrac{1}{2} \times \tfrac{1}{2}}$$
$$= 3$$

We again deal with the stages of the test in the following order:

(a) **Claim.** The claim is that there is **no improvement** in A's play and that the players are still of approximately equal ability.

(b) **Decision rule.** We will reject B's claim if A wins a significantly large number of games. If 36 games are played and A wins more than a critical number c, we reject B's claim and conclude that A is significantly better than B.

Notice that we are interested only in the **right-hand tail** of the distribution.

Suppose that, as in two-tail tests, we reject when we obtain a score in an extreme region where it has a 5% probability of falling by chance. Then we must find the score c above which 5% of the scores will lie.

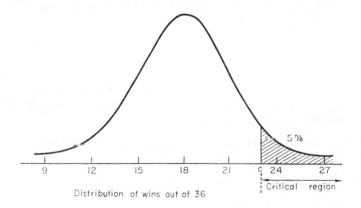

Distribution of wins out of 36

Fig. 11.11

Verify that 5% of the scores of a normal distribution lie above a z-score of 1·65. Then:

$$c = \mu + 1\cdot65\sigma = 18 + (1\cdot65 \times 3)$$
$$= 18 + 4\cdot95$$
$$= 22\cdot95$$

Hence if A beat B 23 times or more out of 36, we would argue that, since this is such an unexpected outcome for players of equal ability, the players were no longer of equal ability and that A was better than B. Notice, however, that we would expect such a decision to be wrong approximately 5% of the time. Hence our decision rule for the 0·05 level of significance is:

(i) Reject B's claim if A wins 23 or more games out of 36, and
(ii) Accept B's claim otherwise.

Verify that 1% of the scores of a normal distribution lie above a z-score of 2·33. Then our critical value k this time would be

$$k = \mu + 2\cdot33\sigma = 18 + (2\cdot33 \times 3)$$
$$= 18 + 6\cdot99$$
$$= 24\cdot99$$

If A beat B 25 times or more out of 36, we would argue that this was an even more unexpected outcome for players of equal ability than that discussed above. We would again conclude that A was better than B and on this occasion expect the probability of a wrong decision to be 0·01.

Our decision rule for the 0·01 level of significance is:

(i) Reject B's claim if A wins 25 or more games out of 36, and
(ii) Accept B's claim otherwise.

(c) **Experiment.** The experiment has revealed in this case that A won 24 games out of 36.

(d) **Conclusion.** If we chose a 0·05 level of significance, we would **reject** B's claim and conclude that A had improved significantly. If, on the other hand we chose a 0·01 level of significance, we would **accept** B's claim.

Alternative method. The test may again be carried out using z-scores. We convert 24 to a z-score:

$$\frac{x - \mu}{\sigma} = \frac{24 - 18}{3} = \frac{-6}{3} = -2$$

Since $2 > 1\cdot65$, we reject B's claim at the 0·05 level.
Since $2 < 2\cdot33$, we accept B's claim at the 0·01 level.

Note. In example 1, we were interested only in the right-hand tail of the distribution. In another problem, we may be interested only in the left-hand tail. Consider:

Example 2. Suppose that, some time later, it is suspected that due to lack of practice, A has become a poorer player than B, and in 36 matches taken at random, wins only 17 times. In this problem we will conclude that A is indeed a poorer player than B if he wins **less** than a certain number of matches out of 36. Is 17 a small enough number? In this case, we would be interested only in the left-hand tail of the distribution.

Definition. Tests of significance which have one tail only of the distribution as region of rejection are called **one-tail tests.** The following is a summary, using the right-hand tail only, for tests using a 0·05 or 0·01 level of significance:

The 0·05 level of significance

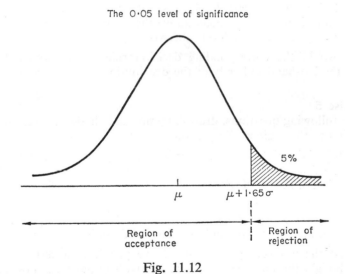

Fig. 11.12

Our decision rule for the 0·05 level is:

(a) Reject at the 0·05 level of significance if a random sample score is more than $1·65\sigma$ above the mean, and

(b) Accept at the 0·05 level otherwise.

0·01 level of significance

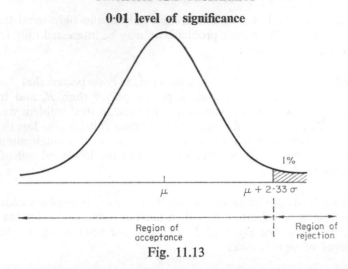

Fig. 11.13

Our decision rule for the 0·01 level is:

    (*a*) Reject at the 0·01 level of significance if a random sample score is more than 2·33σ above the mean, and

    (*b*) Accept at the 0·01 level otherwise.

What would the corresponding decision rules be for one-tail tests using the left-hand tail only of the distribution?

Exercise 5

In the following questions, draw diagrams and shade the areas corresponding to the regions of rejection.

    (1) It is claimed that a certain die is fair, but you suspect that, in fact, too few sixes are occurring for the die to be fair. Would you reject or accept the claim if, in 180 tosses, the following number of sixes occurred?

        (*a*) 23, (*b*) 22, (*c*) 21, (*d*) 20, (*e*) 19, (*f*) 18, (*g*) 17.

        Consider both 0·05 and 0·01 levels of significance.

    (2) At the last survey, two out of five people in a certain district bought the local newspaper regularly. The publisher now claims that **more people than ever** buy the paper regularly. Would you reject that the number who bought the paper was still two out of five (and accept the publisher's claim) if a random sample of 150 revealed the following number of readers: $\mu = 60, \sigma = 6$

        (*a*) 68, (*b*) 69, (*c*) 70, (*d*) 72, (*e*) 73, (*f*) 76, (*g*) 78, (*h*) 54?

        Consider both 0·05 and 0·01 levels of significance.

·05: 69·87   R = reject publishers claim [answer says accept]

·01: 73·98

(3) Three out of four pupils in a school prefer pop group A to pop group B. Later, it is suspected that the popularity of A has declined relative to B. Make decision rules, using both 0·05 and 0·01 levels of significance to test this suspicion if a random sample of 48 is taken.

(4) A manufacturer claims that 95% of the goods which leave his factory conform to specifications. Would you reject this claim if a random sample of 100 revealed: $\sigma = \frac{1}{2}\sqrt{19} = 2\cdot18$

    (a) 3, (b) 4, (c) 5, (d) 6, (e) 7, (f) 8 faulty items?

Consider 0·05 and 0·01 levels of significance.

(5) A manufacturer claims that four out of five housewives use his product in preference to those of his competitors. Make decision rules, using both 0·05 and 0·01 levels of significance, to test the claim if a random sample of 100 is taken.

(6) In a certain district, two out of three people who voted cast their votes for party A, while the remainder voted for party B. Later it was stated that the popularity of A had increased still further relative to B. Would you reject that two out of three people still favoured A (and conclude that the proportion was even higher) if a random sample of 72 was taken and:

    (a) 52, (b) 48, (c) 55, (d) 56, (e) 57, (f) 58, (g) 62, (h) 44

people indicated that they would vote for A rather than B? Use both 0·05 and 0·01 levels of significance.

11.8 One-tail tests: distribution of means

Let us now consider one-tail tests using the distribution of means of samples.

Example. A manufacturer makes ropes with mean breaking strength 2 000 kg and standard deviation 44 kg. A cheaper manufacturing process is claimed to give ropes with the same performance as that of ropes manufactured by the old process. The manufacturer wishes to guard against the possibility that the cheaper ropes in fact have a significantly lower breaking strength, and he takes a random sample of 64 ropes. These are found to have a mean breaking strength 1 989 kg. Should the manufacturer reject that the cheaper process is up to standard and conclude that the cheaper ropes have a significantly smaller breaking strength?

Note that since we are dealing with the **mean** breaking strength of a sample of 64, we are concerned with the distribution of means of samples of 64:

$$\mu_{\bar{X}} = \mu \quad \text{and} \quad \sigma_{\bar{X}} = \frac{\sigma}{\sqrt{N}} \ (N = \text{sample size})$$

$$= 2\,000 \qquad\qquad = \frac{44}{\sqrt{64}}$$

$$= 5 \cdot 5$$

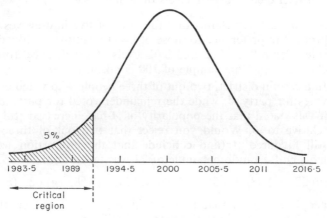

Distribution of means of samples of 64

Fig. 11.14

If the mean breaking strength of the 64 ropes is significantly less than a critical value c, we will reject that the cheaper ropes have the same performance as the others and conclude that they have a breaking strength which is significantly less. Hence our region of rejection is the left-hand tail only of the distribution so that our test is a **one-tail test.**

At the 0·05 level of significance

$$c = \mu_{\bar{X}} - 1 \cdot 65\sigma_{\bar{X}} = 2\,000 - (1 \cdot 65 \times 5 \cdot 5)$$

$$= 1\,990 \cdot 925 \doteqdot 1\,990 \cdot 9$$

At the 0·01 level of significance

$$c = \mu_{\bar{X}} - 2 \cdot 33\sigma_{\bar{X}} = 1\,987 \cdot 185 \doteqdot 1\,987 \cdot 2$$

Hence we can again perform the test as follows:

(a) **Claim.** The claim is that the cheaper ropes have the same mean breaking strength as the others. We wish to guard against the possibility that their mean breaking strength is actually smaller.

(b) **Decision rule.** The decision rule for the 0·05 level is:

(i) Reject that the cheaper ropes have the same breaking strength as the other ropes (and conclude that their breaking strength is in fact less) if the sample of 64 has mean less than 1 990·9 kg, and

(ii) Accept that they have the same breaking strength otherwise.

The decision rule for the 0·01 level is:

(i) Reject that the cheaper ropes have the same breaking strength as the other ropes (and conclude that their breaking strength is in fact less) if the sample of 64 has mean less than 1 987·2 kg, and

(ii) Accept that they have the same breaking strength otherwise.

(c) **Experiment.** The experiment has revealed a mean breaking strength of 1 989 kg.

(d) **Conclusion.** We reject the claim at the 0·05 level, but accept it at the 0·01 level.

Exercise 6

(1) A company makes ropes with mean breaking strength 1 800 kg and standard deviation 36 kg. It is claimed that, when different materials are used, the mean breaking strength is left unaltered. Make decision rules to test, at both 0·05 and 0·01 levels of significance, the possibility that the mean breaking strength is in fact significantly less, if a sample of: (a) 64, (b) 36 is taken and the mean found.

(2) It is thought that a variable has mean 9·5 g and the standard deviation is 0·3 g. Make decision rules, using both 0·05 and 0·01 levels of significance to test the possibility that the mean is actually significantly less than 9·5 g if a sample of 400 is taken and the mean calculated.

(3) A machine turns out components with a mean length 9·75 cm and standard deviation 0·06 cm. It is suspected that, after an overhaul, the machine has been set too high. Would you conclude that the machine was now making components which were too long if a random sample of 36 had a mean length of:

(a) 9·76 cm, (b) 9·77 cm, (c) 9·79 cm, (d) 9·80 cm?

Use both a 0·05 and a 0·01 level of significance.

(4) The owner of a turkey farm sells turkeys which have mean weight 8·0 kg and standard deviation 1·5 kg. It is thought that another diet increases the mean weight of the turkeys. Having used this diet on a random sample of 100 turkeys, he finds that they then have a mean weight of 8·3 kg. Would you reject the old diet in favour of the new one at the (a) 0·05, (b) 0·01 level of significance?

(5) A manufacturer makes a special kind of light bulb which has mean life 120 hours and standard deviation 8 hours. After complaints that bulbs are not lasting as long as advertised, he tests a random sample of 100. Should he conclude that the bulbs had a significantly shorter mean life than he first thought if the sample had a mean of:

(a) 119 hours, (b) 118·5 hours, (c) 118·3 hours, (d) 118 hours?

Consider 0·05 and 0·01 levels of significance.

Revision Examples II

(1) The table shows the distribution of the ages (to the nearest year) of some children in a housing area.

Age in years	Number of children
1—2	150
3—4	123
5—6	116
7—8	91
9—10	100
11—12	95
13—14	75

Indicate whether each of the following statements is **true or false**:

(a) The class interval size is 2 years,

(b) The modal class is 7—8 years,

(c) 20% of the children are under $2\frac{1}{2}$ years of age,

(d) The relative frequency of the 9—10 years class is 0·1.

[S.C.E.E.B.]

(2) The numbers of sparking plugs issued each day from stock in a garage for the 30 days of a month are:

75	72	81	91	101	108	61	72	83	92
74	83	76	62	100	99	96	76	58	73
102	56	68	57	83	81	79	102	97	69

Using groups 55—59, 60—64, etc., draw up the frequency distribution table. From this table, estimate the mean and median. [U.C.L.E.S.]

(3) One hundred investigators each chose three persons at random and questioned them as to whether they take their tea with or without sugar. Assuming that one person in every five takes tea without sugar, what is the number of investigators who may be expected to report that:

(i) Only one of the three persons questioned takes tea without sugar;

(ii) At least two of the three persons take sugar? [S.C.E.E.B.]

(4) 500 candidates sat an examination in which the marks were normally distributed with a mean score of 50 marks and a standard deviation of 10 marks:

(a) How many candidates scored:

(i) 65 marks or less,
(ii) 35 marks or less,
(iii) More than 70 marks,
(iv) 30 marks or less?

(b) If the pass mark is taken to be 45, how many candidates pass this examination?

(c) The top 12 candidates are awarded scholarships. Calculate what percentage of the candidates gain scholarships and hence find (as closely as your tables will allow) the minimum score needed to gain a scholarship.

(5) At a public meeting attended by 1 600 adults, 860 men were present. Test the claim that equal numbers of men and women would attend the meeting. State the levels of significance being considered.

Set 2

(1) The table shows a frequency distribution of the lifetimes (to the nearest hour) of 300 electric bulbs tested by the manufacturer.

Lifetime in hours	Number of bulbs
300—349	18
350—399	28
400—449	46
450—499	62
500—549	50
550—599	42
600—649	24
650—699	18
700—749	12

Indicate whether each of the following statements is **true** or **false**:

(a) The class boundaries of the third class are 339·5 and 450·5,
(b) The class interval size is 49,
(c) The relative frequency of the fifth class is $\frac{1}{6}$,
(d) Approximately 51·3% of the bulbs have a lifetime of less than 499·5 hours,
(e) Approximately 65·7% of the bulbs have a lifetime between 399·5 and 599·5 hours.

(2) A loch containing no fish is stocked with five types of fish as shown in the table. The number of fish put in, and their percentage increase each year, is also given:

Type of fish	I	II	III	IV	V
Number of fish put in	100	200	300	400	500
Percentage increase each year	20	15	10	5	$2\frac{1}{2}$

  (i) Calculate the approximate number of fish of each type in the loch after two years,
  (ii) Show on a bargraph the number of fish of each type

  (a) Immediately after stocking, and (b) After two years.

  (iii) What is the probability that a fish caught after two years will be of type I? [S.C.E.E.B.]

(3) The table gives the grouped frequency distribution of the lifetimes, measured to the nearest hour, of 300 electronic tubes.

Lifetime (hours)	Number of tubes
501—600	12
601—700	44
701—800	56
801—900	83
901—1 000	60
1 001—1 200	36
1 201—1 500	9

Draw, on graph paper, the cumulative frequency polygon of the distribution.
From your graph, estimate

  (i) The median tube lifetime,
  (ii) The percentage of tubes with lifetimes between 750 and 1 050 hours. [J.M.B.]

(4) If the probability that a child is left-handed is 0·15, find the probability that in a school with a roll of 1 500 the number of left-handed pupils is

  (a) Less than 200,
  (b) More than 255,
  (c) Less than 210.

(5) It is claimed that at least 2 out of 5 families go abroad for their summer holidays. In a sample of 150 families taken at random it was found that 50 families intended to go abroad on holiday. Is this finding consistent with the claim?
Discuss levels of significance and whether a one-tailed or a two-tailed test is being used.

Set 3

(1) Indicate whether each of the following statements is **true** or **false**:

(a) The area under the standard normal curve to the right of $z = 1.72$ is equal to that to the left of $z = -1.72$.

(b) If the area under the standard normal curve between 0 and z is 0·490, then z is approximately ± 2.33.

(c) For a set of scores normally distributed with mean 75 and standard deviation 5, a raw score of 72 becomes a standard score of 0·6.

(d) When a pack of playing cards is cut twice, the probability of obtaining two diamond cards is $\frac{3}{8}$.

(e) If a set of scores is normally distributed with mean 235 and if 245 corresponds to a standard score of 3, then the standard deviation of the distribution is 5.

(2) Three coins are tossed together a number of times, giving the following frequency distribution:

Number of heads	0	1	2	3
Frequency	3	13	12	4

How many times were the three coins tossed together?
Use the information in the table to calculate the mean number of heads thrown and the standard deviation. If the number of tails had been recorded instead of the number of heads, write down the corresponding frequency distribution.

Find the mean and standard deviation of the number of tails obtained. Discuss your answer.

(3) The table shows the frequency distribution of the annual salaries of 120 male employees at a certain factory:

Salary (£)		Number of employees
Exceeding	Not exceeding	
400	500	11
500	700	29
700	900	50
900	1 100	17
1 100	1 400	9
1 400	1 800	4

(i) Calculate the arithmetic mean of the distribution.
(ii) Exhibit the data on graph paper in the form of a histogram. Estimate the median salary and describe the method you have used.

[J.M.B.]

(4) Intelligence tests produce a normal frequency distribution of scores with mean 100 and standard deviation 15. If children who score less than 80 in such a test are given special education, calculate the percentage of such children in the whole population. If it is decided that 15% of children (those with the highest score in any intelligence test) should be sent to schools which prepare pupils for university entrance, find the lowest mark which would entitle a child to enrol in such a school.

(5) It was found one year that 2 out of 5 families went abroad for their summer holidays. The following year a survey was made to see if this proportion had changed significantly. State your conclusions if in a random sample of 150 families the following numbers went abroad for their holidays:
(a) 50, (b) 70, (c) 90, (d) 40.
Discuss levels of significance and whether a one-tailed or a two-tailed test is being used.

Set 4

(1) Indicate whether each of the following statements is true or false.

(a) The mean of 4, 1, 3, 9, 4, 6, 8 is greater than the median.

(b) In the table of areas under the standard normal curve, the area to the right of $z = a$ is equal to the area to the left of $z = -a$.

(c) Given that the area under the standard normal curve between 0 and z is 0·475, then the values of z are $\pm 1·96$.

(d) There are five ways in which a total of 6 can be thrown using two dice.

(e) If a census is taken of the number of families with two children, and one of these families is selected at random, the probability that it contains two boys is 1.

[S.C.E.E.B.]

(2) The profit of a company in 1964 was £72 000 000. This profit was used in the following ways, each amount being given in millions of £:

U.K. Taxation	Overseas Taxation	Reserves	Pref. Dividends	Ordinary Dividends
5·5	32·9	13·4	0·6	19·6

Draw a pie chart to illustrate the disposal of the profits.
What are the advantages of using a pie chart to represent these figures?

[U.C.L.E.S.]

(3) In an examination 87·5% of the pupils passed. Assuming a normal distribution with mean 48·9 and standard deviation 6, calculate:

(a) What percentage of passes lies to the right of the mean,
(b) What percentage of passes lies to the left of the mean,
(c) The standard score which corresponds to the pass mark, and
(d) The actual pass mark.

If the pass mark was raised to 55, what percentage of pupils would pass?

(4) 1 person in 6 drives his own car.

(a) If a random sample of size six is taken, find the probability that:

(i) All six drive their own car,
(ii) At least five drive their own car,

(b) If a random sample of size 180 is taken, find the probability that:

(i) Less than 20 drive their own car,
(ii) Between 23 and 30 (inclusive) drive their own car,
(iii) More than 33 drive their own car.

Indicate in each case whether the **binomial expansion** or the **normal approximation to the binomial distribution** is being used. Give reasons.

(5) It is believed that half the people who sit a driving test fail the test at their first attempt. In a random sample of 200 drivers taking the test it was found that 112 passed at their first attempt. Test the assumption that the probability of a driver passing at the first attempt is $\frac{1}{2}$.

Discuss levels of significance and whether a one-tailed or two-tailed test is being used.

Set 5

(1) Indicate whether each of the following statements is **true** or **false**:

(a) The area under the standard normal curve to the left of $z = 0 \cdot 67$ is approximately $1 \cdot 25$.

(b) 3% of the area under the standard normal curve lies to the right of $z = 2 \cdot 17$.

(c) If the mean and standard deviation of a normal distribution are 50 and 12 respectively, a score of 71 becomes a standard score of $1 \cdot 75$.

(d) In a class examination, a score of 50 in Latin (class average 45) is relatively better than a score of 70 in French (class average 70).

(e) If the probability of success in one trial for an event is exactly $0 \cdot 25$, then in 12 trials I shall have 3 successes.

[S.C.E.E.B.]

(2) The table below gives the lengths of time in months that 200 men were employed by a firm of contractors.

Centre of Interval	3	9	15	21	27	33	39	45
Number	109	50	20	9	3	4	2	3

Illustrate these figures by drawing:

(i) A histogram,
(ii) A cumulative frequency curve.

From these graphs estimate the median, the 9th decile and the percentage of the population of men employed for more than 22 months.

[O.C.S.E.B.]

(**Note.** The 9th decile is the score below which nine-tenths of the scores of the distribution lie.)

(3) Tins of fruit juice are sold marked 530 g net weight. The mean

weight of a consignment of tins is 532·33 g. If the weights of the tins are distributed normally, and no more than 1% of the tins are underweight, calculate:

(a) The percentage number of tins with weights greater than 532·33 g,

(b) The percentage number of tins with weights greater than 530·00 g,

(c) The standard score for a weight of 530·00 g, and

(d) The standard deviation for this distribution.

(4) Explain briefly what is meant by 'the standard error of the mean'. In a practical examination 20 candidates attempted to measure a physical constant with the following results:

Centre of interval	21·75	22·25	22·75	23·25
Number	2	5	5	3

Centre of interval	23·75	24·25	24·75	25·25
Number	1	1	2	1

(i) Find the mean and standard error of the mean.

(ii) Find 99% confidence limits for the mean and show that they include the true value of 22·6 although the 95% confidence limits do not.

[O.C.S.E.B.]

(5) (a) Six tulip bulbs, of which only two produce yellow flowers, are planted in a row. What is the probability that the yellow tulips will be next to each other?

(b) Four dice are thrown simultaneously. What is the probability that there will be

(i) One and only one six,

(ii) More than one six? [LOND.]

Set 6

(1) Indicate whether each of the following statements is **true** or **false**:

(a) The area of a relative frequency histogram is 1.

(b) The standard deviation of a set of scores is unaltered when each score is decreased by the same constant.

(c) Two fair dice are tossed together. The probability of obtaining a total of 5 is equal to the probability of obtaining a total of 9.

(d) In the binomial expansion of $(q+p)^5$, there is an even number of terms,

(e) The area under the standard normal curve between $z = -3$ and $z = +3$ is 1·00.

(2) To assist an outfitter who sells boys' raincoats, the heights (in metres, to the nearest 0·01 m) of a group of schoolboys were measured and noted as follows:

1·42	1·50	1·52	1·48	1·62	1·52	1·58	1·55
1·40	1·42	1·50	1·45	1·60	1·48	1·50	1·45
1·55	1·58	1·62	1·55	1·50	1·52	1·48	1·55
1·58	1·50	1·52	1·48	1·60	1·52	1·50	1·45
1·48	1·55	1·58	1·50	1·60	1·48	1·58	1·55
1·45	1·58	1·50	1·52	1·55	1·48	1·52	1·60

Make a frequency table of the heights using class intervals 1·40—1·42, 1·43—1·45, etc., and calculate the mean height.

Assuming that this sample is representative of 1 200 boys in the same age group in the district and that raincoats are sold thus:

Size 1 for heights 1·40—1·45 m,
Size 2 for heights 1·46—1·51 m,
Size 3 for heights 1·52—1·57 m, and
Size 4 for heights 1·58—1·63 m,

find how many coats of each size the outfitter would require to stock in order to be in a position to supply all boys of this age group in the district.

(3) The marks in an examination are normally distributed with mean μ and standard deviation σ. 50% of the scores (i.e. 25% on either side of the mean) lie between 49 and 61. Calculate the mean score and the standard deviation.

If the top 20% of the examination candidates are awarded scholarships, what is the least mark required to gain a scholarship?

If the bottom 40% of the candidates are considered to have failed, what is the lowest mark required to pass the examination?

(4) 625 investigators each visited 4 garages and tested the accuracy of the tyre pressure gauges. If 2 out of 5 garages had faulty instruments what would be the number of investigators expected to report that:

(a) Only one garage had an accurate gauge,
(b) All four garages had accurate gauges,
(c) Two garages had inaccurate gauges,
(d) Not more than two garages had accurate gauges?

(5) From a large population with a normal distribution, a sample of 100 observations has a mean of 14·15 metres and a standard deviation of 1·35 metres,

(a) Calculate the standard error of the mean, and say how you would use it to estimate limits between which the mean of the whole population may be expected to lie.

(b) What would you expect the standard deviation of the whole population to be?

(c) How many observations would be required to make the standard error of the mean 0·15 metres?

[W.J.E.C.] Amended

Set 7

(1) The table shows a frequency distribution of the lifetimes (to the nearest hour) of 200 radio valves tested by the manufacturer.

Lifetime in hours	Number of valves
200—299	6
300—399	24
400—499	30
500—599	44
600—699	40
700—799	32
800—899	20
900—999	4

Indicate whether each of the following statements is **true** or **false**:

(a) The class boundaries of the first class are 199·5 and 299·5.

(b) The class interval size is 99 hours.

(c) The relative frequency of the third class is 0·15.

(d) 72% of the valves have a lifetime of less than 700 hours.

(e) 57% of the valves have a lifetime of at least 300 hours, but less than 700 hours.

[S.C.E.E.B.]

(2) Investigation of 1 000 successive weighings showed them to be normally distributed with a mean of 50 kg and a standard deviation of 10 kg.

Use the table of areas under the normal curve to show that the frequencies for the class intervals 77·5—72·5, 72·5—67·5, 67·5—62·5, 62·5—57·5, 57·5—52·5 (kg) are approximately 9, 28, 66, 121, 174 respectively. Give the frequencies for similar intervals as far as 27·5—22·5 kg, and draw the histogram which represents the distribution (Scales: 1 cm to 1 class interval on the horizontal axis, 1 cm to a frequency of 10 on the vertical axis).

[S.C.E.E.B.]

(3) The number of casts of steel that can be made in an ingot mould before it becomes unusable is called the **life** of the mould. The lives of 90 ingot moulds are shown in the table below:

Life	80—84	85—89	90—94	95—99
Number	2	5	16	32

Life	100—104	105—109	110—114	115—119
Number	20	11	3	1

(i) Find the average life and the standard deviation.
(ii) Assuming these moulds to be representative of a larger population with the same mean and standard deviation, find what percentage of moulds have a life of more than 110 casts.
(iii) What life is exceeded by 95% of the moulds?

[O.C.S.E.B.]

(4) A new variety of plant is developed in which 75% of the plants will have double flowers while the remainder will have single flowers. When a customer buys 200 young plants what is the probability that this purchase will contain the following number of plants with double flowers:

(a) More than 150,
(b) Exactly 150,
(c) Between 140 and 150 (inclusive),
(d) Less than 130?

(5) String made by a manufacturer has a mean breaking strength of 19·8 kg and a standard deviation of 3·1 kg, the breaking strengths being normally distributed. A new method of manufacture is tried and from a sample of eleven pieces of string the following breaking strengths were measured:

20·1, 22·8, 21·4, 22·2, 18·4, 23·4, 24·1, 20·4, 20·8, 19·3, 20·3.

Does the new form of manufacture produce a string with a greater breaking strength? Give statistical reasons for your answer.

[A.E.B.] Amended

Set 8

(1) Indicate whether each of the following statements is **true** or **false**:

(a) If a set of scores has mean 16 and standard deviation 5, the distribution cannot be binomial.
(b) When each score in a list is halved, the mean and standard deviation of the new list are half those of the first list.

(c) Two fair dice are tossed together. The probability that the same score will appear on each is $\frac{1}{6}$.

(d) A large number of samples of size 25 are drawn from a certain population. If the standard error of the mean is 5, then the standard deviation of the population is approximately 25.

(e) In a set of scores with a normal distribution, the scores 75 and 59 have standard scores of $+2$ and -2 respectively. The standard deviation of this distribution is 4.

(2) A student took three examinations. He scored 72 in mathematics, 83 in Latin and 60 in French. The average mark was 78 in mathematics, 90 in Latin and 65 in French: the standard deviations in the marks for the three examinations were 6·0, 4·0 and 7·0 respectively. Assuming that the distributions of marks were approximately normal, compare his standing in the three examinations.

What mark would the student have to score in Latin to make his standing in that subject equivalent to his standing in mathematics? [S.C.E.E.B.]

(3) The mean daily output of operatives in a spinning factory is normally distributed with a mean of 540 metres and a standard deviation of 17 metres. The management are introducing more modern machines but will only train workers whose mean daily output is already 525 metres or more to use them. What percentage of the factory force can expect re-training?

[INST. OF STAT.] Amended

(4) (a) Five in every six pupils at a school do not appreciate classical music. What is the probability that, in a set of three pupils taken at random, all will appreciate classical music?

(b) A Briton, a Swede, a Dane and a German, competitors in the five events of the Pentathlon, have the same chance of winning any of the events. What is the probability that the Briton wins two events?

(c) In a certain restaurant, four people in five usually have coffee after their meal.

Estimate how many tables will order coffee for three when there are eighty diners, all seated at tables for four.

(5) A lady who claims to be able to tell margarine from butter is given three things to taste—one margarine and two kinds of butter. If she can detect the margarine 5 times in 6 trials, is her claim justified at the 5% level of significance?

State briefly any important precautions you would take in carrying out such an experiment. [S.C.E.E.B.]

Set 9

(1) Classify the following into continuous and discrete variables:
  (a) The barometric heights at Kiev over a period.
  (b) Number of persons visiting the local cinema per day for a month.
  (c) The tension in an elastic string when stretched beyond its natural length.
  (d) The number of goals scored per match by the school football team in a season.
  (e) The number of boys per family in a given district.
[A.E.B.]

(2) In a certain intelligence test, boys and girls both had normally distributed I.Q. scores with mean 100 and with standard deviations of 20 and 15 respectively.
  (a) If pupils with I.Q. below 70 go to a special school, estimate the number of boys and girls, out of 1 000 boys and 1 000 girls, you would expect to find in the special school.
  (b) If the top 20% of the boys are put in the top stream of a school, what I.Q. score would allow a boy into this stream?
[S.C.E.E.B.]

(3) 243 persons were asked five questions each. One gave five wrong answers, and 32 gave completely correct answers. The others gave answers as follows:

Number of correct answers	1	2	3	4
Number of persons	10	40	80	80

  (a) Show that this is a binomial distribution.
  (b) What is the probability that one particular answer is correct?
[W.J.E.C.]

(4) A pupil scored 56% in mathematics and 87% in Latin. If the average marks in these subjects were 47% and 83% respectively, and the respective standard deviations were 6 and 8, compare his performance in these two subjects. What mark would he have required to score in mathematics to make his standing equivalent to his Latin mark?

(5) Measurements on items drawn from the same (large) batch have a normal distribution, with a standard deviation of 10 units. The mean value of the batches, however, varies erratically about the target value of 100 units. All items with a value greater than 120 units are regarded as defective.
Show that the mean of the batch must be less than 103·6 units if fewer than 5% defectives are to occur in the batch.
[INST. OF STAT.]

Set 10

(1) Indicate whether each of the following statements is **true** or **false**:

    (*a*) The standard deviation of the four scores 2, 5, 8, 11 is smaller than the standard deviation of the scores 24, 26, 28, 30.

    (*b*) The median of the marks 52, 49, 63, 60, 68, is 63.

    (*c*) If in a class consisting of 15 boys and 10 girls the mean mark scored by the boys is 40 and by the girls is 60, then the mean mark of the whole class is 48.

    (*d*) Given that the mean and standard deviation of the weekly wages of six office employees earning £8, £9, £12, £12, £12, £19 are £12 and £3·51 respectively, then, if each employee receives an increase of £1 per week, the mean and standard deviation of the new wage distribution will be £13 and £3·51.

    (*e*) If the area under the standard normal curve to the right of $z = a$ is 0·15, then the area to the left of $z = a$ is 0·_5.

[S.C.E.E.B.]

(2) 10% of the production of a glass factory is below the required standard. Before leaving the factory, articles produced are carefully examined in batches of 3. If inspectors examine 300 batches each day, how many batches would be expected to contain

    (i) No article below standard?

    (ii) At most 1 article below standard?   [S.C.E.E.B.]

(3) Calculate the arithmetic mean and the standard deviation of the distribution in the table:

Variable x	Frequency
2·5—	14
7·5—	30
12·5—	67
17·5—	123
22·5—	177
27·5—	200
32·5—	178
37·5—	122
42·5—	68
47·5—	29
52·5—62·5	16

Draw an ogive of the distribution and use it to determine the proportion of frequencies between

(i) The arithmetic mean $\pm$ one standard deviation,
(ii) The arithmetic mean $\pm$ two standard deviations.

[A.E.B.]

(4) (a) Explain what is meant by **standard error of the mean.**
   (b) When a random sample of 225 is taken from a population, the sample is found to have mean 45·6 and standard deviation 5·75. Use 5·75 as an estimate of the population standard deviation to find

   (i) 95%, (ii) 99%, confidence limits for the mean of the population.
   (c) It is subsequently established that the population mean and standard deviation are 45·8 and 5·80 respectively. Find the probability that a sample of 25 will have a mean greater than 47·0.

(5) The table shows the grouped frequency distribution of lifetimes, measured to the nearest hour, of 400 electric light bulbs.

Lifetime (hours)	700–	800–	900–	1000–	1100–
Number of bulbs	14	46	58	76	68

Lifetime (hours)	1200–	1300–	1400–	1500–1599
Number of bulbs	62	48	22	6

(a) Which is the modal group of the distribution?
(b) Draw an appropriate graph and from it estimate the median and the semi-interquartile range of the distribution.
(c) The manufacturer of these bulbs offers a 120-days money back guarantee. Assuming the above bulbs are a truly representative sample from the manufacturer's production, estimate the probability that the manufacturer will have to refund the money on a bulb which, on average, is in use for seven hours per day.

[J.M.B.]

K

Set 11

(1) Indicate whether each of the following statements is **true** or **false**:

    (*a*) The percentage of scores less than a standard score of 1 is 84·1, correct to three significant figures.

    (*b*) If seven boys are born consecutively at a nursing home, then the probability that the next birth will be a girl is much greater than 0·5.

    (*c*) Given that in a distribution with standard deviation 12 the value 424 of the variable corresponds to a standard score of 2·0, then the mean of the distribution is 448.

    (*d*) If the probability of a defective article being produced is 0·05, then the most likely number of defective articles in a batch of 144 is 7.

    (*e*) The mean and standard deviation of an infinite population are 50 and 12 respectively. If a sample of 100 is drawn from this population, then the probability that the mean of the sample lies between $50 \pm 1\cdot2$ is 0·682, correct to three significant figures.

                                                          [S.C.E.E.B.]

(2) An engineering firm selects apprentices on the basis of an examination in English, Mathematics and Engineering Drawing. The marks scored by the four top candidates are given in the following table, which also shows the mean and standard deviation of the marks scored in each subject.

Candidate	English	Mathematics	Engineering Drawing
A	64	63	73
B	50	57	93
C	52	81	67
D	75	57	68
Mean	50	45	61
Standard deviation	10	15	12

Standardise each score and hence place the candidates in order of merit, giving the same weight to each subject.   [S.C.E.E.B.]

(3) A machine produces rods whose diameters are required to be within the tolerance limits 0·988 cm to 1·012 cm. A sample of 150 rods, measured to the nearest thousandth of a centimetre, gave the following distribution:

Diameter (centimetres)	0·976 to 0·981	0·982 to 0·987	0·988 to 0·993	0·994 to 0·999	1·000 to 1·005	1·006 to 1·011	1·012 to 1·017
Number of rods	1	5	30	71	34	7	2

   (a) Construct the cumulative frequency curve for the rods,
   (b) Calculate the percentage number of rods outside the tolerance limits.

[A.E.B.] Amended

(4) The average daily temperatures for February for a certain city form a distribution which is approximately normal. The mean and standard deviation of this distribution are 5·0°C and 2·5°C. What is the probability of having in that city in February an average daily temperature

   (i) Greater than 8·7°C?
   (ii) Lower than −0·2°C?
   (iii) Within the range 3·7°C to 6·3°C?

(5) (a) One person in seven buys frozen foods. Find the mean and standard deviation for the distribution of people buying frozen foods among ninety-eight people.

   (b) Three people in five prefer to rent a television set rather than buy one. Ten branches of a large firm each delivered four sets on a certain morning. Estimate how many of the branches have made arrangements to rent two of the four sets delivered that morning.

TABLES OF SQUARES, SQUARE ROOTS, AND THE AREA UNDER THE STANDARD NORMAL CURVE

Squares from 1 to 10

	0	1	2	3	4	5	6	7	8	9
1·0	1·00	1·02	1·04	1·06	1·08	1·10	1·12	1·14	1·17	1·19
1·1	1·21	1·23	1·25	1·28	1·30	1·32	1·35	1·37	1·39	1·42
1·2	1·44	1·46	1·49	1·51	1·54	1·56	1·59	1·61	1·64	1·66
1·3	1·69	1·72	1·74	1·77	1·80	1·82	1·85	1·88	1·90	1·93
1·4	1·96	1·99	2·02	2·04	2·07	2·10	2·13	2·16	2·19	2·22
1·5	2·25	2·28	2·31	2·34	2·37	2·40	2·43	2·46	2·50	2·53
1·6	2·56	2·59	2·62	2·66	2·69	2·72	2·76	2·79	2·82	2·86
1·7	2·89	2·92	2·96	2·99	3·03	3·06	3·10	3·13	3·17	3·20
1·8	3·24	3·28	3·31	3·35	3·39	3·42	3·46	3·50	3·53	3·57
1·9	3·61	3·65	3·69	3·72	3·76	3·80	3·84	3·88	3·92	3·96
2·0	4·00	4·04	4·08	4·12	4·16	4·20	4·24	4·28	4·33	4·37
2·1	4·41	4·45	4·49	4·54	4·58	4·62	4·67	4·71	4·75	4·80
2·2	4·84	4·88	4·93	4·97	5·02	5·06	5·11	5·15	5·20	5·24
2·3	5·29	5·34	5·38	5·43	5·48	5·52	5·57	5·62	5·66	5·71
2·4	5·76	5·81	5·86	5·90	5·95	6·00	6·05	6·10	6·15	6·20
2·5	6·25	6·30	6·35	6·40	6·45	6·50	6·55	6·60	6·66	6·71
2·6	6·76	6·81	6·86	6·92	6·97	7·02	7·08	7·13	7·18	7·24
2·7	7·29	7·34	7·40	7·45	7·51	7·56	7·62	7·67	7·73	7·78
2·8	7·84	7·90	7·95	8·01	8·07	8·12	8·18	8·24	8·29	8·35
2·9	8·41	8·47	8·53	8·58	8·64	8·70	8·76	8·82	8·88	8·94
3·0	9·00	9·06	9·12	9·18	9·24	9·30	9·36	9·42	9·49	9·55
3·1	9·61	9·67	9·73	9·80	9·86	9·92	9·99	10·05	10·11	10·18
3·2	10·24	10·30	10·37	10·43	10·50	10·56	10·63	10·69	10·76	10·82
3·3	10·89	10·96	11·02	11·09	11·16	11·22	11·29	11·36	11·42	11·49
3·4	11·56	11·63	11·70	11·76	11·83	11·90	11·97	12·04	12·11	12·18
3·5	12·25	12·32	12·39	12·46	12·53	12·60	12·67	12·74	12·82	12·89
3·6	12·96	13·03	13·10	13·18	13·25	13·32	13·40	13·47	13·54	13·62
3·7	13·69	13·76	13·84	13·91	13·99	14·06	14·14	14·21	14·29	14·36
3·8	14·44	14·52	14·59	14·67	14·75	14·82	14·90	14·98	15·05	15·13
3·9	15·21	15·29	15·37	15·44	15 52	15·60	15·68	15·76	15·84	15·92
4·0	16·00	16·08	16·16	16·24	16·32	16·40	16·48	16·56	16·65	16·73
4·1	16·81	16·89	16·97	17·06	17·14	17·22	17 31	17·39	17·47	17·56
4·2	17·64	17·72	17·81	17·89	17·98	18·06	18·15	18·23	18·32	18·40
4·3	18·49	18·58	18·66	18·75	18·84	18·92	19·01	19·10	19·18	19·27
4·4	19·36	19·45	19·54	19·62	19·71	19·80	19·89	19·98	20·07	20·16
4·5	20·25	20·34	20·43	20·52	20·61	20·70	20·79	20·88	20·98	21·07
4·6	21·16	21·25	21·34	21·44	21·53	21·62	21·72	21·81	21·90	22·00
4·7	22·09	22·18	22·28	22·37	22·47	22·56	22·66	22·75	22·85	22·94
4·8	23·04	23·14	23·23	23·33	23·43	23·52	23·62	23·72	23·81	23·91
4·9	24·01	24·11	24·21	24·30	24·40	24·50	24·60	24·70	24·80	24·90
5·0	25·00	25·10	25·20	25·30	25·40	25·50	25·60	25·70	25·81	25·91
5·1	26·01	26·11	26·21	26·32	26·42	26·52	26·63	26·73	26·83	26·94
5·2	27·04	27·14	27·25	27·35	27·46	27·56	27·67	27·77	27·88	27·98
5·3	28 09	28·20	28·30	28·41	28·52	28·62	28·73	28·84	28·94	29·05
5·4	29·16	29·27	29·38	29·48	29·59	29·70	29·81	29·92	30·03	30·14

Squares from 1 to 10

	0	1	2	3	4	5	6	7	8	9
5·5	30·25	30·36	30·47	30·58	30·69	30·80	30·91	31·02	31·14	31·25
5·6	31·36	31·47	31·58	31·70	31·81	31·92	32·04	32·15	32·26	32·38
5·7	32·49	32·60	32·72	32·83	32·95	33·06	33·18	33·29	33·41	33·52
5·8	33·64	33·76	33·87	33·99	34·11	34·22	34·34	34·46	34·57	34·69
5·9	34·81	34·93	35·05	35·16	35·28	35·40	35·52	35·64	35·76	35·88
6·0	36·00	36·12	36·24	36·36	36·48	36·60	36·72	36·84	36·97	37·09
6·1	37·21	37·33	37·45	37·58	37·70	37·82	37·95	38·07	38·19	38·32
6·2	38·44	38·56	38·69	38·81	38·94	39·06	39·19	39·31	39·44	39·56
6·3	39·69	39·82	39·94	40·07	40·20	40·32	40·45	40·58	40·70	40·83
6·4	40·96	41·09	41·22	41·34	41·47	41·60	41·73	41·86	41·99	42·12
6·5	42·25	42·38	42·51	42·66	42·77	42·90	43·03	43·16	43·30	43·43
6·6	43·56	43·69	43·82	43·96	44·09	44·22	44·36	44·49	44·62	44·76
6·7	44·89	45·02	45·16	45·29	45·43	45·56	45·70	45·83	45·97	46·10
6·8	46·24	46·38	46·51	46·65	46·79	46·92	47·06	47·20	47·33	47·47
6·9	47·61	47·75	47·89	48·02	48·16	48·30	48·44	48·58	48·72	48·86
7·0	49·00	49·14	49·28	49·42	49·56	49·70	49·84	49·98	50·13	50·27
7·1	50·41	50·55	50·69	50·84	50·98	51·12	51·27	51·41	51·55	51·70
7·2	51·84	51·98	52·13	52·27	52·42	52·56	52·71	52·85	53·00	53·14
7·3	53·29	53·44	53·58	53·73	53·88	54·02	54·17	54·32	54·46	54·61
7·4	54·76	54·91	55·06	55·20	55·35	55·50	55·65	55·80	55·95	56·10
7·5	56·25	56·40	56·55	56·70	56·85	57·00	57·15	57·30	57·46	57·61
7·6	57·76	57·91	58·06	58·22	58·37	58·52	58·68	58·83	58·98	59·14
7·7	59·29	59·44	59·60	59·75	59·91	60·06	60·22	60·37	60·53	60·68
7·8	60·84	61·00	61·15	61·31	61·47	61·62	61·78	61·94	62·09	62·25
7·9	62·41	62·57	62·73	62·88	63·04	63·20	63·36	63·52	63·68	63·84
8·0	64·00	64·16	64·32	64·48	64·64	64·80	64·96	65·12	65·29	65·45
8·1	65·61	65·77	65·93	66·10	66·26	66·42	66·59	66·75	66·91	67·08
8·2	67·24	67·40	67·57	67·73	67·90	68·06	68·23	68·39	68·56	68·72
8·3	68·89	69·06	69·22	69·39	69·56	69·72	69·89	70·06	70·22	70·39
8·4	70·56	70·73	70·90	71·06	71·23	71·40	71·57	71·74	71·91	72·08
8·5	72·25	72·42	72·59	72·76	72·93	73·10	73·27	73·44	73·62	73·79
8·6	73·96	74·13	74·30	74·48	74·65	74·82	75·00	75·17	75·35	75·52
8·7	75·69	75·86	76·04	76·21	76·39	76·56	76·74	76·91	77·09	77·26
8·8	77·44	77·62	77·79	77·97	78·15	78·32	78·50	78·68	78·85	79·03
8·9	79·21	79·39	79·57	79·74	79·92	80·10	80·28	80·46	80·64	80·82
9·0	81·00	81·18	81·36	81·54	81·72	81·90	82·08	82·26	82·45	82·63
9·1	82·81	82·99	83·17	83·36	83·54	83·72	83·91	84·09	84·27	84·46
9·2	84·64	84·82	85·01	85·19	85·38	85·56	85·75	85·93	86·12	86·30
9·3	86·49	86·68	86·86	87·05	87·24	87·42	87·61	87·80	87·98	88·17
9·4	88·36	88·55	88·74	88·92	89·11	89·30	89·49	89·68	89·87	90·06
9·5	90 25	90·44	90·63	90·82	91·01	91·20	91·39	91·58	91·78	91·97
9·6	92·16	92·35	92·54	92·74	92·93	93·12	93·32	93·51	93·70	93·90
9·7	94·09	94·28	94·48	94·67	94·87	95·06	95·26	95·45	95·65	95·84
9·8	96·04	96·24	96·43	96·63	96·83	97·02	97·22	97·42	97·61	97·81
9·9	98·01	98·21	98·41	98·60	98·80	99·00	99·20	99·40	99·60	99·80

Square Roots from 1 to 10

	0	1	2	3	4	5	6	7	8	9
1·0	1·00	1·00	1·01	1·01	1·02	1·02	1·03	1·03	1·04	1·04
1·1	1·05	1·05	1·06	1·06	1·07	1·07	1·08	1·08	1·09	1·09
1·2	1·10	1·10	1·10	1·11	1·11	1·12	1·12	1·13	1·13	1·14
1·3	1·14	1·14	1·15	1·15	1·16	1·16	1·17	1·17	1·17	1·18
1·4	1·18	1·19	1·19	1·20	1·20	1·20	1·21	1·21	1·22	1·22
1·5	1·22	1·23	1·23	1·24	1·24	1·24	1·25	1·25	1·26	1·26
1·6	1·26	1·27	1·27	1·28	1·28	1·28	1·29	1·29	1·30	1·30
1·7	1·30	1·31	1·31	1·32	1·32	1·32	1·33	1·33	1·33	1·34
1·8	1·34	1·35	1·35	1·35	1·36	1·36	1·36	1·37	1·37	1·37
1·9	1·38	1·38	1·39	1·39	1·39	1·40	1·40	1·40	1·41	1·41
2·0	1·41	1·42	1·42	1·42	1·43	1·43	1·44	1·44	1·44	1.45
2·1	1·45	1·45	1·46	1·46	1·46	1·47	1·47	1·47	1·48	1·48
2·2	1·48	1·49	1·49	1·49	1·50	1·50	1·50	1·51	1·51	1·51
2·3	1·52	1·52	1·52	1·53	1·53	1·53	1·54	1·54	1·54	1·55
2·4	1·55	1·55	1·56	1·56	1·56	1·57	1·57	1·57	1·57	1·58
2·5	1·58	1·58	1·59	1·59	1·59	1·60	1·60	1·60	1·61	1.61
2·6	1·61	1·62	1·62	1·62	1·62	1·63	1·63	1·63	1·64	1.64
2·7	1·64	1·65	1·65	1·65	1·66	1·66	1·66	1·66	1·67	1.67
2·8	1·67	1·68	1·68	1·68	1·69	1·69	1·69	1·69	1·70	1.70
2·9	1·70	1·71	1·71	1·71	1·71	1·72	1·72	1·72	1·73	1·73
3·0	1·73	1·73	1·74	1·74	1·74	1·75	1·75	1·75	1·75	1·76
3·1	1·76	1·76	1·77	1·77	1·77	1·77	1·78	1·78	1·78	1·79
3·2	1·79	1·79	1·79	1·80	1·80	1·80	1·81	1·81	1·81	1·81
3·3	1·82	1·82	1·82	1·82	1·83	1·83	1·83	1·84	1·84	1·84
3·4	1·84	1·85	1·85	1·85	1·85	1·86	1·86	1·86	1·87	1·87
3·5	1·87	1·87	1·88	1·88	1·88	1·88	1·89	1·89	1·89	1·89
3·6	1·90	1·90	1·90	1·91	1·91	1·91	1·91	1·92	1·92	1·92
3·7	1·92	1·93	1·93	1·93	1·93	1·94	1·94	1·94	1·94	1·95
3·8	1·95	1·95	1·95	1·96	1·96	1·96	1·96	1·97	1·97	1·97
3·9	1·97	1·98	1·98	1·98	1·98	1·99	1·99	1·99	1·99	2·00
4·0	2·00	2·00	2·00	2·01	2·01	2·01	2·01	2·02	2·02	2·02
4·1	2·02	2·03	2·03	2·03	2·03	2·04	2·04	2·04	2·04	2·05
4·2	2·05	2·05	2·05	2·06	2·06	2·06	2·06	2·07	2·07	2·07
4·3	2·07	2·08	2·08	2·08	2·08	2·09	2·09	2·09	2·09	2·10
4·4	2·10	2·10	2·10	2·10	2·11	2·11	2·11	2·11	2·12	2·12
4·5	2·12	2·12	2·13	2·13	2·13	2·13	2·14	2·14	2·14	2·14
4·6	2·14	2·15	2·15	2·15	2·15	2·16	2·16	2·16	2·16	2·17
4·7	2·17	2·17	2·17	2·17	2·18	2·18	2·18	2·18	2·19	2·19
4·8	2·19	2·19	2·20	2·20	2·20	2·20	2·20	2·21	2·21	2·21
4·9	2·21	2·22	2·22	2·22	2·22	2·22	2·23	2·23	2·23	2·23
5·0	2·24	2·24	2·24	2·24	2·24	2·25	2·25	2·25	2·25	2·26
5·1	2·26	2·26	2·26	2·26	2·27	2·27	2·27	2·27	2·28	2·28
5·2	2·28	2·28	2·28	2·29	2·29	2·29	2·29	2·30	2·30	2·30
5·3	2·30	2·30	2·31	2·31	2·31	2·31	2·32	2·32	2·32	2·32
5·4	2·32	2·33	2·33	2·33	2·33	2·33	2·34	2·34	2·34	2·34

Square Roots from 1 to 10

	0	1	2	3	4	5	6	7	8	9
5·5	2·35	2·35	2·35	2·35	2·35	2·36	2·36	2·36	2·36	2·36
5·6	2·37	2·37	2·37	2·37	2·37	2·38	2·38	2·38	2·38	2·39
5·7	2·39	2·39	2·39	2·39	2·40	2·40	2·40	2·40	2·40	2·41
5·8	2·41	2·41	2·41	2·41	2·42	2·42	2·42	2·42	2·42	2·43
5·9	2·43	2·43	2·43	2·44	2·44	2·44	2·44	2·44	2·45	2·45
6·0	2·45	2·45	2·45	2·46	2·46	2·46	2·46	2·46	2·47	2·47
6·1	2·47	2·47	2·47	2·48	2·48	2·48	2·48	2·48	2·49	2·49
6·2	2·49	2·49	2·49	2·50	2·50	2·50	2·50	2·50	2·51	2·51
6·3	2·51	2·51	2·51	2·52	2·52	2·52	2·52	2·52	2·53	2·53
6·4	2·53	2·53	2·53	2·54	2·54	2·54	2·54	2·54	2·55	2·55
6·5	2·55	2·55	2·55	2·56	2·56	2·56	2·56	2·56	2·57	2·57
6·6	2·57	2·57	2·57	2·57	2·58	2·58	2·58	2·58	2·58	2·59
6·7	2·59	2·59	2·59	2·59	2·60	2·60	2·60	2·60	2·60	2·61
6·8	2·61	2·61	2·61	2·61	2·62	2·62	2·62	2·62	2·62	2·62
6·9	2·63	2·63	2·63	2·63	2·63	2·64	2·64	2·64	2·64	2·64
7·0	2·65	2·65	2·65	2·65	2·65	2·66	2·66	2·66	2·66	2·66
7·1	2·66	2·67	2·67	2·67	2·67	2·67	2·68	2·68	2·68	2·68
7·2	2·68	2·69	2·69	2·69	2·69	2·69	2·69	2·70	2·70	2·70
7·3	2·70	2·70	2·71	2·71	2·71	2·71	2·71	2·71	2·72	2·72
7·4	2·72	2·72	2·72	2·73	2·73	2·73	2·73	2·73	2·73	2·74
7·5	2·74	2·74	2·74	2·74	2·75	2·75	2·75	2·75	2·75	2·75
7·6	2·76	2·76	2·76	2·76	2·76	2·77	2·77	2·77	2·77	2·77
7·7	2·77	2·78	2·78	2·78	2·78	2·78	2·79	2·79	2·79	2·79
7·8	2·79	2·79	2·80	2·80	2·80	2·80	2·80	2·81	2·81	2·81
7·9	2·81	2·81	2·81	2·82	2·82	2·82	2·82	2·82	2·82	2·83
8·0	2·83	2·83	2·83	2·83	2·84	2·84	2·84	2·84	2·84	2·84
8·1	2·85	2·85	2·85	2·85	2·85	2·85	2·86	2·86	2·86	2·86
8·2	2·86	2·87	2·87	2·87	2·87	2·87	2·87	2·88	2·88	2·88
8·3	2·88	2·88	2·88	2·89	2·89	2·89	2·89	2·89	2·89	2·90
8·4	2·90	2·90	2·90	2·90	2·91	2·91	2·91	2·91	2·91	2·91
8·5	2·92	2·92	2·92	2·92	2·92	2·92	2·93	2·93	2·93	2·93
8·6	2·93	2·93	2·94	2·94	2·94	2·94	2·94	2·94	2·95	2·95
8·7	2·95	2·95	2·95	2·95	2·96	2·96	2·96	2·96	2·96	2·96
8·8	2·97	2·97	2·97	2·97	2·97	2·97	2·98	2·98	2·98	2·98
8·9	2·98	2·98	2·99	2·99	2·99	2·99	2·99	2·99	3·00	3·00
9·0	3·00	3·00	3·00	3·00	3·01	3·01	3·01	3·01	3·01	3·01
9·1	3·02	3·02	3·02	3·02	3·02	3·02	3·03	3·03	3·03	3·03
9·2	3·03	3·03	3·04	3·04	3·04	3·04	3·04	3·04	3·05	3·05
9·3	3·05	3·05	3·05	3·05	3·06	3·06	3·06	3·06	3·06	3·06
9·4	3·07	3·07	3·07	3·07	3·07	3·07	3·08	3·08	3·08	3·08
9·5	3·08	3·08	3·09	3·09	3·09	3·09	3·09	3·09	3·10	3·10
9·6	3·10	3·10	3·10	3·10	3·10	3·11	3·11	3·11	3·11	3·11
9·7	3·11	3·12	3·12	3·12	3·12	3·12	3·12	3·13	3·13	3·13
9·8	3·13	3·13	3·13	3·14	3·14	3·14	3·14	3·14	3·14	3·14
9·9	3·15	3·15	3·15	3·15	3·15	3·15	3·16	3·16	3·16	3·16

Square Roots from 10 to 100

	·0	·1	·2	·3	·4	·5	·6	·7	·8	·9
10	3·16	3·18	3·19	3·21	3·22	3·24	3·26	3·27	3·29	3·30
11	3·32	3·33	3·35	3·36	3·38	3·39	3·41	3·42	3·44	3·45
12	3·46	3·48	3·49	3·51	3·52	3·54	3·55	3·56	3·58	3·59
13	3·61	3·62	3·63	3·65	3·66	3·67	3·69	3·70	3·71	3·73
14	3·74	3·75	3·77	3·78	3·79	3·81	3·82	3·83	2·85	3·86
15	3·87	3·89	3·90	3·91	3·92	3·94	3·95	3·96	3·97	3·99
16	4·00	4·01	4·02	4·04	4·05	4·06	4·07	4·09	4·10	4·11
17	4·12	4·14	4·15	4·16	4·17	4·18	4·20	4·21	4·22	4·23
18	4·24	4·25	4·27	4·28	4·29	4·30	4·31	4·32	4·34	4·35
19	4·36	4·37	4·38	4·39	4·40	4·42	4·43	4·44	4·45	4·46
20	4·47	4·48	4·49	4·51	4·52	4·53	4·54	4·55	4·56	4·57
21	4·58	4·59	4·60	5·62	4·63	4·64	4·65	4·66	4·67	4·68
22	4·69	4·70	4·71	4·72	4·73	4·74	4·75	4·76	4·77	4·79
23	4·80	4·81	4·82	4·83	4·84	4·85	4·86	4·87	4·88	4·89
24	4·90	4·91	4·92	4·93	4·94	4·95	4·96	4·97	4·98	4·99
25	5·00	5·01	5·02	5·03	5·04	5·05	5·06	5·07	5·08	5·09
26	5·10	5·11	5·12	5·13	5·14	5·15	5·16	5·17	5·18	5·19
27	5·20	5·21	5 22	5·22	5·23	5·24	5·25	5·26	5·27	5·28
28	5·29	5·30	5·31	5·32	5·33	5·34	5·35	5·36	5·37	5·38
29	5·39	5·39	5·40	5·41	5·42	5·43	5·44	5·45	5·46	5·47
30	5·48	5·49	5·50	5·50	5·51	5·52	5·53	5·54	5·55	5·56
31	5·57	5·58	5·59	5·59	5·60	5·61	5·62	5·63	5·64	5·65
32	5·66	5·67	5·67	5·68	5·69	5·70	5·71	5·72	5·73	5·74
33	5·74	5·75	5·76	5·77	5·78	5·79	5·80	5·81	5·81	5·82
34	5·83	5·84	5·85	5·86	5·87	5·87	5·88	5·89	5·90	5·91
35	5·92	5·92	5·93	5·94	5·95	5·96	5·97	5·97	5·98	5·99
36	6·00	6·01	6·02	6·02	6·03	6·04	6·05	6·06	6·07	6·07
37	6·08	6·09	6·10	6·11	6·12	6·12	6·13	6·14	6·15	6·16
38	6·16	6·17	6·18	6·19	6·20	6·20	6·21	6·22	6·23	6·24
39	6·24	6·25	6·26	6·27	6·28	6·28	6·29	6·30	6·31	6·32
40	6·32	6·33	6·34	6·35	6·36	6·36	6·37	6·38	6·39	6·40
41	6·40	6·41	6·42	6·43	6·43	6·44	6·45	6·46	6·47	6·47
42	6·48	6·49	6·50	6·50	6·51	6·52	6·53	6·53	6·54	6·55
43	6·56	6·57	6·57	6·58	6·59	6·60	6·60	6·61	6·62	6·63
44	6·63	6·64	6·65	6·66	6·66	6·67	6·68	6·69	6·69	6·70
45	6·71	6·72	6·72	6·73	6·74	6·75	6·75	6·76	6·77	6·77
46	6·78	6·79	6·80	6·80	6·81	6·82	6·83	6·83	6·84	6·85
47	6·86	6·86	6·87	6·88	6·88	6·89	6·90	6·91	6·91	6·92
48	6·93	6·94	6·94	6·95	6·96	6·96	6·97	6·98	6·99	6·99
49	7·00	7·01	7·01	7·02	7·03	7·04	7·04	7·05	7·06	7·06
50	7·07	7·08	7·09	7·09	7·10	7·11	7·11	7·12	7·13	7·13
51	7·14	7·15	7·16	7·16	7·17	7·18	7·18	7·19	7·20	7·20
52	7·21	7·22	7·22	7·23	7·24	7·25	7·25	7·26	7·27	7·27
53	7·28	7·29	7·29	7·30	7·31	7·31	7·32	7·33	7·33	7·34
54	7·35	7·36	7·36	7·37	7·38	7·38	7·39	7·40	7·40	7·41

Square Roots from 10 to 100

	·0	·1	·2	·3	·4	·5	·6	·7	·8	·9
55	7·42	7·42	7·43	7·44	7·44	7·45	7·46	7·46	7·47	7·48
56	7·48	7·49	7·50	7·50	7·51	7·52	7·52	7·53	7·54	7·54
57	7·55	7·56	7·56	7·57	7·58	7·58	7·59	7·60	7·60	7·61
58	7·62	7·62	7·63	7·64	7·64	7·65	7·66	7·66	7·67	7·67
59	7·68	7·69	7·69	7·70	7·71	7·71	7·72	7·73	7·73	7·74
60	7·75	7·75	7·76	7·77	7·77	7·78	7·78	7·79	7·80	7·80
61	7·81	7·82	7·82	7·83	7·84	7·84	7·85	7·85	7·86	7·87
62	7·87	7·88	7·89	7·89	7·90	7·91	7·91	7·92	7·92	7·93
63	7·94	7·94	7·95	7·96	7·96	7·97	7·97	7·98	7·99	7·99
64	8·00	8·01	8·01	8·02	8·02	8·03	8·04	8·04	8·05	8·06
65	8·06	8·07	8·07	8·08	8·09	8·09	8·10	8·11	8·11	8·12
66	8·12	8·13	8·14	8·14	8·15	8·15	8·16	8·17	8·17	8·18
67	8·19	8·19	8·20	8·20	8·21	8·22	8·22	8·23	8·23	8·24
68	8·25	8·25	8·26	8·26	8·27	8·28	8·28	8·29	8·29	8·30
69	8·31	8·31	8·32	8·32	8·33	8·34	8·34	8·35	8·35	8·36
70	8·37	8·37	8·38	8·38	8·39	8·40	8·40	8·41	8·41	8·42
71	8·43	8·43	8·44	8·44	8·45	8·46	8·46	8·47	8·47	8·48
72	8·49	8·49	8·50	8·50	8·51	8·51	8·52	8·53	8·53	8·54
73	8·54	8·55	8·56	8·56	8·57	8·57	8·58	8·58	8·59	8·60
74	8·60	8·61	8·61	8·62	8·63	8·63	8·64	8·64	8·65	8·65
75	8·66	8·67	8·67	8·68	8·68	8·69	8·69	8·70	8·71	8·71
76	8·72	8·72	8·73	8·73	8·74	8·75	8·75	8·76	8·76	8·77
77	8·77	8·78	8·79	8·79	8·80	8·80	8·81	8·81	8·82	8·83
78	8·83	8·84	8·84	8·85	8·85	8·86	8·87	8·87	8·88	8·88
79	8·89	8·89	8·90	8·91	8·91	8·92	8·92	8·93	8·93	8·94
80	8·94	8·95	8·96	8·96	8·97	8·97	8·98	8·98	8·99	8·99
81	9·00	9·01	9·01	9·02	9·02	9·03	9·03	9·04	9·04	9·05
82	9·06	9·06	9·07	9·07	9·08	9·08	9·09	9·09	9·10	9·10
83	9·11	9·12	9·12	9·13	9·13	9·14	9·14	9·15	9·15	9·16
84	9·17	9·17	9·18	9·18	9·19	9·19	9·20	9·20	9·21	9·21
85	9·22	9·22	9·23	9·24	9·24	9·25	9·25	9·26	9·26	9·27
86	9·27	9·28	9·28	9·29	9·30	9·30	9·31	9·31	9·32	9·32
87	9·33	9·33	9·34	9·34	9·35	9·35	9·36	9·36	9·37	9·38
88	9·38	9·39	9·39	9·40	9·40	9·41	9·41	9·42	9·42	9·43
89	9·43	9·44	9·44	9·45	9·46	9·46	9·47	9·47	9·48	9·48
90	9·49	9·49	9·50	9·50	9·51	9·51	9·52	9·52	9·53	9·53
91	9·54	9·54	9·55	9·56	9·56	9·57	9·57	9·58	9·58	9·59
92	9·59	9·60	9·60	9·61	9·61	9·62	9·62	9·63	9·63	9·64
93	9·64	9·65	9·65	9·66	9·66	9·67	9·67	9·68	9·69	9·69
94	9·70	9·70	9·71	9·71	9·72	9·72	9·73	9·73	9·74	9·74
95	9·75	9·75	9·76	9·76	9·77	9·77	9·78	9·78	9·79	9·79
96	9·80	9·80	9·81	9·81	9·82	9·82	9·83	9·83	9·84	9·84
97	9·85	9·85	9·86	9·86	9·87	9·87	9·88	9·88	9·89	9·89
98	9·90	9·90	9·91	9·91	9·92	9·92	9·93	9·93	9·94	9·94
99	9·95	9·95	9·96	9·96	9·97	9·97	9·98	9·98	9·99	9·99

Area under the standard normal curve

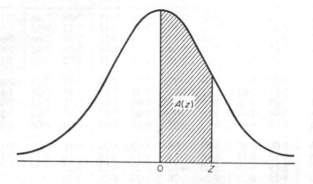

The table gives the values of the area $A(z)$ from $z = 0\cdot00$ to $z = 3\cdot39$

z	$A(z)$	z	$A(z)$	z	$A(z)$	z	$A(z)$
0·00	0·000	0·25	0·099	0·50	0·191	0·75	0·273
0·01	0·004	0·26	0·103	0·51	0·195	0·76	0·276
0·02	0·008	0·27	0·106	0·52	0·198	0·77	0·279
0·03	0·012	0·28	0·110	0·53	0·202	0·78	0·282
0·04	0·016	0·29	0·114	0·54	0·205	0·79	0·285
0·05	0·020	0·30	0·118	0·55	0·209	0·80	0·288
0·06	0·024	0·31	0·122	0·56	0·212	0·81	0·291
0·07	0·028	0·32	0·126	0·57	0·216	0·82	0·294
0·08	0·032	0·33	0·129	0·58	0·219	0·83	0·297
0·09	0·036	0·34	0·133	0·59	0·222	0·84	0·300
0·10	0·040	0·35	0·137	0·60	0·226	0·85	0·302
0·11	0·044	0·36	0·141	0·61	0·229	0·86	0·305
0·12	0·048	0·37	0·144	0·62	0·232	0·87	0·308
0·13	0·052	0·38	0·148	0·63	0·236	0·88	0·311
0·14	0·056	0·39	0·152	0·64	0·239	0·89	0·313
0·15	0·060	0·40	0·155	0·65	0·242	0·90	0·316
0·16	0·064	0·41	0·159	0·66	0·245	0·91	0·319
0·17	0·067	0·42	0·163	0·67	0·249	0·92	0·321
0·18	0·071	0·43	0·166	0·68	0·252	0·93	0·324
0·19	0·075	0·44	0·170	0·69	0·255	0·94	0·326
0·20	0·079	0·45	0·174	0·70	0·258	0·95	0·329
0·21	0·083	0·46	0·177	0·71	0·261	0·96	0·331
0·22	0·087	0·47	0·181	0·72	0·264	0·97	0·334
0·23	0·091	0·48	0·184	0·73	0·267	0·98	0·336
0·24	0·095	0·49	0·188	0·74	0·270	0·99	0·339

z	$A(z)$	z	$A(z)$	z	$A(z)$	z	$A(z)$
1·00	0·341	1·45	0·426	1·90	0·471	2·35	0·491
1·01	0·344	1·46	0·428	1·91	0·472	2·36	0·491
1·02	0·346	1·47	0·429	1·92	0·473	2·37	0·491
1·03	0·348	1·48	0·431	1·93	0·473	2·38	0·491
1·04	0·351	1·49	0·432	1·94	0·474	2·39	0·492
1·05	0·353	1·50	0·433	1·95	0·474	2·40	0·492
1·06	0·355	1·51	0·434	1·96	0·475	2·41	0·492
1·07	0·358	1·52	0·436	1·97	0·476	2·42	0·492
1·08	0·360	1·53	0·437	1·98	0·476	2·43	0·492
1·09	0·362	1·54	0·438	1·99	0·477	2·44	0·493
1·10	0·364	1·55	0·439	2·00	0·477	2·45	0·493
1·11	0·367	1·56	0·441	2·01	0·478	2·46	0·493
1·12	0·369	1·57	0·442	2·02	0·478	2·47	0·493
1·13	0·371	1·58	0·443	2·03	0·479	2·48	0·493
1·14	0·373	1·59	0·444	2·04	0·479	2·49	0·494
1·15	0·375	1·60	0·445	2·05	0·480	2·50	0·494
1·16	0·377	1·61	0·446	2·06	0·480	2·51	0·494
1·17	0·379	1·62	0·447	2·07	0·481	2·52	0·494
1·18	0·381	1·63	0·448	2·08	0·481	2·53	0·494
1·19	0·383	1·64	0·449	2·09	0·482	2·54	0·494
1·20	0·385	1·65	0·451	2·10	0·482	2·55	0·495
1·21	0·387	1·66	0·452	2·11	0·483	2·56	0·495
1·22	0·389	1·67	0·453	2·12	0·483	2·57	0·495
1·23	0·391	1·68	0·454	2·13	0·483	2·58	0·495
1·24	0·393	1·69	0·454	2·14	0·484	2·59	0·495
1·25	0·394	1·70	0·455	2·15	0·484	2·60	0·495
1·26	0·396	1·71	0·456	2·16	0·485	2·61	0·495
1·27	0·398	1·72	0·457	2·17	0·485	2·62	0·496
1·28	0·400	1·73	0·458	2·18	0·485	2·63	0·496
1·29	0·401	1·74	0·459	2·19	0·486	2·64	0·496
1·30	0·403	1·75	0·460	2·20	0·486	2·65	0·496
1·31	0·405	1·76	0·461	2·21	0·486	2·66	0·496
1·32	0·407	1·77	0·462	2·22	0·487	2·67	0·496
1·33	0·408	1·78	0·462	2·23	0·487	2·68	0·496
1·34	0·410	1·79	0·463	2·24	0·487	2·69	0·496
1·35	0·411	1·80	0·464	2·25	0·488	2·70	0·497
1·36	0·413	1·81	0·465	2·26	0·488	2·71	0·497
1·37	0·415	1·82	0·466	2·27	0·488	2·72	0·497
1·38	0·416	1·83	0·466	2·28	0·489	2·73	0·497
1·39	0·418	1·84	0·467	2·29	0·489	2·74	0·497
1·40	0·419	1·85	0·468	2·30	0·489	2·75	0·497
1·41	0·421	1·86	0·469	2·31	0·490	2·76	0·497
1·42	0·422	1·87	0·469	2·32	0·490	2·77	0·497
1·43	0·424	1·88	0·470	2·33	0·490	2·78	0·497
1·44	0·425	1·89	0·471	2·34	0·490	2·79	0·497

z	A(z)	z	A(z)	z	A(z)	z	A(z)
2·80	0·497	2·95	0·498	3·10	0·499	3·25	0·499
2·81	0·498	2·96	0·498	3·11	0·499	3·26	0·499
2·82	0·498	2·97	0·499	3·12	0·499	3·27	0·499
2·83	0·498	2·98	0·499	3·13	0·499	3·28	0·499
2·84	0·498	2·99	0·499	3·14	0·499	3·29	0·499
2·85	0·498	3·00	0·499	3·15	0·499	3·30	0·500
2·86	0·498	3·01	0·499	3·16	0·499	3·31	0·500
2·87	0·498	3·02	0·499	3·17	0·499	3·32	0·500
2·88	0·498	3·03	0·499	3·18	0·499	3·33	0·500
2·89	0·498	3·04	0·499	3·19	0·499	3·34	0·500
2·90	0·498	3·05	0·499	3·20	0·499	3·35	0·500
2·91	0·498	3·06	0·499	3·21	0·499	3·36	0·500
2·92	0·498	3·07	0·499	3·22	0·499	3·37	0·500
2·93	0·498	3·08	0·499	3·23	0·499	3·38	0·500
2·94	0·498	3·09	0·499	3·24	0·499	3·39	0·500

Answers

Note. Where examples involve the use of class intervals, there may be slight variations in the answers obtained, depending upon the choice of intervals.

CHAPTER 1
Exercise 1, page 7

(3) Skid, 15%, 150; loss of control, 10%, 100; bad overtaking, 25%, 250; other causes, 30%, 300; not known 20%, 200.

(6) Actual sales (thousands) 168, 187, 182, 171, 171, 184.

(7) U.S.A. 61 million tons.

(8) (*a*) 1960, 450 sets; (*b*) 1962; (*c*) (i) 60%, (ii) 40%; (*d*) (i) 150, (ii) 700.

(9) Arts, 40·5%; Diploma, $\frac{5}{8}$.

(10) (*a*) 8 a.m., 12 noon, 6 p.m.
 (*c*) 325 000 kw.
 (*d*) (i) 6 a.m., (ii) 6 p.m. At 6 a.m. (before full power available) 110 000 kw unused; with full power, 310 000 kw unused. At 6 p.m. 10 000 kw unused.

Exercise 2, page 14

(1) (*a*) Impression conveyed of large increase in mileage; dotted to show future, proposed building.
 (*b*) The 1965 to 1970 interval should not be the same length as the other intervals.
 (*c*) 13 miles per year (approx.); $13\frac{1}{2}$ miles per year (approx.).

(2) (*a*) Equal lengths represent unequal time intervals.
 (*b*) Scale changes from £2 million per interval to £1 million.
 (*c*) £4 million; £14·3 million; no, prices have risen greatly.

(3) 1939: 1·02, 0·45, 0·48, 0·21, 0·15, 0·24, 0·45;
 1960: 1·44, 1·89, 1·26, 0·63, 0·81, 0·54, 2·43.
 No, the tonnage has increased; Britain's share of the world tonnage has declined.

(4) The rise in numbers achieved is over-emphasised.

CHAPTER 2
Exercise 1, page 21

(1) Samples contain too many young people, who generally prefer pop music.

(2) Samples contain too many theatre goers who obviously enjoy the theatre.

(3) Samples, composed entirely of car owners, do not include any other sections of the public.

(4) Samples, composed entirely of young people, take no account of the opinions of older people.

Exercise 3, page 26

(1) (a) Continuous, (b) Discrete, (c) Discrete, (d) Continuous, (e) Discrete, (f) Discrete, (g) Continuous.

(2) 2, 3, 4, . . . 12; discrete.

(3) Discrete: (a), (b) (d), (g).
Continuous: (c), (e), (f).

CHAPTER 3

Exercise 1, page 30

(3) (b) Four years, (c) 81, (d) Modal score = 1.

(4) (b) 40, (c) 10, (d) 25%, (e) 118, (f) 3 passes.

(6) (b) 50, (c) 464·7 g, (d) 40%.

(7) (b) $42\frac{1}{2}\%$, (c) 0 defective transistors.

(8) (b) 50, (c) 10%, (d) $\frac{19}{50}$.

Exercise 2, page 34

(1) The distributions of exercise 2 have shapes as follows:
(3) asymmetric, (4) bell shaped, (5) rectangular, (6) asymmetric, (7) J-shaped, (8) bell shaped.

Exercise 3, page 36

(1) (a) 19 and 15, (b) 20–24.

(2) (a) 28 (c) 15 and 19; 25 and 29, (d) 5 goals.

(3) (a) Range 87 marks; nine classes (c) 52% (d) 50–59.

Exercise 4, page 40

(1) $\Sigma f = 40$; $\Sigma fX = 2\,658$; Σfx represents the total weight of all forty recruits.

(2) $\Sigma fX = 2\,656$.

(3) (a) 15 (b) 19 (c) 26 (d) 6·5 and 9·5 (e) £3 (f) 8%.

(4) (a) £32, 55, 126, 272, 240, 69, 26,
(b) £820; using mid values leads to loss of accuracy.

(5) Ten classes
(a) 3·8–4·0, 5·0–5·2, (b) 3·75–4·05, 4·95–5·25,
Modal class, 4·1–4·3.

Exercise 5, page 48

(2)

Time (seconds)	176	177	178	179	180	181	182	183	184
Frequency	2	0	3	11	15	12	3	2	2

(3)

Weight (kilogrammes)	53–56	57–60	61–64	65–68	69–72	73–76	77–80
Frequency	1	3	12	13	4	5	2

(4) Class boundaries: 0·65–0·95, 0·95–1·25, 1·25–1·55, 1·55–1·85, 1·85–2·15, 2·15–2·45, 2·45–2·75, 2·75–3·05,
Mid values: 0·8, 1·1, 1·4, 1·7, 2·0, 2·3, 2·6, 2·9.
(5) (a) Range, 5·4 hours (b) $\Sigma fX = 476·5$.

Exercise 6, page 51
(1) (a) Relative frequencies: 0·250, 0·271, 0·250, 0·125, 0·042, 0·042, 0·021.
  (b) 0·250, 0·105, (c) 1·001 = 1·00 to two decimal places.
(2) (a) Relative frequencies: 0·06, 0·08, 0·24, 0·26, 0·20, 0·12, 0·04,
  (b) 0·38, 0·36, (c) 1·00.

Exercise 7, page 55
(1) Relative frequencies: 0·08, 0·10, 0·18, 0·32, 0·24, 0·06, 0·02.
(2) 0·117, 0·133, 0·167, 0·350, 0·183, 0·050.
(3) (a) 0·24, (b) 0·37, (c) (i) 42, (ii) 24.
  (d) frequencies: 8, 14, 24, 28, 36, 48, 42, $\Sigma fX = 157·82$.
(4) Histograms not suitable because the factories employ different numbers of people.
  Relative frequencies:
  Table 1, 0·172, 0·260, 0·280, 0·150, 0·108, 0·030;
  Table 2, 0·220, 0·284, 0·296, 0·116, 0·064, 0·020.
  Relative frequency histograms are suitable.
  Birmingham factory has smaller proportion of employees in three lowest wage intervals, and larger proportion in three highest.

(5) Relative frequencies: 0·02, 0·18, 0·21, 0·20, 0·09, 0·07, 0·07, 0·04, 0·08, 0·01, 0·01, 0·02.
(a) 0·09, (b) 0·16.

(6) $\Sigma fX = 2\,280$, total games played in the tournament, approximate. Relative frequencies: 0·250, 0·383, 0·167, 0·083, 0·050, 0·033, 0·017, 0·017.

CHAPTER 4

Exercise 1, page 61

(1) (a)z $\bar{X} = 23$, (b) $\mu = 8·1$, (c) $\bar{X} = 0·039$.
(2) 44.4, 6 girls.
(3) 36·2, 28·2, 39·8; Brown, Green, White.

Exercise 2, page 64

(1) (a) $\bar{X} = 14·2$, median = 16, mode = 17,
(b) $\mu = 5·2$, median = 5, no mode,
(c) $\bar{X} = 57·8$, median = 60, no mode,
(d) $\bar{X} = 8·0$, median = 8·5, no mode.
(2) (a) $\mu = 53·9$, median = 54, mode = 43. Median.
(b) $\mu = 54·5$, median = 49, mode = 49. Median or mode.
(c) $\bar{X} = 21·5$, median = 20·5, no mode. Mean or median.
(3) Mode.

Exercise 3, page 66

(1) $\bar{X} = 7·5$, mode = 8.
(2) $\Sigma fX = 820$, $\mu = 16·4$.
(4) $\bar{X} = 60$, mode = 60.
(5) $\bar{X} = 4·36$ to two decimal places.
(6) $\bar{X} = 1·82$, modal class 1·3—1·5, mid value 1·4.

Exercise 4, page 70

(1) $\bar{X} = 74·2$, to one decimal place.
(2) $\mu = 15·5$ to one decimal place, mode = 15.
(3) $\bar{X} = 66·2$.
(4) $\bar{X} = 498·1$, mode = 498.
(6) 1 002·1.

Exercise 5, page 72

(1) (a) 7, (b) 21, (c) 56, (d) 70, (e) 140.
(2) Mean of 0, 1, 2, 3, 4 = 2;
(a) 10, (b) 60, (c) 12, (d) 120, (e) 18.

(4) 2 002·5.
(5) 308.
(6) 63.
(7) 359·5.

Exercise 6, page 75

(1) 57·1, to one decimal place.
(2) 540·6, 31 head.
(3) $\bar{X} = 45$, mid value of modal class $= 37$.
(6) 88·80, $\frac{4}{5}$ unsuitable.
(7) Section A, $\bar{X} = 64·7$; section B, $\bar{X} = 61·2$.
Section A better than section B.
In section A, mark of 75 lies between 20th and 30th places.
In section B, mark of 75 lies between 8th and 14th places.

Exercise 7, page 79

(1) (a) 6, (b) 74, (c) 0·37.
(2) Median $= 21$, $\bar{X} = 21·2$.

CHAPTER 5

Exercise 1, page 83

(1) Cumulative frequencies: 1, 6, 13, 18, 21, 22, 22.
(2) (a) Continuous, (c) 17, 69, 52, (d) 41, 97, 56.
(3) Cumulative frequencies: 3, 11, 27, 56, 80, 94, 99, 100.
(4) Cumulative frequencies: 1, 3, 7, 14, 27, 50.
(5) (a) Cumulative frequencies: 22, 35, 45, 52, 58, 61, 63, 64,
(b) 45, (c) 45, (d) 18, (e) 65·6%.
(6) (a) Continuous, (b) class limits, (c) cumulative frequencies:
3, 14, 41, 80, 123, 162, 188, 197, 200, (d) 123, 41, 82, (e) No.

Exercise 2, page 89

(1) (a) 74, (b) 171, (c) 2·36.
(2) (a) 46, (b) 48, (c) 2.
40 pupils made 13 errors or less.

Exercise 3, page 92

(1) (a) 67·1,   (b) 69·1,   (c) 65·3.
(2) (a) 60·03,   (b) 60·27,   (c) 59·80.
(3) (a) 28·2,   (b) 34·5,   (c) 23·3.

Exercise 5, page 99

(1) (a) $\frac{13}{12}$ m², 1 m², (b) Fig. 5·9, area under curve $= 1$.

CHAPTER 6

Exercise 1, page 103
(1) Mean = 13·5, median = 14, range = 15.
(2) $Q = 5·8$.
(3) (b) Median = 1 080, $Q_1 = 890$, $Q_3 = 1\ 300$,
    (c) $Q = 205$.

Exercise 2, page 105
(2) (a) $s = 1·95$, (b) $s = 1·09$, (c) $\sigma = 6·91$.

Exercise 3, page 108
(1) 2·69, 2·53.
(2) 2·66.
(3) $\sigma = 4$.
(4) 6·8, 1·33.

Exercise 4, page 110
(2) Mean = 1·7, median = 1, $s = 1·43$.
(5) 3·25, 1·34.
(6) 3·9, 1·56.
(7) 2·75, 1·33.

Exercise 5, page 113
(1) 60·3, 1·93.
(2) Mean 13 years 0·9 months, $s = 2·1$ months.
(3) 10·7.

Exercise 6, page 115
(1) 498·1, 1·84.
(2) 15·5, 2·09.
(3) Mode = 51, mean = 51·3, $s = 3·07$.
(4) Median = 72, mean = 72·2, $s = 3·07$.

Exercise 7, page 117
(1) (a) 4·2, (b) 12·6.
(2) 1·41, (a) 7·05, (b) 7·05.
(4) 77·5, 5·13.

Exercise 8, page 119
(1) 69·8, 3·16.
(2) $\mu = 29·25$, $\sigma = 8·71$.
(4) Modal class = 25—29, mid value = 27, mean = 32·2, $s = 12·1$.
(5) (a) 540·6, 47·8, (b) 2·28, 0·42, (c) 44·6, 11·5.

Revision Examples I

Set 1, page 126

(2) Mode $= 7\frac{1}{2}$; 324 pairs per 1 000.
(3) (b) 1.
(4) Mean $= 1.5$, standard deviation $= 1.37$.
(5) Median $= 5.85$, $Q_1 = 5.0$, $Q_2 = 6.85$.

Set 2, page 127

(2) (a) A: mean $= £2\ 149.5$; B: mean $= £2\ 269.5$.
　　(b) A: 22%; B: 32%.
　　(c) Company B has higher mean earnings, but a larger proportion
　　　　of workers in the lowest wage group.
(3) (a) 25.2 mins, (b) 1.2 mins, (c) 35%, (d) 0.5 mins.
(4) Mean $= 7.1$, standard deviation $= 2.44$.
(5) A: mean $= 6$, standard deviation $= 1.44$.
　　B: mean $= 6$, standard deviation $= 2.74$.
　　(i) Same mean, (ii) differently dispersed.

Set 3, page 130

(1) West Germany, 0.047; U.S.S.R., 0.001.
(2) Class limits, 95 and 104; class boundaries 94.5 and 104.5;
　　(a) 101, (b) 8.5, (c) 53%.
(3) $\bar{X} = 0.82$, $s = 0.98$.
(5) Mid value $= 5.37$, $\bar{X} = 5.30$, $s = 0.342$.

Set 4, page 132

(2) Modal class $= 46-55$, estimate of modal age $= 52$, estimate
　　of median age $= 51$.
(3) (i) 16, (ii) 16, (iii) 16.0, (iv) 4.93; 26 questions.
(4) 64, $\bar{X} = 3.0$, $s = 1.26$;
　　(i) 32.8%, (ii) 10.9%, (iii) 76.6%, (iv) 95.3%, (v) 100%.
(5) (a) $\mu = 6$, $\sigma = 3$.

Set 5, page 134

(1) Depreciation £300, miscellaneous £2 000, rates and insurance, £1 300, maintenance and repairs £2 600. Total, £10 000.
(2) Mean = 46·2, standard deviation = 17·1.
(3) (a) 46, (b) 42, (c) 11.
(4) 22 seconds, 7·0 seconds.
(5) Median = 89·9 cm, S.I.Q.R. = 0·13 cm, Adjustment = 3 mm.

Set 6, page 136

(2) (a) Modal class: 9 and less than 10 c.c.; better estimate = 9·4 c.c.
    (b) Median volume = 9·4 c.c.
(3) $\bar{X}$ = 6·4, s = 2·53.
(4) (i) £14·5, (ii) £12·5 to £16·3, (iii) 70%, (iv) 80%.
(5) $\bar{X}$ = 31·6, s = 9·31.

Set 7, page 137

(1) (a) (i) Line graph (or bar graph), (ii) pie chart, (iii) bar graph.
(2) (a) Road junction, observe private cars, record sex of driver, and make of car.
    (b) Car park; ask: 'Do you drive? If so, what make?' Question all persons, drivers and passengers.
    (c) Method, (b) ask 'Which make do you prefer?'
(3) (a) 44, (b) 61, (c) 11·5.
(4) Exact mean = 7·85; with intervals 1—5, 6—10, . . .
    mean = 8·35.
(5) (i) $\bar{X}$ = 48·2, s = 15·3,
    (ii) $\bar{X}$ = 241·0, s = 76·5.

Set 8, page 139

(1) (b) $\frac{3029}{12316}$.
(2) 76, 62.
(3) Mean = 52·0, standard deviation = 3·96.
(4) (a) Relative frequencies: 0·02, 0·09, 0·18, 0·41, 0·25, 0·05,
    (b) (i) 1 398, (ii) 241.
(5) Mean = 10, standard deviation = 5·74.
    (a) Mean = 5·5, standard deviation = 2·87.
    (b) Mean = 19, standard deviation = 5·74.

CHAPTER 7

Exercise 1, page 149

(1) (a) $Pr(A) = Pr(B) = Pr(C) = Pr(D) = Pr(E) = 0.20$,
   (b) $Pr(P) = 0.19$, $Pr(Q) = 0.23$, $Pr(R) = 0.20$, $Pr(S) = 0.17$,
   $Pr(T) = 0.21$.
(2) (a) $\frac{2812}{5352} = 0.525$,
   (b) $\frac{1227}{5352} = 0.229$,
   (c) $\frac{1313}{5352} = 0.245$,
   Not equally likely,
   1966–67: $Pr(H) = \frac{1391}{2714} = 0.513$,
   $Pr(A) = \frac{652}{2714} = 0.240$, $Pr(D) = \frac{671}{2714} = 0.247$.
(3) (a) 0.47, (b) 0.44, (c) 0.37.
(4) (a) 0.515, 0.514, 0.515,
   (b) 0.485, 0.486, 0.485,
   (c) (i) 0.512, (ii) 0.488,
   (d) (i) 0.519, (ii) 0.481,
   (e) (i) 0.514, (ii) 0.486,
   (f) Not equally likely events.

Exercise 2, page 154

(1) (b), (e).
(3) Relative frequencies: $A = 0.224$, $B = 0.217$, $C = 0.218$,
   $D = 0.221$, $Y = 0.059$, $Z = 0.062$.
   Probability model: $A, B, C, D, Pr = 0.22$; $Y, Z, Pr = 0.06$.

Exercise 3, page 157

(1) 0.86.
(2) 0.37.
(3) (a) 0.51, (b) 0.34, (c) 1.
(4) (a) 0.46, (b) 0.54, (c) 0.66.
(5) (a) 0.64, (b) 0.06, (c) 0.77.

Exercise 4, page 158

(1) (a) 16, (b) 102, (c) 99.
(2) 1 429.
(3) 0.52; (a) 33, (b) 15, (c) 16.

Exercise 5, page 161

(1) (a) 0·010, (b) 0·217.
(2) 0·241; 0·759.
(3) (a) 0·190, (b) 0·095, 0·905, 3 approximately.
(4) (a) 0·204, (b) 0·122, 0·878, 4 approximately.
(5) (a) 0·037, (b) 0·222, (c) 0·111, 4 approximately.

Exercise 6, page 166

(1) (a) (i) 0·36, (ii) 0·86, (iii) 0·05; 32 approximately.
   (b) (i) 0·83, (ii) 0·68, (iii) 0·15; 14 approximately.
(2) (a) 0·5, (b) 0·28, (c) 0·28.
(3) (a) Grade 1, 0·35; grade 2, 0·57; grade 3, 0·08,
   (b) 88, 142, 20.
(4) (a) 0·22, (b) 0·58, (c) 0·16, (d) 24 approximately.
   (e) 1 approximately.

CHAPTER 8

Exercise 1, page 171

(1) (a) $x^2+2xy+y^2$,
   (b) $q^4+4q^3p+6q^2p^2+4qp^2+p^4$,
   (c) $q^3+3q^2p+3qp^2+p^3$,
   (d) $a^6+6a^5b+15a^4b^2+20a^3b^3+15a^2b^4+6ab^5+b^6$,
   (e) $q^5+5q^4p+10q^3p^2+10q^2p^3+5qp^4+p^5$,
   (f) $a^2+a+\frac{1}{4}$,
   (g) $\frac{1}{16}+\frac{1}{2}b+b^2$,
   (h) $x^3+x^2+\frac{1}{3}x+\frac{1}{27}$,
   (i) $\frac{1}{16}+\frac{1}{4}+\frac{3}{8}+\frac{1}{4}+\frac{1}{16}$,
   (j) $\frac{1}{64}+\frac{9}{64}+\frac{27}{64}+\frac{27}{64}$,
   (k) $\frac{16}{25}+\frac{8}{25}+\frac{1}{25}$,
   (l) $\frac{64}{729}+\frac{192}{729}+\frac{240}{729}+\frac{160}{729}+\frac{60}{729}+\frac{12}{729}+\frac{1}{729}$,
(2) (a) $3q^2p$, (b) $4qp^3$, (c) $\frac{3}{8}$, (d) $\frac{1}{3125}$, (e) $\frac{2}{9}$.

Exercise 2, page 181

(1) $\frac{216}{625}$, (2) (a) $\frac{256}{625}$, (b) $\frac{96}{625}$, (c) $\frac{512}{625}$.
(3) $\frac{80}{243}$, (4) $\frac{1029}{2500}$, (5) $\frac{335}{343}$, (6) $\frac{328}{625}$.

Exercise 3, page 182

(Answers to the nearest whole number).

(1) 8, (2) 58, (3) 26, (4) 1, (5) 22, (6) 2, (7) 4.

Exercise 4, page 186

(1) $\mu = 80, \sigma = 4\sqrt{3}.$

(2) $\mu = 60, \sigma = 2\sqrt{6}$

(3) $\mu = 25, \sigma = 5\dfrac{\sqrt{3}}{2}$

(4) $\mu = 5, \sigma = \dfrac{\sqrt{30}}{7}$

(5) $\mu = 14, \sigma = \sqrt{10}.$

CHAPTER 9

Exercise 1, page 194

(1) (a) 46, (b) 34, (c) 52, (d) 28, (e) 58, (f) 22, (g) 682, (h) 954,
   (i) 998.

(2)

Score	28	33	38	43	48
Deviation from mean	-2σ	$-\sigma$	0	σ	2σ

(3) (a) 50%, 0·5, (b) 50%, 0·5.
(4) (a) 0·841, (b) 0·159.
(5) 0·159.
(6) (a) 47·7% or 0·477, (b) 97·7% or 0·977, (c) 2·3% or 0·023.
(7) 0·136.   (8) 0·136.
(9) (a) 0·499, (b) 0·999, (c) 0·001,
    (d) 0·499, (e) 0·001, (f) 0·099.
(10) (a) 0·022, (b) 0·022.
(11) (a) 0·841, (b) 0·159.
(12) (a) 0·159, (b) 0·841, (c) 0·682.
(13) (a) 0·999, (b) 0·001, (c) 0·001, (d) 0·999, (e) 0·998.
(14) (a) 0·841, (b) 0·159.
(15) (a) 0·159, (b) 0·841, (c) 0·682.
(16) (a) 0·999, (b) 0·001, (c) 0·001, (d) 0·999, (e) 0·998.
(17) (a) 841, (b) 136, (c) 1, (d) 1.

Exercise 2, page 201

(1) 1·6, (2) 1·25, (3) 1·00, (4) 1·00.
(5) (a) 58, (b) 66, (c) 62, (d) 42, (e) 34, (f) 38.
(6) Zero mean, unit standard deviation.
(7) Zero mean, unit standard deviation.

Exercise 3, page 204

(1) (a) 0·933, (b) 0·067, (c) 0·067, (d) 0·933,
(e) 0·242, (f) 0·242, (g) 0·061, (h) 0·061.
(2) (a) 0·067, 670, (b) 230, (c) 0·382, 3 820.
(d) (i) 3 300 hours, (ii) 3 600 hours, (e) 4 500 hours.
(3) (a) $z_1 = 1$, $z_2 = 1\frac{1}{2}$, (b) in second test, (c) 65.
(5) (a) Mathematics better, (b) 91, (c) 29.
(6) (a) 44, 68, (b) 50, 62, (c) 32, 80, (d) 20, 92.
(7) Mean 175 cm standard deviation 7·5 cm.

Exercise 4, page 208

(1) (a) 0·159, (b) 0·255, (c) 0·353, (d) 0·454,
(e) 0·487, (f) 0·499, (g) 0·499, (h) 0·491.
(2) (a) 0·84, (b) 1·81, (c) 2·16, 2·17, 2·18,
(d) 0·42, (e) 0·19, (f) 2·44 to 2·48,
(g) 2·05, 2·06, (h) 0·12.
(3) (a) 81·8, (b) 38·2, (c) 81·8, (d) 46·0,
(e) 46·0, (f) 45·2.
(4) (a) 0·341, (b) 0·629, (c) 0·858, (d) 0·079, (e) 0·642.
(5) 0·01.
(6) (a) 995, (b) 7, (c) 24.
(7) (a) 97·6%, (b) 42·7%, (c) 9·4%, (d) 90 to 110,
(e) 83 to 117.

Exercise 5, page 216

(1) (a) 0·246, 0·249, (b) 0·410, 0·408, (c) 0·164, 0·159,
(d) 0·498, 0·496, (e) 0·500, 0·499, (f) 0·252, 0·247,
(g) 0·252, 0·247.
(2) 0·011.
(3) (a) 0·196, 0·198, (b) 0·122, 0·121, (c) 0·122, 0·121,
(d) 0·546, 0·546, (e) 0·364, 0·361, (f) 0·297, 0·295,
(4) 0·048.

(5) (a) 0·048, (b) 0·864, (c) 0·184,
$\qquad$ 1·048 = 1·000+0·048.
(6) (a) 0·132, 0·134, $\qquad$ (b) 0·106, 0·106,
$\quad$ (c) 0·106, 0·106, $\qquad$ (d) 0·382, 0·382,
$\quad$ (e) 0·363, 0·364, $\qquad$ (f) 0·231, 0·230.
(7) (a) 0·011, $\quad$ (b) 0·982, $\quad$ (c) 0·029.
(8) (a) 0·047, $\quad$ (b) 0·149, $\quad$ (c) 0·898,
$\quad$ (d) 0·102, $\quad$ (e) 0·102, $\quad$ (f) 0·796.

CHAPTER 10

Exercise 1, page 232

(1) 3. (2) 10. (3) 1. (4) 12.
(5) $2\frac{2}{3}$, (6) 2. (7) 960 hours, 6 hours.
(8) 64 kg, $\frac{3}{4}$ kg. (9) 960 hours, 60 hours.

Exercise 2, page 232

(1) 20 000 km, 2 000 km. (2) 180 kg, 5 kg.
(3) £60, £7·07. (4) 12 volts, 0·2 volts.

CHAPTER 11

Exercise 1, page 238

(1) 95%: 46·32 and 77·68, 6·06 and 11·94, 0·8108 and 0·8892, 40·2 and 59·8,
99%: 41·36 and 82·64, 5·13 and 12·87, 0·7984 and 0·9016, 37·1 and 62·9.
(2) (a) 97·06 and 102·94 ohms, (b) 96·13 and 103·87 ohms,
(i) 89% confidence interval, (ii) 77% confidence interval,
(iii) 25·8% confidence interval.
(3) (a) 10·995 and 13·005 km/l, (b) 10·275 and 13·725 km/l,
(c) 9·525 and 14·475 km/l, (d) 8·13 and 15·87 km/l.
(4) (a) 59 and 77, (b) 58 and 78, (c) 55 and 81.
(5) (a) 4 minutes 20·79 seconds and 4 minutes 33·21 seconds,
(b) 4 minutes 19·22 seconds and 4 minutes 34·78 seconds,
(c) 4 minutes 16·42 seconds and 4 minutes 37·58 seconds.
(6) $\mu = 1\,000$, $\sigma = 75$; 806·5 and 1 193·5.
(7) Means: 7·00, 5·20, 84·5, 11·0, 26·0;
standard deviations: 1·00, 0·204, 0·969, 1·55, 0·408;
95% limits: 82·6 and 86·4, 7·96 and 14·04,
99% limits: 4·42 and 9·58, 4·47 and 5·73, 24·95 and 27·05.

Exercise 2, page 241

(1) (*a*) 11·2 and 12·8; 11·0 and 13·0,
    (*b*) 11·0 and 13·0; 10·7 and 13·3,
    (*c*) 11·6 and 13·4; 11·5 and 12·5,
    (*d*) 11·4 and 12·6; 11·1 and 12·9.
(2) (*a*) 1 175·25 and 1 224·75 hours.
    (*b*) 1 170·6 and 1 229·4 hours.
    (*c*) 1 161·3 and 1 238·7 hours.
(3) (*a*) (i) 1 989·7 and 2 010·3 kg.
      (ii) 1 993·1 and 2 006·9 kg.
     (iii) 1 995·9 and 2 004·1 kg.
    (*b*) (i) 1 987·8 and 2 012·2 kg.
      (ii) 1 991·8 and 2 008·2 kg.
     (iii) 1 995·1 and 2 004·9 kg.
    (*c*) (i) 1 983·9 and 2 016·1 kg.
      (ii) 1 988·2 and 2 004·8 kg.
     (iii) 1 993·6 and 2 006·4 kg.
(4) (*a*) 985·3 and 1 014·7 hours.
    (*b*) 992·6 and 1 007·4 hours.
    (*c*) 975·5 and 1 024·5 hours.
(5) (*a*) 1·95 and 2·05 kg, 1·96 and 2·04 kg.
    (*b*) 1·94 and 2·06 kg, 1·95 and 2·05 kg.
(6) (*a*) 80·02 and 83·98,   (*b*) 79·65 and 84·35,
    (*c*) 78·90 and 85·10.
(7) (*a*) 229·67 and 230·33,   (*b*) 229·61 and 230·39,
    (*c*) 229·48 and 230·52.

Exercise 3, page 248

(1) $\mu = 48$, $\sigma = 4$,
    (*a*) 41 to 55, (*b*) 38 to 58.
(2) 0·05 level: reject (i), (iv), (v), (vi), (viii), (ix), (x),
    0·01 level: reject (i), (vi).
(3) 0·05 level: less than 7 or more than 17,
    0·01 level: less than 5 or more than 19.
(4) (*a*) Reject at 0·05 level if less than 21 or more than 39, accept
       otherwise,
    (*b*) Reject at 0·01 level if less than 18 or more than 42, accept
       otherwise,
    0·05 level: reject (ii), (iii), (iv), (v), (vi), (vii), (viii), (x),
    0·01 level: reject (iv), (v), (x).

(5) (*a*) Reject fairness at 0·05 level if less than 41 or more than 59 heads, accept otherwise,
(*b*) Reject fairness at 0·01 level if less than 38 or more than 62 heads, accept otherwise.
(6) 0·05 level: reject (i), (iii), (iv), (vi), (vii), (x),
0·01 level: reject (iv), (vi), (x).

Exercise 4, page 252

(1) 0·01 level: (*a*) reject (iii), (*b*) reject (iii),
0·05 level: (*a*) reject (ii), (iii), (iv), (*b*) reject (ii), (iii), (iv).
(2) 0·01 level: reject (v), (vi), (vii),
0·05 level: reject (ii), (iii), (v), (vi), (vii).
(3) 0·05 level: reject in (i), (ii), (iii), (iv),
0·01 level: reject in (ii), (iv).
(4) 99·63 to 100·37 ohms; the range 99·52 to 99·63 and 100·37 to 100·48 ohms.

Exercise 5, page 256

(1) 0·05 level: reject in (*c*), (*d*), (*e*), (*f*), (*g*),
0·01 level: reject in (*f*), (*g*).
(2) 0·05 level: reject in (*c*), (*d*), (*e*), (*f*), (*g*),
0·01 level: reject in (*f*), (*g*).
(3) (*a*) 0·05 level: reject if less than 32 prefer *A* to *B*, accept otherwise,
(*b*) 0·01 level: reject if less than 30 prefer *A* to *B*, accept otherwise.
(4) 0·05 level: no, no, no, no, no, no.
0·01 level: no, no, no, no, no, no.
(5) 0·05 level: reject if less than 74, accept otherwise,
0·01 level: reject if less than 71, accept otherwise.
(6) 0·05 level: reject in (*c*), (*d*), (*e*), (*f*), (*g*).
0·01 level: reject in (*f*), (*g*).

Exercise 6, page 259

(1) 0·05 *level:*
(*a*) Reject if mean is less than 1 792·58 kg (and conclude that breaking strength is less), accept otherwise,
(*b*) Reject if mean is less than 1 790·10 kg (and conclude that breaking strength is less), accept otherwise.

0·01 *level:*

(a) Reject if mean is less than 1 789·52 (and conclude that breaking strength is less), accept otherwise,

(b) Reject if mean is less than 1 786·02 (and conclude that breaking strength is less), accept otherwise.

(2) 0·05 level: reject if sample mean is less than 9·475 g, accept otherwise,

0·01 level: reject if sample mean is less than 9·465 g, accept otherwise.

(3) 0·05 level: no, yes, yes, yes,

0·01 level: no, no, yes, yes.

(4) (a) yes, (b) no.

(5) 0·05 level: no, yes, yes, yes,

0·01 level: no, no, no, yes.

Revision Examples II

Set 1, page 261

(1) (a) T, (b) F, (c) T, (d) F.

(2) Mean = 80·8, Median = 79·5.

(3) (i) 38, (ii) 90.

(4) (a) (i) 469, (ii) 37, (iii) 10, (iv) 13,

(b) 354,

(c) 70.

(5) Reject claim at both 0·05 and 0·01 levels.

Set 2, page 262

(1) (a) F, (b) F, (c) T, (d) T, (e) F.

(2) (i) 144, 265, 363, 441, 525,

(ii) 0·08 to one significant figure.

(3) (i) 850,

(ii) 62%.

(4) (a) 0·032, (b) 0·014, (c) 0·131.

(5) One tail test.

Reject at 0·05 level, but accept at 0·01 level.

Set 3, page 264

(1) (*a*) **T**, (*b*) **T**, (*c*) F, (*d*) F, (*e*) F.
(2) 32 times $\bar{X} = 1.53$, $s = 0.83$,
$\bar{X} = 1.47$, $s = 0.83$.
(3) (i) £808·3, (ii) £785.
(4) 8·5%, 116.
(5) Two-tail test,
Reject (*c*), (*d*) at both 0·05 and 0·01 levels.

Set 4, page 265

(1) (*a*) **T**, (*b*) **T**, (*c*) **T**, (*d*) **T**, (*e*) F.
(3) (*a*) 50%, (*b*) 37·5%, (*c*) −1·15, (*d*) 42, 15·4%.
(4) (*a*) (i) $(\frac{1}{6})^6$, (ii) $\frac{31}{6^6}$,
(*b*) (i) 0·018, (ii) £0·473, (iii) 0·242.
(5) Two-tail test.
Accept at both 0·05 and 0·01 levels.

Set 5, page 267

(1) (*a*) F, (*b*) F, (*c*) **T**, (*d*) **T**, (*e*) F.
(2) Median = 5, Ninth decile = 19, 7·5%.
(3) (*a*) 50%, (*b*) 99%, (*c*) −2·33, (*d*) 1.
(4) (i) 23·05, 0·22, (ii) 99% limits: 22·48, 23·62,
95% limits: 22·62, 23·48.
(5) (*a*) $\frac{1}{3}$, (*b*) (i)$\frac{125}{324}$, (ii) $\frac{171}{1296}$.

Set 6, page 268

(1) (*a*) **T**, (*b*) **T**, (*c*) **T**, (*d*) **T**, (*e*) F.
(2) Mean = 1·522, Size 1: 175, Size 2: 375,
Size 3: 350, Size 4: 300.
(3) 55, 9; 63; 53.
(4) (*a*) 96, (*b*) 81, (*c*) 216, (*d*) 328.
(5) (*a*) 0·135. 95% confidence limits for population mean: 13·885,
14·415, 99% confidence limits for population mean: 13·802,
14·498.
(*b*) Approximately 1·35,
(*c*) 81.

Set 7, page 270

   (1) (*a*) **T,** (*b*) **F,** (*c*) **T,** (*d*) **T,** (*e*) **F.**
   (2) 9, 28, 66, 121, 174, 198.
   (3) (i) 98·3, 6·56, (ii) 3·1%, (iii) 87·5.
   (4) (*a*) 0·468, (*b*) 0·064, (*c*) 0·488, (*d*) 0·000.
   (5) One-tail test: $\mu_{\bar{X}} = 19\cdot8$, $\sigma_{\bar{X}} = 0\cdot93$.
      Mean 21·2 not significant at either 0·05 or 0·01 levels.

Set 8, page 271

   (1) (*a*) **T,** (*b*) **F,** (*c*) **T,** (*d*) **T,** (*e*) **T.**
   (2) 86.
   (3) 81·9%.
   (4) (*a*) $\frac{1}{216}$, (*b*) $\frac{135}{512}$, (*c*) 8.
   (5) Yes. *Pr* (5 correct) $= \frac{4}{245} \doteqdot 0\cdot016 < 0\cdot05$.

Set 9, page 273

   (1) Continuous: (*a*), (*c*); discrete: (*b*), (*d*), (*e*).
   (2) (*a*) 64 boys, 21 girls, (*b*) 117.
   (3) (*a*) $p = \frac{2}{3}$, $q = \frac{1}{3}$, $n = 5$, $N = 243$; expected frequencies:
       1, 10, 40, 80, 80, 32.
     (*b*) $\frac{2}{3}$.
   (4) Mathematics, $z = 1\cdot5$, Latin $z = 0\cdot5$.
      50% in mathematics equivalent to 87% in Latin.

Set 10, page 274

   (1) (*a*) **F,** (*q*) **F,** (*c*) **T,** (*d*) **T,** (*e*) **F.**
   (2) (i) 219, (ii) 292.
   (3) Mean = 30·1, standard deviation = 10·28,
      (i) 0·69, (ii) 0·96.
   (4) (*b*) 95%: 44·85 and 46·35; 99%: 44·61 and 46·59. (*c*) 0·152.
   (5) (*a*) 1 000—1 099, (*b*) $Q_2 = 1\ 110$ hours, $Q = 145$ hours,
      (*c*) 0·075.

Set 11, page 276

(1) (a) **T,** (b) **F,** (c) **F,** (d) **T,** (e) **T.**
(2) Standard scores, English, Mathematics, Drawing, respectively:
    A 1·40, 1·20, 1·00, total 3·60,
    B 0·00, 0·80, 2·67, total 3·47,
    C 0·20, 2·40, 0·50, total 3·10,
    D 2·50, 0·80, 0·58, total 3·88.
    Order of merit, *D, A, B, C.*
(3) (b) 5%.
(4) (i) 0·067, (ii) 0·018, (iii) 0·410.
(5) (a) $\mu = 14$, $\sigma = 2\sqrt{3}$, (b) 3.